Reference Guide

Office Te

D0088103

Preface

When I began the updating and revising of *The Secretary's Handbook* for its fourth edition, it was suggested that perhaps the title was no longer appropriate and should be changed. However, it soon became apparent that the title does indeed show what the book covers and, more importantly, for whom the book is intended; it is the concept of a secretary that has changed. Because the word *secretary* is now used in a more general sense to cover a broader range of office duties, the title of *The Secretary's Handbook* was expanded to reflect this change. A subtitle, *A Manual for Office Personnel*, has been added.

Some of the changes in the secretarial profession are semantic. The titles *stenographer* and *clerk-typist* have gone the way of the manual typewriter. Word processing has further qualified the title of *secretary* by adding *administrative* and *correspondence* to its name. Since secretaries are becoming increasingly difficult to find, employers have changed their demands to such euphemisms as *administrative assistant* and *executive assistant*—with the qualification of ability to type! Help-wanted columns show the title of *transcriptionist* and such specializations as *medical transcriptionist* and *technical* (or *medical* or *legal*) *secretary*. All of them perform secretarial duties.

Along with title changes, there have also been qualification changes. Perhaps the most significant change has been that many employers no longer require shorthand skills; in fact, only about 10 percent of the secretarial help-wanted ads ask for such skills. Rarely, too, are specific requirements, such as typing speed of 75 words per minute or a dictation speed of 100 words per minute, listed. However, emphasis is placed on communication skills and such personal qualifications as initiative and ability to get along with others.

The people who become secretaries are also changing. Because of the great demand, secretaries are being recruited from the ranks of reentry women, minorities (in secretarial work, men are the sexual minority), handicapped, and older workers. Employers are accepting less highly trained secretaries and often training them on the job.

FOURTH EDITION

The Secretary's Handbook

A MANUAL FOR OFFICE PERSONNEL

Doris H. Whalen, *Professor Emeritus*
College of Marin

Business Books from
HBJ Media Systems Corporation
A Subsidiary of Harcourt Brace Jovanovich, Inc.

Requests for permission to make copies of any part of the work should be mailed to: Permissions, HBJ Media Systems Corporation, 757 Third Avenue, New York, N.Y. 10017
ISBN: 0-15-579301-2
Library of Congress Catalog Card Number: 82-83787

Printed in the United States of America
05-793013 / 10   9   8   7   6   5   4   3   2   1

11-23-87
cjs

Contents

Therefore, the *Handbook* was revised to help all of those who perform the great range of office duties—from routine tasks to administrative and supervisory jobs. None of the secretaries have been overlooked: the *Handbook* is for word processing secretaries, for those who are supervisors or administrators, for those who still take shorthand dictation and those who now transcribe from machine dictation, and for all of those who do the vast variety of duties that every secretary encounters.

Like the earlier editions, the Fourth Edition is a dual-purpose book. On the one hand, it is intended to serve as a textbook and reference manual in secretarial and other business courses—especially when used in conjunction with the exercises and answers that are provided. On the other hand, it will admirably serve the secretary and office worker already on the job, both as a ready reference manual of acceptable office and language skills and as a means of reinforcing and updating previous training.

Approximately half of the text (excluding the exercises) deals with office procedures and the various aspects of office typing; the remainder is devoted to grammar, punctuation, style, and word usage. Because this is a handbook, the material is arranged primarily for ease of topic location. Rules are stated clearly and concisely so that their application becomes a matter of mechanics and not decision-making. In cases where opinions differ among various authorities, common business usage prevails.

The sixty exercises with answers at the back of the book review the points of grammar, punctuation, spelling, word usage, and style discussed in the text. These exercises will be particularly effective in courses where this manual is used as a textbook, but they will also be of value to the office worker and secretarial student as a means of self-testing and review.

Ease of finding and using information has been a major concern in the physical organization and design of the book. The comprehensive Index and the Table of Contents have been organized to help the user locate specific subjects, rules, and terms quickly; the Glossary in the Appendix gives instant definitions. The marginal sideheads that pinpoint the material are designed to speed location of topics. Within the text itself many cross-references clarify related topics. Charts, examples, and "warnings" have been given graphic treatment. A number of sample letters and envelopes illustrating a variety of current styles have been included, with all of the sample letters conforming to Postal Service recommendations.

The Fourth Edition of *The Secretary's Handbook* has been thoroughly updated and revised to reflect the many recent changes in the business world and to prepare for the rather rapid movement toward the electronic office. This edition has continued to avoid sexist connotations and stereotypes of all kinds. Although all aspects of the book have been revised to bring them up-to-date, major changes and additions include:

- an updated and significantly expanded section on word processing
- a new section on maintaining office files
- a new section on writing business letters and reports
- a revised section on communications incorporating practical information on such recent innovations as electronic mail and "800" WATS lines
- an expanded section on dictation and transcription, including greater emphasis on machine dictation
- addition of a section on proofreading as a further technique toward finding and correcting errors
- reorganization of three chapters of the Third Edition—capitalization, numbers, and abbreviations—into a more consolidated and accessible chapter called "Style or Mechanics"
- a new spiral binding that helps the book to lie flat and makes it easier to use

I cannot possibly list all of those who contributed in so many ways to the publication of this handbook. I do wish to thank those who in the planning process reviewed the book: Rosemarie McCauley, Montclair State College; Patricia Parzych, Hostos Community College; and Brian Wilson, College of Marin. I am grateful to my students and colleagues at the College of Marin, to the many business educators who made excellent suggestions, to the reference librarians who assisted greatly in locating information, and to the staff members at Harcourt Brace Jovanovich who have contributed in so many ways toward making this edition better in every aspect.

DORIS H. WHALEN

I. Office Techniques and Procedures

DICTATION AND TRANSCRIPTION

Dictation and transcription are the twin skills used to produce business letters and other office documents; these skills can be accomplished through a variety of methods. The traditional method has been to dictate to a secretary who records the dictation in shorthand and then transcribes it. However, the rapid expansion of word processing centers and the increasing use of dictation equipment are changing procedures in many offices. Secretaries may also transcribe from longhand, from corrected rough drafts, from telephone dictation, and sometimes directly on the typewriter. In many offices dictation and transcription are produced by more than one method. These various dictation and transcription methods with helpful suggestions for their performance are discussed here.

Transcribing Machine Dictation

Dictation given to a machine is recorded electronically on belts, tapes, cassettes, or discs. The material is then transcribed by a secretary from a transcription machine. Machine dictation is valuable for the person who must dictate when a secretary is not available or is busy with other work. Other advantages are that machine transcription does not require two people and that the dictation can be given out of the office. There are, in fact, pocket-sized dictation units available for on-the-spot use. Machine dictation is replacing shorthand dictation in many offices.

For the person transcribing from machine dictation, the chief difference is that you must type what you *hear* rather than what you see.

Use these suggestions to help you transcribe machine dictation:

1

1. Learn to use the transcription equipment and to handle the medium used for dictation (belt, tape, cassette, disc, or magnetic card). Read the user's manual for the machine. (If one is unavailable, obtain a copy from the vendor.)

2. Check the company's procedures or style manual, if one is available.

3. Before you begin transcription, assemble all supplies (for example, letterheads, second sheets, carbon paper, and correcting supplies) that you will need.

4. Check names, addresses, facts, figures, spelling, and any other details that you anticipate you will need to know. Collect correspondence that is being answered if it is available. Check the dictator's index slip to see which items should be transcribed first and if there are any special instructions.

5. Learn to judge letter length from a marked index slip and from previous experience with the dictator's voice speed. You will need to get used to the dictator's voice and to learn to type and listen at the same time. (You can already read and type at the same time.) Check letter placement charts on page 36 to help set typewriter margin stops.

6. Play back as much of the material as you can remember; then stop the machine and type. While you are typing the last few words, start the machine again so that you can listen to the next portion. Do not pause in your typing. You can, of course, replay the dictation; however, this greatly slows down the transcription. Try to avoid typing rough drafts of material; however, it may be necessary to do so if the material is long or technical.

7. Correct errors as you are transcribing, using the correction method best suited to your particular needs.

8. To improve hearing, use headphones rather than an earpiece if the work area is noisy. It may also be necessary to ask the dictator to speak more distinctly if you are having difficulty understanding the recording. If the dictation still sounds garbled or indistinct, check the equipment itself.

9. Keep a dictionary nearby to check spellings and word division.

10. Always proofread a page before taking it from the typewriter (see page 29).

11. Confidential or top-secret material should be transcribed when other employees are not nearby. The original and carbon copy should be given to the dictator immediately or covered so that it cannot be seen. If the carbon paper can be read, destroy it. Do not leave partially typed confidential material in the typewriter. Erase the dictation medium.

12. Erase or file the dictation medium.

Taking Dictation in Shorthand

Your dictation supplies should be kept in one place where they can be picked up quickly whenever you are asked to take dictation. You will need a shorthand notebook, pens and pencils, a file folder, and paper clips.

Suggestions for using the shorthand notebook:

Shorthand notebook

1. Use a rubber band to hold the used pages.
2. If you take dictation from more than one person, keep a notebook for each dictator.
3. Always write in the notebook in one direction (one side of the page only); then reverse the notebook and write on the back pages. It is important that, as you take dictation, you always find the next page blank.
4. Do not use your notebook for anything but shorthand dictation.
5. Take an extra notebook with you, if the one you are using is almost filled, so that you do not run out of space.
6. Many firms file shorthand notebooks so that they will be available if questions arise. Show the dates of the material that the notebook contains on the front cover.

Example: June 1, 1984, to October 10, 1984

Suggestions for using pens and pencils:

Pens and pencils

1. Use a pen for dictation; it requires less effort and your notes will be more legible. Dark-colored ink—either blue or black—provides better contrast with the notebook paper. Always carry a spare.
2. Carry several well-sharpened No. 2 pencils to make notes that can be erased later and some colored pencils to use for jotting down notations that can be quickly found after dictation.

Suggestions for using the file folder and paper clips:

File folder and paper clips

1. The folder is used to hold correspondence that is being answered as well as other papers that the dictator may give you.
2. Use paper clips for markers in the shorthand notebook. For example, clip pages where you have dictation to be transcribed immediately. In the file folder use clips to keep related papers together.

Suggestions for taking dictation:

1. Discuss with the dictator the possibility of setting a regular time for dictation, such as after the day's mail is delivered. This makes it easier to schedule appointments and to plan other work.

2. Open the notebook to the first blank page—the used pages are behind the rubber band—and write the day's date at the bottom of the page, preferably in red.

3. Number each item that is dictated. If you are given a letter that the dictator is answering, put the corresponding number on it in pencil. This can eliminate the employer's dictating and your having to write the inside address. Assemble the correspondence in the same order as the dictation and put it into a file folder. If there are several documents pertaining to one letter, clip them together.

4. Do not try to squeeze a change or an addition into shorthand notes. Put a colored letter (such as A, B, C) at the point where the addition is made. Put the corresponding letter with the change where you have room to write. If the dictator makes frequent changes, leave one column of each notebook page blank for these changes.

5. There will be times when you will use longhand in your notes, particularly for proper nouns (personal, trade, or geographic names, for example), as there can be a great variety of ways to spell such nouns.

6. Be sure to mark the end of each item of dictation; a couple of blank lines or a distinctive symbol, such as a wavy line or a crosshatch, will serve the purpose.

7. Write down all special instructions from the dictator. Don't trust your memory!

8. If there is something that should be transcribed first, mark that dictation *Rush* in color; then either turn the corner of the page back so that it extends beyond the notebook or put a paper clip on the page.

9. Try to avoid interrupting while the dictation is being given. If you are losing the dictation, ask that the dictation be given more slowly; otherwise, wait until the dictation is finished before you check on a word or ask a question. Read back the sentence where the question occurs to make it easier for the dictator to answer your question.

10. Use any time when the dictator is interrupted to read back on notes, correct outlines, insert paragraph marks, and add punctuation. To help the dictator resume his or her train of thought after the interruption, it may be necessary to read back the last sentence dictated.

11. At the end of the dictation, check with the dictator about dates, spellings, and any other information that might not be found in files or in reference sources. Do not guess or bluff on such information.

Transcribing Shorthand Dictation

Use these suggestions for helping you transcribe dictation:

1. Transcribe as soon as you can after dictation. Your memory will be better, and you will be able to get the dictation completed more quickly.

2. Before transcribing: check your supplies (letterheads, second sheets, and carbon paper, for example); assemble from the files any information that you will need; check names, addresses, facts, figures, spellings, and any other details; check to see which items should be transcribed first and if there are any special instructions, such as *send an extra copy to the Sales Department.*

3. Plan your transcription before you begin typing. Do such things as: estimate the length of the letter, determine the number of carbon copies needed, check to see where sentences break, and verify spellings.

4. Glance through your notes before you begin transcription. This does not mean reading every word or writing longhand above the shorthand. Transcribe from your notes, reading ahead as you type. Do not type a rough draft before you type a final copy on letterhead unless the dictator wants an item of the dictation typed in rough draft.

5. It is easier to read a letter that is broken into small typewritten blocks, so paragraph frequently. Try to have no more than seven or eight lines in each paragraph; however, avoid numerous short paragraphs of three lines or less.

6. If you are interrupted during transcription, place a colored mark next to the last outline you have transcribed.

7. Confidential or top-secret material should be transcribed when other employees are not nearby. The original and carbon copy should be given to the dictator immediately, and the shorthand notes may need to be destroyed. If the carbon paper can be read, destroy it too. Do not leave partially typed confidential material in the typewriter.

8. Correct errors as you are typing, using the correction method best suited to what you are typing and the kind of machine you are using (see page 30).

9. Keep a dictionary nearby to check spellings and word division.

10. Always proofread a page before taking it out of the typewriter (see page 29).

11. Cancel shorthand notes by drawing a colored pencil line through *each item* after it is transcribed. When you have finished all of the transcription, check the notebook pages to be sure that you have not overlooked any of the notes, then put the transcribed pages behind the rubber band.

12. When you have finished transcribing, check supplies so that they will be ready for the next dictation session: used pages of the notebook behind the band, pencils sharpened, pens with adequate ink supplies, and clips and file folder available. Return the supplies to their usual place so you will be ready to take the next dictation.

Transcribing Other Dictation

You may be asked to take dictation over the telephone or directly on the typewriter. There may be times when dictation is given at your desk or while you are standing or working elsewhere with inadequate writing space. You may be asked to transcribe from rough-draft or longhand copy.

Telephone dictation

Suggestions for telephone dictation:

1. When taking telephone dictation, you will have only one free hand so you will write more slowly.

2. Since the dictator cannot see how fast you are writing, say *yes* after you have completed taking down a sentence or phrase. You may have to ask to have words or phrases repeated.

3. Read back the entire dictation to the dictator before ending the conversation.

4. If you are monitoring a telephone call, take down the main points rather than attempting to make a word-for-word transcript.

5. Transcribe as soon as you can while the conversation is still fresh in your mind.

Dictation on the typewriter

Suggestions for dictation on the typewriter:

1. If you are asked to take dictation directly on the typewriter, ask first about dictation length to help determine placement on the page.

2. Do not stop to correct errors as you are typing; instead, do any correcting when the dictation is finished.

3. Retyping will often be necessary in this kind of dictation because any addition of material makes it difficult to type the desired copy the first time and to place the letter attractively.

Suggestions for transcribing rough-draft or longhand material: **Rough-draft or longhand material**

1. Transcription of rough-draft or longhand material is a matter of reading and understanding the handwriting and markings. Read through rough-draft or longhand material before transcription to be sure that markings and handwriting are understandable and legible.

2. Become familiar with standard proofreaders' marks (see page 222).

3. If you have any questions, ask; do not guess or bluff.

If dictation is given at your desk or when you are using another   **Dictation in unusual area**
work area, it may be necessary to write while standing or by putting your notebook on your knees. Practice writing while standing or with your notebook in your lap. Sometimes you may have to write on any paper that is available. Practice writing on unlined paper. If your notes are written on paper other than in a shorthand notebook, after transcription, fold the notes to fit your notebook and staple the paper to it.

WARNING:

Accurate transcription is not just important, it is essential. There are several things a secretary can do to insure accuracy:

1. *Verify all names, figures, and unusual or technical terms. If you have checked information sources—file copies, dictionaries, reference books, telephone and other directories—and still are not able to confirm information, check with the dictator or your supervisor.*
2. *Keep your own lists of names, addresses, and telephone numbers.*
3. *Keep a calendar/diary of meetings, deadlines, and similar information.*
4. *Proofread any typing before you take it from the typewriter and before you submit it to the dictator.*
5. *Never guess at or fake any information.*

Arranging Transcription for Signature

When transcription is finished, follow these steps to arrange the work for presentation to the dictator for signature:

1. When letters are typed and ready to be signed, assemble each letter and any enclosures under the flap of the envelope, with the address side of the envelope on top. (*Rush* transcription was submitted when it was completed.)

2. If a carbon copy is being sent, place the copy and its addressed envelope underneath the original letter.

3. File copies and any incoming correspondence that you have will not go to the dictator but will be kept separate.

4. If the dictator is temporarily away from the desk when you complete the transcription, put the letters in a folder or lay them face down. You may prefer always to use a folder for the completed dictation.

5. Discuss with the dictator what procedure you should follow when the correspondence is signed. Usually it is your responsibility to fold letters and insert them in envelopes. The filled envelopes are then either sent to the mail room or run through the postage meter.

WORD PROCESSING

Word processing is something that secretaries have been doing for a long time—that is, producing high-quality transcription of dictation. The actual method, though, has been drastically improved by the introduction of sophisticated text-editing equipment and the formation of word processing centers that both speed transcription and improve its quality. Since word processing was introduced in the mid-1960s, such dramatic technological changes have taken place that it is difficult to write a current description of word processing equipment. However, the implications, purposes, and principles of word processing seem to remain constant, with improvements occurring in the areas of equipment versatility and ease of operation.

Definition

Word processing has been defined broadly as the automation of document production. A more generalized definition is that word processing combines three elements—specialized personnel, modern equipment, and standardized procedures—to produce high-quality communications rapidly and at low cost. The word processor itself is a truly all-purpose piece of equipment that enables the operator to write, edit, rewrite, revise, correct, and store (file) copy for instant recall.

Word Processing Center

The word processing center consists of the space, personnel, and equipment allocated to word processing. It replaces the old steno pool, where secretaries worked in one room transcribing dictation from various dictators. The center can be as small as two persons (one correspondence secretary and one administrative secretary) and one text-editing (automatic) typewriter; or it can consist of a number of secretaries, machine dictation equipment, text-editing stations, and administrative support work stations. There are one-person word processing stations within small firms or in divisions of large companies. The organization and setup of a word processing center are determined by the needs of a company or organization.

The secretarial jobs in a word processing center are divided into two categories: *correspondence secretary,* who does the typing (keyboarding) and *administrative secretary,* who is responsible for the non-typing jobs, such as handling mail, filing, phones; performing clerical duties; and composing and editing correspondence. There are further breakdowns within each of these classifications: Correspondence secretary (entry level), senior correspondence secretary, executive correspondence secretary, and word processing center supervisor. Administrative secretary (entry level), senior administrative secretary, executive administrative secretary, and administrative support center supervisor.

Word Processing System

A word processing system is the combination of equipment and trained personnel working in an environment of job specialization and supervisory controls so that documents are produced in a routine, cost-efficient manner. The difference between word processing and a word processing system is that word processing systems contain job specialization and supervisory controls.

The following are the steps in a word processing system:

1. *Input.* The dictator is called the *word originator.* Material for transcription is "originated" by longhand writing, from edited rough-draft material, by shorthand dictation, or, most commonly,

Steps in word processing systems

through machine dictation. *Input,* therefore, is the creation of material to be transcribed.

2. *Delivery.* Input to the transcriber (*correspondence secretary*) can be face-to-face, delivered by messenger, or sent over telephone wires to recording equipment in the word processing center.

3. *Output.* The typing in a word processing center is done on text-editing (automatic) typewriters that record on magnetic tape, cards, discs, or cassettes. The material that is being typed (*output*) can be seen either on paper, as in a conventional typewriter, or on a display screen, similar to a small television screen. Errors are corrected by backspacing and striking over. It is easy to make additions and deletions, as well as move the order of material—even from page to page. The machine will then play back what has been recorded at speeds that can go as high as several hundred words per minute. The dictation media (card, disc or diskette, or cassette) can be erased or stored for future use. In addition, material can be retrieved from filed tapes or discs and played back for transcription. It is also possible to merge material from several media sources to produce one document.

Machine transcription in a word processing center follows the same procedures as in other machine transcription (see page 1). Very often the correspondence secretary in the word processing center does not see the word originator, since material recorded on the tape or disc may have been dictated from a distance and transmitted over wires to the center. The correspondence secretary types at rough-draft speeds and corrects errors by backspacing and striking over. The copy must be carefully proofread before the draft is played back by the automatic typewriter. If the copy is not in final form, it is edited by proofreaders, word originators, or administrative secretaries (see page 222).

Procedure for transcribing dictation in a word processing center is very important. To keep work flowing smoothly, each correspondence secretary must follow identical procedures, such as order in which material is transcribed, what is done with transcribed material, and filing or erasing of transcribed tapes or discs.

4. *Review.* The typed material is checked and reviewed—first by the administrative secretary, then by the word originator.

5. *Distribution.* The document is mailed or delivered. Copies are retained for files.

Implications for Secretaries

The implications of word processing for the secretary are many. Word processing has taken a great deal of the drudgery out of typing. No longer does the secretary need to erase errors or to re-type pages to change words and phrases or to add or delete sentences and paragraphs—all of these revision tasks can be accomplished by backspacing and retyping or by striking special function keys that can add or delete. Repeated typing of the same document is not necessary—the typewriter automatically types as many copies as are wanted. Forms and form letters can be stored for future use and played back whenever needed. Word processing, however, has greatly intensified the importance of the secretary's language and communication skills. Such skills as grammar, spelling, syntax, punctuation, proofreading, and ability to use a dictionary have always been important secretarial skills; however, the volume and speed with which material is produced from a word processing center make such skills, if possible, of even greater importance.

Secretarial jobs have always provided opportunities for promotion, both within the company and outside of it. Often promotions are to administrative positions. Certainly word processing secretaries are offered equal career opportunities.

Increasingly, office typing will be done on electronic equipment with word processing functions. In between the electric typewriter and the word processor is the electronic typewriter. This is a computerized machine with memory and limited word processing functions. Presently these machines can store approximately 12 to 15 pages of typing. It is expected that manufacturers in the future will expand the word processing functions and increase the memory of the electronic typewriter so that word processing and electronic typing will be combined in one machine. It is also expected that the electronic typewriter will replace the conventional electromechanical machine.

HANDLING MAIL

Handling mail involves processing the incoming mail so that it is sent to the proper departments or persons for answering and getting the outgoing mail ready for the post office.

Incoming Mail

In large firms mail arrives at the mail room for its first sorting. Anything addressed to the company is opened in the mail room and sent to the appropriate persons or departments; anything addressed to persons or departments is sent unopened to those individuals or offices. In a small office it is often the secretary who handles all mail and sends it to the persons who will answer it.

Some offices keep a register or record of important mail (not advertisements, circulars, or bulk mail). Such a register includes date received, date of item, sender's name, addressee's name, and when and how disposed.

Whether you process all mail or only your employer's, these are the steps in processing incoming mail:

SORTING
INCOMING
MAIL

Sort the incoming mail into these categories: (1) mailgrams, first-class and special-service (certified, special delivery) mail, international mail, interoffice memoranda; (2) priority (air parcel post); (3) second-class (newspapers and magazines); (4) third-class (circulars, catalogs, and other printed matter); and (5) fourth-class (parcel post).

OPENING
MAIL

Unless you are instructed otherwise, do not open mail marked "Personal" or "Confidential" (if such a letter is opened, mark it "Opened by mistake" and reseal it with tape). Use a letter opener or scissors if an automatic letter opener is not available. Remove *everything* from the envelope and check to see that all listed enclosures are included. Make a note on the letter if an enclosure is missing. If possible, clip or staple enclosures to the letter. If you are not required to save envelopes (some firms want this done), do check to be sure that the return address is given in the letter and that the letter does not vary greatly in time length from its date to the postmark.

DATING MAIL

Use a date stamp to date all mail as it is opened. If a stamp is not available, write the date on the mail.

SEPARATING
MAIL

Separate the opened mail for your employer. Arrange it in order of importance; that is, such items as mailgrams or special delivery or certified mail on top and circulars or advertisements on the bottom.

READING
AND ROUTING
MAIL

If you are asked to read the mail, underline the important points and make notes in the margins or on the back of the letter. Gather additional files and information that would be helpful in answering the letter.

If it is necessary to send mail to others, either photocopy the letter or use a routing slip (a slip with a listing of names; the recipient initials his or her name after reading the mail and passes it on to the next person on the list) attached to the letter.

Outgoing Mail

The size of the office determines the secretary's duties in handling outgoing mail. If a firm has a mail clerk, the secretary's responsibilities end with giving the signed mail and its envelopes to a mail clerk. In smaller offices, the secretary may prepare the mail for the mail room or have sole responsibility for preparing the mail for the post office.

These are the steps in preparing outgoing mail:

Before mail is folded and inserted into envelopes, check dates, addresses, mailing notations, signatures, enclosures, and carbon-copy notations of all mail. Be sure that there are addressed labels if mail is being sent in large envelopes or packages.

CHECKING MAIL

There are machines that fold and seal mail. If you are doing these tasks manually, fold the letters and insert them into envelopes, then place the envelopes face down, flatten the flaps, and arrange the envelopes in a line so that the gummed edges are visible. Put the envelopes over a blotter to absorb any excess water. With a moistener—a plastic tube or ceramic wheel but never your tongue!—moisten all of the edges at once. Then seal the envelope nearest you, lay it aside face up, and continue up the line of envelopes.

FOLDING AND SEALING MAIL

A postage meter saves in many ways and should, except perhaps in very small offices, be used. Weigh mail with a postage scale to determine the correct postage. If you do use stamps, lay the envelopes face up in a line leaving the stamp edge visible. Take a strip of stamps, moisten one at a time, and place the stamps on the envelopes, tearing them off as you stamp.

STAMPING MAIL

Outgoing mail will be processed at the post office much faster if it is sorted into bundles such as *local, out-of-town,* and *precanceled* and labeled as to category. Bulk mail (third-class) must be bundled and labeled or the Postal Service will not accept it for delivery.

SORTING OUT-GOING MAIL

MAINTAINING FILES AND RECORDS

Supplying information when it is needed is an important secretarial duty. In order to supply such information quickly, it is essential that well-organized files be kept. The discussion here is based on the filing system maintained by the secretary, not on the automated central files maintained by the records management department. In large offices the records management department maintains central files in one location and, increasingly, in computers and magnetic storage devices. In smaller offices where the secretary maintains all of the files, they, too, may be automated. Another system allows departmental files to be located within each department, with centralized control kept in the records management department. In any situation, however, the secretary will have filing responsibilities—to what extent depends on the office.

Automated equipment—replacing the traditional cabinets, folders, and guides—is moving businesses toward the "paperless" office. Once an automatic system has been installed, the savings in time, money, and space are enormous. No longer, for example, do checked-out files have to be found; retrieval involves a printout or a display on a screen with the file itself never leaving storage.

Although there are many systems for maintaining files—geographic, subject, numeric, and alphabetic—all files are to some degree based on an alphabetic system. Since it is estimated that at least 80 percent of all filing systems are alphabetic, this is the system that will be discussed here. Consult records management texts (see page 229) or the Association of Records Managers and Administrators (ARMA) for information concerning other systems.

Notice that alphabetic filing rules vary from one authority to another. Determine the rules that are best for your company—if this is your responsibility—and follow them carefully. It might be well to have the rules listed in a notebook so that everyone follows the same filing rules.

Steps in filing

Any filing system is based on following these steps:

1. *Collecting* in one place all of the correspondence to be filed.

2. *Checking* each piece of correspondence to see that it is ready to be filed; usually correspondence that is ready to be filed has a release mark on it.

3. *Indexing and Coding* each piece of correspondence by determining the title under which it will be filed and underlining (usually in color) that name.

4. *Sorting* the material to be filed in the sequence required by the filing system.

5. *Storing* the correspondence in file folders in cabinets.

Any materials that could be filed under more than one name should be cross-referenced. Usually a cross-reference sheet is placed in the file to show the name under which the file is actually maintained.

Example: Is <u>Betty Miller</u> a nickname for <u>Elizabeth Miller</u>? If so, cross-reference with <u>See Elizabeth Miller</u>.

Alphabetic Filing Rules

The rules for filing are based on an alphabetic order. Names to be indexed are divided into names of individuals and names of businesses or groups. Each part of any name is considered to be an indexing unit. Therefore, if the first units of two names are identical, it is necessary to check the second, third, or fourth units until a difference is reached.

Example: Johnson Automotive Repair Shop
      Unit: 1   2   3   4

      Johnson Automotive Sales Company
      Unit: 1   2   3   4

It is necessary to go to the third unit before a difference is reached.

The names with fewer units are indexed first, as nothing goes before something.

Example: Anderson, J.
Anderson, Jane
Anderson, Jane T.

Here are the rules:

1. *Indexing Order.* In individual names, the name is transposed so that the surname (last name) is the first filing unit, followed by the first name and the middle name or initial. If the first units of two or more names are identical, it will be necessary to go to further units (such as *junior* or *senior* or a part of an address).

Names of individuals

Examples: *Filed as:*
          M. Walter   Walter, M.
          Marian Walter   Walter, Marian
          Walters, Carol   Walters, Carol
          Thomas R. Walters, Jr.   Walters, Thomas R. (Jr.)
          Thomas R. Walters, Sr.   Walters, Thomas R. (Sr.)

WARNING:

When the indexing units of unusual or foreign names are not distinguishable—that is, it is not known which is the surname—file in the usual manner. It may be necessary to cross-reference.

Examples:	*Filed as:*
Nga Chu	Chu, Nga
Jon Chung	Chung, Jon
Kai Wong Chung	Chung, Kai Wong

In Spanish names, very often the middle name is the surname. In the example *Jose Lopez Portillo* (former president of Mexico), he is referred to as *Lopez Portillo*. Cross-referencing would be necessary.

   2. *Names with Prefixes.* A name with a prefix, such as *D', De, Del, Du, El, Il, La, Le, Los, Mac, Mc, Van,* and *Von,* is considered to be one indexing unit. Whether the name is spelled as one word or more than one word is not significant.

Examples:	*Filed as:*
Howard Demaris	Demaris, Howard
Robert DeMartin	DeMartin, Robert
Jean Macmillan	Macmillan, Jean
James McMillan	McMillan, James

   3. *Hyphenated Names.* Hyphenated individual names are treated as separate indexing units.

Examples: Harold Burke   Burke, Harold
            Unit: 1   2

        Harold Burke-Jones   Burke-Jones, Harold
            Unit: 1   2   3

WARNING:

Cross-referencing may be necessary when indexing hyphenated names. Many times a person with a hyphenated surname uses only the second part of the name; that is, Margaret Bailey-Jones *may be known as Mrs. Jones. Cross-referencing in this instance would be needed.*

   4. *Titles or Degrees.* Personal or professional titles or degrees are not usually considered in filing unless the title is required for

identification. If the name consists of a title and one name—*Father Felix,* for example—file it as written.

When a name with a title is written in index form, the title is usually abbreviated and placed in parentheses at the end of the name.

Examples: *Filed as:*

Dean Richard R. Ames	Ames, Richard R. (Dean)
Rev. Dwight T. Hill	Hill, Dwight T. (Rev.)
Capt. Helen Naylor	Naylor, Helen (Capt.)
Prince Charles	Prince Charles

Appendages, identifying elements such as seniority titles (*Jr., Sr., III, IV*) and professional degrees (*M.D., Ph.D.*), are considered identifying, not filing, units and are placed in parentheses after the names. If names are identical, the identifying units are considered; they are filed in abbreviated form with numerical terms in numerical sequence.

Examples: *Filed as:*

Richard Daniels	Daniels, Richard
Richard Daniels, Jr.	Daniels, Richard (Jr.)
Richard Daniels, M.D.	Daniels, Richard (M.D.)
Richard Daniels, III	Daniels, Richard (III)
Richard Daniels, IV	Daniels, Richard (IV)

5. *Names of Married Women.* The name of a married woman is indexed according to her legal name, which is first name; middle name, middle initial, or maiden name; and husband's surname. *Mrs.* is disregarded, but it may be placed in parentheses after the legal name. If known, the husband's name may also be shown in parentheses. If a married woman uses her maiden name, index the name as she signs it.

Examples: *Filed as:*

Mrs. Linda T. Kaye	Kaye, Linda T. (Mrs.)
Mrs. Martin (Linda T.) Kaye	Kaye, Linda T. (Martin)
Linda R. Thomas (maiden name)	Thomas, Linda R.

6. *Indexing Order.* Names of businesses or groups are indexed as written. If the name contains one name and a title (such as *Mrs. Brown's Restaurant*), file it as written. If the firm name contains the full name of an individual, such as *Roger Wilson School of Design,* the surname is the first indexing unit, followed by the first name or initial, middle name or initial, and the rest of the name.

Names of businesses and groups

Examples:	*Filed as:*
Wilton Publishing Company	Wilton Publishing Company
R. Wilton Publishing Com- pany	Wilton, R., Publishing Com- pany
Roger Wilton Publishing Com- pany	Wilton, Roger, Publishing Company

WARNING:

When a business name that contains an individual's name becomes so well-known that transposing it would cause confusion, the name is indexed as written.

Examples: Marshall Field & Company
Mark Hopkins Hotel
Montgomery Ward (&) Company

7. *Ampersand, Articles, Conjunctions, and Prepositions.* The ampersand, &; the articles, *a, an,* and *the;* conjunctions, such as *and* or *or;* and prepositions, such as *of, by, in,* and *for,* are disregarded in filing. They are often placed in parentheses to assist the person doing the filing in recognizing the name. A beginning *the* is placed in parentheses after the last unit.

Examples:	*Filed as:*
The New Yorker	*New Yorker (The)*
Oscar of the Waldorf	Oscar (of the) Waldorf
Williams & Associates	Williams (&) Associates

8. *Possessives.* When filing names containing apostrophes, disregard the apostrophe and index the name as it appears.

Examples:	*Filed as:*
Ander's Photo Supplies	Anders Photo Supplies
Anders Radio Shop	Anders Radio Shop
Ray Howard	Howard, Ray
Howard's Auto Equipment	Howards Auto Equipment

9. *Hyphenated Names.* Hyphenated words, including personal names and coined words, in a firm name are indexed as separate units.

Examples	*Filed as:*			
Robert Burke-Jones	Burke-Jones,	Robert,	Company	
Company	Unit: 1	2	3	4

Coin-op Cleaners	Coin-op Cleaners
	Unit: 1 2 3
Flex-Kleen Control	Flex-Kleen Control Company
Company	Unit: 1 2 3 4

10. *Single Letters, Abbreviations, and Titles in Names.* When a single letter is part of a firm name, whether it is an initial or a coined name, it is indexed as a separate unit. A known abbreviation (with the exception of *Mr.* and *Mrs.*) is indexed as if it were spelled in full. A firm name that includes a title followed by a one-word name is indexed in the order written.

Examples: *Filed as:*

A.P.A. Agency
A P A Agency
Unit: 1 2 3   4

IBM
International Business Machines
Unit: 1   2   3

K Mart Corporation
K Mart Corporation
Unit: 1 2   3

KOIT (radio station)
K O I T
Unit: 1 2 3 4

Mrs. Lee's Chocolates
Mrs. Lees Chocolates
Unit: 1   2   3

11. *Numbers in Names.* When the firm name contains numbers, spell out the number and index it as one unit. Spell out numbers larger than 99 by breaking them into the number of hundreds followed by the rest of the number (5650 is spelled *fifty-six fifty*).

Examples: *Filed as:*

Four Sixty Four Restaurant
FourSixtyFour Restaurant
Unit: 1   2

One-Hour Martinizing
One-Hour Martinizing
Unit: 1   2   3

Lew's 365 Club
Lews ThreeSixtyFive Club
Unit: 1   2   3

12. *Compound Words as One or Two Units.*

a. Compound words written separately or with a hyphen but shown as one word in the dictionary should be indexed as one word. This includes compound compass points, such as *northeast* or *southwest*.

Examples:	*Filed as:*
North East Charter Flights	Northeast Charter Flights

Unit: 1   2   3

North-west Airlines	Northwest Airlines

Unit: 1   2

Swift Air Lines	Swift Airlines

Unit: 1   2

Swift Airways	Swift Airways

Unit: 1   2

b. In names containing compound geographic names, each word is considered a separate filing unit.

Examples:	*Filed as:*
San Francisco Coin Company	San Francisco Coin Company

Unit: 1   2   3   4

Sanford Trading Company	Sanford Trading Company

Unit: 1   2   3

New York Times	New York Times

Unit: 1   2   3

Newcomb Service Company	Newcomb Service Company

Unit: 1   2   3

13. *Identical Names.* Identical names of businesses are indexed alphabetically by address. If the identical names also have identical cities, arrange the names by streets. If streets are identical, arrange numerically by house number.

Examples:	*Filed as:*
Jameson Answering Service, San Jose	Jameson Answering Service San Jose
Jameson Answering Service, Santa Clara	Jameson Answering Service Santa Clara
Jameson Answering Service, 402 First Street, Santa Cruz	Jameson Answering Service Santa Cruz First 402
Jameson Answering Service, 511 First Street, Santa Cruz	Jameson Answering Service Santa Cruz First 511

14. *Federal Governmental Names.* Federal governmental names are indexed in this order: *United States Government* (first three filing units), then subdivided by word or words in the title of the department, bureau, division, commission, or board.

Examples:	*Filed as:*			
FBI	United States Government Justice			
	Unit: 1	2	3	4
	Department (of) Federal Bureau (of)			
	Unit: 5		6	7
	Investigation			
	Unit: 8			
Social Security	United States Government Health			
Administration	Unit: 1	2	3	4
	Education (and) Welfare Social			
	Unit: 5		6	7
	Security Administration			
	Unit: 8	9		

WARNINGS:

1. *Obviously, cross-references will be needed for names that are commonly referred to, such as the* FBI *and* IRS.

Example: United States Government, Treasury Department (of) Internal Revenue Service

Cross-reference: IRS, See: United States Government, Treasury, etc.

2. *It is sometimes difficult to know the major division or department that an agency is a part of. Telephone directories, United States Government publications, and office files can frequently provide such information.*

15. *Other Governmental Names.* Other governmental names (state, county, city, town, or village) are indexed in this order: principal word or words in the name, followed by its governmental classification (state, county, or city) then the principal word or words in the name of the agency (department, board, or bureau).

Examples:	*Filed as:*		
California Department of	California State (of)		
Transportation	Unit: 1	2	
	Transportation Department (of)		
	Unit: 3		4
Marin County Housing	Marin County (of) Housing		
Authority	Unit: 1	2	3

		Authority	
	Unit:	4	

Mill Valley Parks and	Mill Valley City (of) Parks

Recreation Department	Unit:	1	2	3	4
		(and) Recreation Department (of)
	Unit:	5	6

16. *Foreign Governmental Names.* Foreign-language names are translated into English for indexing with the distinctive English name becoming the first filing unit, followed by the rest of the formal name of the government. Divisions are considered the same way as are United States governmental names.

Examples: **Filed as:**

Dominion of Canada,	Canada Dominion (of) Education
Department of	Unit:	1	2	3
Education	

		Department (of)
	Unit:	4

Republique Francaise,	France Republic (of) Air
Armee de l'Air	Unit:	1	2	3

		Force
	Unit:	4

17. *Names of Institutions and Organizations.* Names of institutions and organizations (colleges, universities, elementary and high schools, hotels and motels, and financial institutions), and names of associations, organizations, and unions are indexed and filed according to the distinctive words in the names. When the official name is not in common use, file by the commonly used name and cross-reference the official name. If names are the same, addresses will need to be considered.

Examples: *Filed as:*

Bank of Marin, Mill Valley	Bank (of) Marin Mill Valley
Bank of Marin, San Rafael	Bank (of) Marin San Rafael
Katherine Branson School	Branson Katherine School
Hotel Brown	Brown Hotel
CIO	C I O
	Cross-reference: Congress (of) Industrial Organizations
Eastern Illinois University	Eastern Illinois University

St. John Ursuline High School   Saint John Ursuline High
                                     School

St. Johns Lutheran School   Saint Johns Lutheran School

Follow these suggestions to help maintain files and records:

1. Keep filing up-to-date; do not allow papers to accumulate unfiled. Use odd moments to file.

2. Do not allow borrowed files to stay out for long periods of time. Devise a system to show who has each file and when it was borrowed; check to see that files are returned promptly.

3. Set up and file according to consistent rules. Authorities do not agree on many of the filing rules. Therefore, office files need to be maintained by following one set of rules; otherwise, there will be a great deal of confusion and difficulty in locating papers.

4. Follow a policy for either destroying or transferring inactive records. The length of time that material is retained in files is determined by the type of business or profession (the needs of the organization where the files are maintained) and legal considerations (the statute of limitations for accounts, for example).

5. Access to files by other office workers should be limited in order to preserve confidentiality of the files and to prevent records from being misfiled.

6. Replace dog-eared or worn folders; retype labels if they become illegible.

7. Store permanent records in fireproof files. It may be necessary to rent a bank safe deposit for little-used permanent records, such as deeds or car registrations.

8. Some secretaries use a tickler file, in addition to a desk calendar, to keep track of deadlines. Usually a tickler file is a card file arranged chronologically by months and days. The secretary checks the reminders in the daily guides at the beginning of each day and, as they are acted upon, removes the cards and places them in the back of the file.

Retrieval

There would be no point in storing information and records if they were not available to office workers when needed. Therefore, the process of locating information—retrieval—is an important phase of records control.

When the secretary removes documents from the file, it involves knowing which file is wanted (the label under which it is filed), finding and removing the document, and showing in the file that something has been removed and where it is.

When a file does not seem to be in its correct location, use these suggestions to help you locate it:

1. Be sure that the spelling of the file name is correct.
2. Check other spellings of the name (*Andersen/Anderson,* for example).
3. Look in folders in front of and behind the correct folder.
4. Look in the space in front of and behind the correct folder.
5. Look through the folder to see if the document is out of order.
6. Look at other filing units of the name. (If the name is *John Anderson,* look at *John* as well as *Anderson.*)
7. Look in your desk trays as well as desk trays of co-workers (ask first!) and your employer.

REPROGRAPHICS

Making more than one copy of a document can be done by one of many processes. The simplest and probably the least expensive method is the use of carbon paper, as it requires no special equipment. Special reprographic equipment—copiers and duplicators—however, is used in most offices. Technological advances in such equipment have increased the speed and ease of operation, improved copy quality, and lowered the cost per copy. When purchasing reprographic equipment, such factors as number of copies needed, quality of copies required, cost per copy, and time needed to make copies should be considered. It is also possible to lease equipment or to have copies made by commercial services.

Carbon Copies

Carbon paper and copying film can be used to make from 1 to 15 copies on the typewriter. Carbon paper for making more than one copy has been available as long as the typewriter and is well-known to all typists. Copying or film carbon is much newer; it is a polyester film coated with solvent ink. It can be used to make as many as 15 copies; carbon paper makes ten. It is more durable than carbon paper and does not wrinkle so easily. It also does not smear or smudge.

Select carbon paper by finish and weight, taking into consideration the number of copies usually made, the kind of typewriter (manual or electric) and the kind of type (pica or elite). Carbon paper comes in weights from four to ten pounds. Lightweight carbons make more copies; heavier papers make fewer copies but are easier to handle and will last longer. Electric typewriters, because they strike harder, usually require carbon paper with a hard finish; manual typewriters, a softer finish. Pica type, because it has larger characters than elite, requires a hard finish.

Carbon copies are usually made on lightweight paper, often colored, and called by various names—onionskin, manifold, or tissue.

A carbon pack—an original and a number of carbons—is assembled by placing a sheet of copy paper on the desk and a piece of carbon paper—glossy side down—on top of that. Add as many sets (paper plus a sheet of carbon paper) as you need. Put the paper for the original on the top of the pack. **Carbon pack**

Hold the pack so that the glossy sides of the carbon paper are toward you. Straighten the edges by tapping the pack. Insert the pack into the typewriter, keeping the glossy side toward you. Release the paper release lever before putting the pack through the machine; then, as the pack begins to show in front of the platen, lock the lever.

If the pack is thick, keep the sheets together by putting the flap of a large envelope or the fold of a sheet of paper over the top of the pack before inserting into the typewriter. Remove when the pack is in the typewriter. If necessary, straighten the carbon pack. To avoid wrinkling the carbon paper, release and reset the paper release lever.

Here are some suggestions for making carbon copies:

1. When several carbon copies are being made, rotate the carbon paper from front to back—the first carbon sheet in the pack becomes the last in the next typing, as the carbon paper nearest the original gets the greatest wear.

2. Use carbon paper that is longer than the original paper; it is easier to handle and can be reversed to distribute the use more evenly so that more copies can be made from the carbon paper.

3. Throw away carbon paper when copies become faint or when carbon paper has wrinkles or "trees" pressed into the paper.

4. Cut opposite corners of carbon paper to make separating easier.

5. Make carbon copies of correspondence rather than photocopies. Even though it is time-consuming to correct errors on car-

bon copies, it actually saves both time and money over making trips to the copying machine. Check with the dictator to see if strikeovers on carbon copies used for file purposes are acceptable.

6. Use the backs of letters that are being answered for the carbon copies of replies. It saves time and file space.

7. Producing carbon copies on a word processor is effortless. Since revisions are made electronically before inserting the carbon pack into the printer (typewriter), no corrections will need to be made on the typed page.

Photocopying

The copying machine has become commonplace in most offices. It quickly reproduces high-quality copy directly from the original, and it can reproduce on plain paper and in color. Although the quality of the copies is high, it is the most expensive way to make copies. The two most frequently used photocopying processes are the thermal and electrostatic.

Most copiers today use the electrostatic process. There are two types, plain paper copiers and coated paper copiers. Although some users believe the coated paper copiers produce better copies, the plain paper copiers are more widely used as they are less expensive to operate and will copy on any paper.

The thermographic machines involve the use of infrared or heat transfer processes. These machines were among the first to be operated; but today are used primarily to prepare stencils, direct-process masters, and overhead projector transparencies and to laminate documents.

Here are some suggestions for making photocopies:

1. Typing errors on copy for photocopying should be corrected by using liquid correction fluid (unless you are using a correcting typewriter). Do not erase, as an erasure will often appear gray when the page is photocopied.

2. Proofread all typing before removing it from the typewriter.

3. Copying forms (such as tax returns or legal documents) saves a great deal of time.

4. Be sure that you are not violating copyright laws when you do photocopying. In addition to copyrighted material, there are other items that may not be copied. They are: automobile registrations, United States currency and coins, certificates of deposit, bonds, postage stamps, passports, drivers' licenses, draft cards, immigration papers, and citizenship or naturalization papers.

5. The per-copy cost of photocopying is quite high, so do not make more copies than are necessary.

6. It may be necessary to keep a log sheet of persons using the copier so that the machine is not used indiscriminately.

7. Use 20-pound paper for best results; lighter-weight paper may create feeding problems.

Stencil Duplicating

The stencil method of duplication (usually called mimeograph) involves four elements: stencil, ink, paper, and stencil duplication machine. The machine prints through the stencil, a wax-coated tissue that allows ink to penetrate into the paper. The stencil is placed on the cylinder of the machine over an inked pad. Ink flows from the cylinder through openings in the stencil that have been cut by typing, handwriting, or drawing. Stencils can also be prepared from typed, printed, or pasted-up copy on an electronic stencil-making machine. Printing is done on thick paper. Several thousand copies can be made from one stencil; the quality of the stencil determines the number of copies it will make. Stencils can be cleaned and stored for future use.

Follow these suggestions for preparing stencils:

1. It may be necessary to prepare a dummy on plain paper before typing the stencil.

2. Before typing a stencil, clean the type of the machine. If typing a number of stencils, it will be necessary to clean the type often, unless the stencil has a plastic cover sheet.

3. Set the ribbon lever for stencil position and move the paper bail rollers to the left and right.

4. Use the plastic sheet over the stencil if you are using an electric machine; an electric typewriter may also require a lower pressure-control setting. Be sure that you place the cushion sheet between the backing sheet and the stencil.

5. Proofread each paragraph as you type because it is easier to align correctly when returning only a short distance.

Liquid or Spirit Duplicating

Spirit duplicators (or dittos) are based on the principle of dye transfer. A master set, consisting of a sheet of special carbon paper attached to a sheet of master paper, is used to make the copies. A thin protective sheet separates the two sheets until the master is written or typed upon. The prepared master is separated from the carbon and placed on the drum of a spirit duplicator. The alcohol-type liquid in the drum moistens the copy paper; and as the paper is fed through the machine, part of the carbon dye is dissolved and a copy is produced. The usual color of the carbon is purple; but other colors, including black, are available. One master will produce up to 300 copies. Ditto masters can also be produced by photocopiers using the thermographic process.

Follow these suggestions for making spirit masters:

1. Make corrections on the carbon side. For an error of a few letters, use a razor blade or sharp knife to scrape the carbon containing the error, then place a small piece of new carbon at the correction point and retype. Be sure to remove the carbon paper. If the error is longer than a few letters, place gummed correction tape over the typing to be corrected, insert new carbon, and retype. A correction pencil is also available. Making corrections on a master is messy and slow under any circumstances.

2. Proofread the master before removing it from the typewriter.

3. Masters can be stored and reused if only a few copies are run at a time. Be sure to put a protective sheet between the carbon and the master before storing.

4. Use special duplicator paper for making copies. Duplicator paper is fairly soft with a smooth surface; ordinary paper will give poor copies.

Offset Duplicating

Offset duplicating and the printing process known as *lithography* are the same process. Although the equipment is expensive and the operator of the machine needs special training, as many as 10,000 high-quality copies can be produced from one master. Recently small tabletop units have become available; this has increased the popularity of the process. Material is typed, written, or drawn on a paper, metal, or plastic master that is then transferred to a plate by a photochemical process. Offset masters can also be produced by certain photocopiers.

Follow these suggestions for preparing offset masters:

1. Because of the coating on the offset master, be very careful about touching the sheet and leaving fingerprints. Oil from hand lo-

tion can also cause smudges or fingerprints that will transfer in the duplicating process.

2. Type or write within the margins indicated on the master.

3. Do not bend or fold the master.

4. When typing a master, use an offset ribbon, offset carbon, or a carbon ribbon. Clean the type and adjust the ribbon pressure of an electric typewriter to a lower setting.

5. Corrections on the master can be made with an ordinary eraser, but a special offset eraser will do a better job. Erase lightly using just enough pressure to remove surface ink but not the coating of the master. Clean the eraser after each stroke to prevent ink from transferring to the master.

6. Always proofread before removing the master from the typewriter.

PROOFREADING AND CORRECTING

Proofreading

Before errors can be corrected, they must be found; this requires careful proofreading and checking. Most secretaries do their own proofreading; but if material is technical, long, or difficult, it may be necessary to proofread with a co-worker.

Proofreading should be done before the page is taken from the typewriter (errors are easier to correct), but a final check should also be made before work is submitted to the dictator or word originator.

Here are the steps that the secretary should follow in proofreading:

Steps in proofreading

1. *Check* the page for format and style, looking for such things as consistently indented paragraphs, uniformly typed headings, and correct horizontal spacing. If errors such as these are found, usually the page will need to be retyped.

2. *Scan* the page for obvious errors such as typographical, spacing, and word division errors.

3. *Read* the page for content and meaning. Errors such as a word omitted or a word typed twice, which are not usually found in scanning, can be found.

4. *Correct* any errors or retype the page if the errors cannot be corrected.

<u>WARNING:</u>

If you have difficulty finding typographical errors, proofread by the paper bail method. To do this, place the paper bail directly below the line you are reading and space a line at a time as you read.

Correcting

Unless you are fortunate enough to be typing on a word processing terminal or on a correcting typewriter, you should know how to make good neat corrections. With this skill, you can avoid much retyping.

There are a variety of correction products available. A trip to a stationery store can introduce you to them, and a little experimentation will show which products you prefer for the kind of work that you do.

For correcting originals and carbon copies, the following products are useful: typing or ink eraser with brush (also available in pencil form), correction fluid, chalk-back paper, soft eraser for carbon copies, erasing shield, erasing guard, chalk.

Steps in correcting errors on carbon copies

If you are correcting an error on a page of typing made with several carbon copies, follow these steps:

1. Roll the paper forward. If the error is at the bottom of the page, carefully roll the paper back so that the line of writing does not slip.

2. Place an eraser guard (a card or a piece of plastic or metal) between the original and the first copy, in front of the carbon sheet. Do not use bits of paper; they can be overlooked, and the carbon copy will then have bald spots on it.

3. Hold the paper firmly and erase the error on the original with the typing eraser. Erase lightly, using short vertical strokes, and erase each letter separately instead of scrubbing the entire error. Brush the eraser crumbs from the paper. If the paper has roughened or turned gray, go over the spot with chalk.

4. Insert the eraser guard between the first and second carbon copies, in front of the carbon sheet. Erase the error on the first carbon, using a soft pencil eraser. Brush the eraser crumbs from the paper. Repeat on each additional carbon.

5. If the eraser becomes dirty, remove the ink or carbon smudges by rubbing the eraser on clean paper. If the ink or smudges do not come off the eraser, use an emery board or sandpaper.

6. Return the paper to the line of writing and strike in the correction, using a lighter pressure-control setting.

7. When erasing errors on paper that has been removed from the typewriter, use an eraser shield (a credit-card-sized piece of plastic or thin steel with various-sized openings). Place one of the openings of the eraser shield over the error and erase through the opening; in this way the correct typing is covered and protected from erasing.

For quick corrections on such materials as rough drafts, use either chalk-back correction paper, following the manufacturer's directions, or correction fluid, which can be painted over the error. The correction fluid usually is white, but it also comes in colors to match colored paper. Although the correction fluid should be used for corrections on material that will be photocopied, it should not be used on original typing as the corrections are quite obvious. The disadvantage of chalk-back paper is that it tends to flake off and the error shows through. Therefore, use other correction methods when the appearance is important.   QUICK CORRECTIONS

A quick method of editing and changing placement of typed material is to cut sections apart and paste in the desired order on another sheet of paper. Typing can also be covered with a gummed correction tape.

Crowding and spreading letters on an electric typewriter with a single element (such as an IBM Selectric) are easily accomplished if the machine has a half-space key (see the instruction manual). If the machine does not have such a key, follow these directions: CROWDING AND SPREADING

Crowding:

If a letter has been omitted in a word—for example, *the* has been typed for *they*—the missing letter can be crowded into the space using these steps:

1. Erase the incorrect word (*the* in this instance).
2. Move the carrier or element to the position of the first letter of the word.
3. With the index finger of the right hand, push the right side of the carrier to the left until it is positioned in the correct spot (about a half space).
4. Type the first letter—*t*.
5. Repeat the procedure for the rest of the word.

Spreading:

If an extra letter has been typed in a word (*they* for *the*), spread the letters in the extra space using these steps:

1. Erase the incorrect word (*they* in this instance).
2. Move the carrier to the position of the first letter of the word.
3. With the index finger of the left hand push the left side of the carrier to the right until it is positioned in the correct spot.
4. Type the first letter—*t*.
5. Repeat the procedure for the rest of the word.

REINSERTING PAGES

Always proofread typed material before removing it from the typewriter; it is much easier to correct, particularly if a number of carbon copies are involved. If it is necessary to reinsert a page, follow these steps:

1. Reinsert the page into the machine.
2. Using the paper release and then the variable line spacer, align the typing on the alignment scale. This can be accomplished by aligning an *i*, an *l*, or a period with the white lines of the scale.
3. Put the ribbon in stencil position and test the alignment with a very light stroke (use the zero setting on an electric typewriter).
4. Adjust the alignment if necessary.
5. Move the ribbon back into typing position and type the correction.

WARNING:

Typewriters vary, so experiment with yours to find the relationship between the typing and the alignment scale. Type a word such as will and see where it positions on the scale.

CARE OF THE TYPEWRITER

A well-maintained typewriter is an important part of any secretary's efficiency. Although the secretary does not ordinarily make mechanical repairs, there are things that a secretary can do to keep the typewriter clean and working well.

Here are some suggestions:

1. Check the typeface daily to see that the type is clean. If the machine has a carbon ribbon, cleaning the type will not be neces-

sary. If the machine has a fabric ribbon and the type appears dirty, use a stiff brush to clean the type. On a machine with a typing element, remove the element in order to brush the type. (See the typewriter instruction booklet.) On a machine with type bars, brush toward you and away from the type basket. Use light easy strokes. Brushing is usually sufficient; but products such as liquids, plastics, and coated sheets can help you clean the type.

2. Dust the typewriter daily. Use a dry, lint-free cloth or a soft brush to dust the exterior parts. Dust under the typewriter as well.

3. Clean the carriage rails and platen once a week. Do not use oil unless the manufacturer of the typewriter recommends it. Cleaners such as denatured alcohol or a coated sheet can be used.

4. Cover the typewriter at the end of the day.

5. Ribbon changing has become greatly simplified because most ribbons are now in cartridge form. The instruction manual of the typewriter shows how to change the ribbon. If a manual is not available and you cannot get one from the manufacturer, draw a diagram of the threading of the ribbon before removing it. Often the packaging for a new ribbon provides a diagram. Then insert a new ribbon in the same position as the old. Be sure the new ribbon is made for your brand and model of typewriter.

6. Arrange with a local agency to service your typewriter after it is no longer covered by warranty.

WARNING:

Liquid type cleaners should be used only on manual typewriters or electric typewriters with type bars. In fact, liquid cleaners can be harmful to many parts of any electric typewriter. Never use a pin to clean carbon from the typeface.

2. Business Communications and Reports

BUSINESS LETTERS, MEMORANDUMS, AND CARDS

Writing Business Letters and Memorandums

Business letters are one of the most common and important ways that businesses communicate. The secretary is often responsible for writing much of the routine correspondence such as letters of acknowledgment, inquiry, transmittal, and order.

The difference between a letter and an interoffice memorandum is that a letter goes outside of a company and a memo is kept within a company, even though an interoffice memo may go to branch offices in other cities. Businesses also use post cards for quick short messages.

The business letter consists of three parts: opening, body, and closing. The opening starts with a clear-cut statement of what the letter is about—it gets to the point immediately. The body of the letter develops the opening and adds any needed details. The closing is a summary of the letter; it is a short and courteous goodbye.

Business letters are written for three purposes: to get the receiver to respond, to give information, and to build goodwill. Some letters serve all three purposes.

The interoffice memo follows the same writing principles as a business letter; however, it differs in format (see page 49).

A business timesaver is the form letter. A form letter is a previously written standardized letter to which the name and address of the recipient have been added (for example, a letter to a new customer thanking that person for opening an account). A form letter can also be composed from a number of previously written paragraphs—usually the paragraphs are numbered, and the secretary or dictator selects the appropriate paragraphs by number. Word processing is an excellent way of producing form letters quickly, with the advantage that each letter is originally typed.

Suggestions for writing business letters and memos:

1. The writing of any piece of business correspondence should be planned. If you are answering a letter, read and mark the letter that is being answered, then gather any information that you will need. If you are initiating the letter, determine the purpose of the letter—why it is being written—then collect all of the necessary background information.

2. Do not make a rough draft of a letter first in longhand; instead learn to dictate or to compose at the typewriter.

3. As you plan the letter, be sure to keep in mind the purpose of the letter.

4. With the exception of bad news letters, get to the point of the letter in the opening sentence. In bad news letters, first explain the bad news and, if possible, offer an alternative.

5. Never tell the reader something that is already known. An opening sentence such as "I have before me your letter of March 28 in which you ask the price of our new calculator" is unnecessary.

6. The closing of a letter should not contain any information that has not already been given.

7. Do not use sentence fragments for either the opening or closing of a letter. Fragments are such things as "In regard to your letter of the 15th" and "Hoping to hear from you soon."

8. Keep sentences and paragraphs short; they are easier to read.

9. Be sure that you have included all necessary information. Be sure that names, addresses, facts, figures, and dates are accurate.

10. The tone of the letter should always be courteous and friendly; never write a letter in anger.

11. Orient the tone of the letter to the reader; use "you" instead of "I" or "we."

12. Make it easy for the reader to reply by telling him or her exactly what kind of reply you would like.

13. The appearance of the letter often determines whether a letter will be read. Be sure the letter is attractively placed on the letterhead, that it contains no strikeovers or typographical errors, and that it looks easy to read—keep paragraphs short and preferably write letters of less than one page.

Typing Business Letters and Memorandums

A well-placed letter must be planned. Before it can be planned, the typist must know the mechanics of the typewriter.

Type size

Know the size of your typewriter. *Elite* type has 12 spaces to an inch of type; *pica* has 10 spaces to an inch of type. Usually, there are 6 vertical lines to an inch. Therefore, an 8½ by 11-inch letter-head sheet has 85 horizontal spaces of pica type or 102 spaces of elite type and 66 vertical lines. If you do not know whether a machine has elite or pica type type 10 or 12 x's and measure or look at the margin scale on the front of the typewriter.

Letter placement

Learn to estimate the number of words written in a column of shorthand notes (handwriting sizes vary) or the length of a letter from the marked index slip of a transcribing machine. Use the chart below to assist you.

| SIZE OF LETTER | WORDS IN LETTER | LENGTH OF LINE | | |
		INCHES	ELITE SPACES	PICA SPACES
Short	Under 100	4	50	40
Medium	100–200	5	60	50
Long	201–300	6	70	60
2-page	Over 300	6	70	60

Such things as variations in paragraphing, the presence of tabulations in the letter, and the addition of attention and subject lines affect the actual length of the letter.

The date is typed two to six lines below the last line of the letterhead (the usual practice is to place it three lines below). Spacing varies with the design of the letterhead, the length of the letter, and company policy. Notice from the chart that a writing line is not less than four inches or more than six.

Many offices save time by using the same length of writing line for all letters. If you wish to do this, follow this chart:

| SIZE OF LETTER | WORDS IN LETTER | LENGTH OF LINE | | | LINES BETWEEN DATE AND INSIDE ADDRESS |
		INCHES	ELITE SPACES	PICA SPACES	
Short	Under 100	5	60	50	10–12
Medium	100–200	5	60	50	6–8
Long	Over 200	5	60	50	3–4

Do not double space the body of the letter unless it is extremely short and consists of only one paragraph.

Letter styles presently used are based on a "block" style. A **Letter styles** *full-block* letter begins every line of the letter at the left margin. *Modified block* centers the date or puts it to the right, blocks or indents the paragraphs of the body of the letter, centers the closing or puts it to the right, and begins all other lines of the letter at the left margin. Examples of these and other letter styles begin on page 50.

The two most frequently used styles of punctuation in business **Punctuation** letters are *mixed* and *open*. In the mixed style, a colon is placed **styles** after the salutation and a comma after the complimentary close; open style means that there is no punctuation after the salutation or complimentary close. The tendency in computer typing of inside addresses is to omit punctuation.

The standard letter-sized stationery measures 8½ by 11 inches. **Stationery** Other sizes include the half-sized letterhead (8½ by 5½ or 5½ by 8½) for very short letters and the 7¼ by 10½ (called Monarch or Executive) used for either personal or professional letters. Envelope sizes are the Nos. 6¾ (3⅝ by 6½ inches) and 10 (4⅛ by 9½ inches) with a No. 7 (3⅞ by 7½ inches) to accompany the Monarch-sized stationery.

Bond paper is used for letters. The weight and the fiber content of the paper determine its cost and quality. Letterhead stationery is usually 16-, 20-, or 24-pound weight with at least 25 percent cotton fiber content.

Snap-out forms are becoming more widely used in business offices. Each pack of forms consists of a letterhead and any number of sheets for carbon copies. The alternate sheets of paper and carbon paper are fastened at the bottom. When something has been typed, the carbon paper is snapped out and discarded. Such forms are available with or without the company letterhead.

Carbon paper is available in various weights and finishes. The number of carbon copies ordinarily made, the weight of the paper, and the kind of typewriter used determine the type of carbon paper needed (see page 24).

Parts of the Business Letter

Because business letters are ordinarily typed on letterhead **Date** stationery that includes the name and address of the firm or person, the date is the only part of the heading that the typist need supply.

The date is usually typed a double space below the last line of the letterhead. The letter style and the letterhead determine where the date is typed on the page: the date may be blocked, centered, begun at center, or typed even with the right margin. There should be at least four line spaces between the date and the next part of the letter.

WARNINGS:

1. *Do not abbreviate the month or use all numbers to express the date (as in 2/14/84). Type it as: February 14, 1984.*
2. *Do not place a period after the date.*
3. *In military correspondence and in correspondence from foreign countries, the day precedes the month and no punctuation is used.*

Example: 14 February 1984

4. *If a letterhead is not used, type the address of the writer above the date, starting approximately two inches from the top of the page.*

Example: 342 Erie Drive
                Chicago, IL 60607
                February 14, 1984

Mailing notation   A mailing notation indicates that a letter is being sent by other than regular first-class mail—for example, *special delivery* or *registered mail*.

The mailing notation is usually typed in all capital letters a double space above the inside address. It may also be placed a double space below the date at the right margin or a double space below the identification initials. It is more noticeable—and therefore preferable—to type the mailing notation at the top of the letter rather than at the bottom. It is also placed on the envelope, usually below the stamp position.

Other notations   Such notations as *Personal, Confidential, Please Forward,* and *Hold for Arrival* are also typed above the inside address. They are usually underscored but not typed in all capitals. Should there be a mailing notation as well as one of these notations, type the mailing notation first and the other notation a double space below it. These notations should also appear on the envelope, either in the upper left corner or after the addressee's name in the address. Do not type a notation in the lower left corner because it will interfere with the machine sorting by the post office.

The inside address includes the complete name and address of **Inside** the person or firm receiving the letter (the addressee). It should agree **address** with the envelope address in style and form. Therefore, the inside address should be typed to conform to the changes required by the scanners used in large post offices for machine sorting of the mail (see page 46).

Follow these suggestions for typing inside addresses:

1. Type the inside address four to six lines below the date. If there are notations, there may be more than six lines between the date and the inside address.

2. Ordinarily the inside address should not contain abbreviations other than *Mr., Mrs., Ms.,* other titles preceding complete names, and the two-letter state abbreviations. Firm names may include abbreviations if the letterhead of the firm contains such abbreviations. (See pages 195–199 for more detailed information on abbreviations.)

3. *All* personal names in inside addresses are preceded by titles; if there is no specific business or professional title, use *Mr., Mrs., Miss,* or *Ms.* (For addressing certain officials, see pages 217–221.)

4. Type ZIP Codes one space after the city and state.

5. If the letter is to be sent within the same city or town from which the letter is written, use the full name of the city or town and its ZIP Code.

6. When addressing mail to foreign countries, be sure to copy the addresses exactly as they are given to you. Many such addresses differ from American styles. In some countries, for example, the house number follows the street name. Type the name of the country on a separate line, preferably in all capitals (which is easier to read). With the exception of U.S.S.R. (Union of Soviet Socialist Republics), do not abbreviate the names of foreign countries. Notice, too, that many foreign addresses now include the equivalent of our ZIP Codes.

Examples:

```
Claridge's              Mr. Vladimir Blok
Brook Street            2/4 Sverdlov Square
London W1A2JQ           Moscow
ENGLAND                 U.S.S.R.
```

WARNINGS:

1. *Always verify the spellings of names and accuracy of addresses. Errors can cause delay in mail delivery.*

2. Try to have the lines of the inside address of equal length. This can often be done by juggling the title of the addressee—which may be placed after the person's name, before the firm name, or on a line by itself.

3. If the addressee's title or the firm name in the inside address is long, either or both may be written on two lines. Indent the second line two spaces.

Examples: Mr. James Allen, Executive Secretary
          and Assistant to the President
     Martin & Simmons, Inc.
     2140 Commonwealth Avenue
     Boston, MA 02109

     The North American Technical
          Data Processing Company
     742 Battery Street
     New York, NY 10001

Attention line   The purpose of the attention line is to speed delivery of the mail by directing it to one person or department within a firm. Use of the attention line is disappearing; it is preferable to address the letter to a person or department within a company.

The attention line may be placed a double space below the inside address or, if the typist needs to save space, to the right of the inside address. It may be blocked or centered. It is preferable to spell out the word *Attention,* and a colon may follow. A title should precede a name in the attention line. Since the attention line is part of the address, it is typed on the envelope under the return address or after the addressee's name.

Example: Davis & Hall, Inc.
     505 Fifth Avenue
     New York, NY 10015

     Attention Mr. John Scott <u>or</u> Attention: Mr. John
     Scott

     Gentlemen:

WARNING:

A letter with an attention line should always be addressed to a firm, and the salutation should be either Gentlemen or Ladies and Gentlemen.

The salutation agrees with the inside address—that is, if the **Salutation** letter is addressed to a firm, the salutation should be *Gentlemen*. (*Dear Sirs* is out of date.) If the letter is addressed to a person, the salutation should be *Dear Mr., Mrs.,* or *Ms. Smith,* rather than *Dear Sir* or *Dear Madam*. Many business people object to the use of the salutation *Gentlemen* to a firm consisting of both men and women. The substitution of *Ladies and Gentlemen* seems to be gaining acceptance, although some people regard it as awkward. If a letter is addressed to an individual whose name and sex are unknown—that is, to a title such as *sales manager* or *personnel director*— the salutation choice again becomes a problem. A substitute such as *Dear Sales Manager* is a suggestion. Another possibility is the elimination of the salutation from the letter as the Administrative Management Society suggests in its Simplified letter style (see page 55). In general, choice of salutation is decided within a firm by those who are authorized to determine letter style and other letter-writing mechanics. In a small office, such things are decided by the employer or the secretary.

Follow these suggestions for typing salutations:

1. The salutation has a double space both above and below it and always begins at the left margin. If mixed punctuation is used, a colon is placed after the salutation.

2. Capitalize the first word of the salutation as well as any proper nouns used in it. Do not abbreviate titles other than *Mr., Mrs., Ms.,* and *Messrs.*

3. This is a list of salutations in order of decreasing formality:

```
Sir
My dear Sir
Dear Sir
My dear Mr. Black
Dear Mr. Black
My dear Paul
Dear Paul
```

See pages 217–221 for salutations used when writing to certain officials and dignitaries.

The subject line tells what the letter is about. It is useful for filing **Subject line** purposes or for quick identification without having to read the letter.

Follow these suggestions for typing subject lines:

1. The subject line goes between the salutation and the body of the letter. It is typed with a double space above and below, but it

may be placed on the same line as the salutation if the typist is try-ing to save space. Like the attention line, it may be blocked, in-dented, or centered.

2. The word *Subject* is followed by a colon. It may be typed in all capitals or with only the first letter capitalized. (Sometimes it is omitted.) If the typist prefers, the entire subject line may be typed in all capitals or underscored. In legal correspondence either *In re* or *Re* may be used in place of the word *Subject*.

Example: Gentlemen:

SUBJECT: Your Order No. 43621 (<u>or</u>
<u>Subject: Your Order No. 43621</u>)

Body The body of the letter is the message. Paragraphs should be short in order to make the letter easier to read. Check the rules of word division (pages 214–215), and punctuate and spell correctly.

Complimentary close The complimentary close is a short courteous phrase used to end a letter.

Follow these suggestions for typing complimentary closes:

1. The complimentary close is placed a double space below the body of the letter. Depending upon the letter style being used, it is blocked, centered, or typed flush with the right margin.

2. Only the first word is capitalized.

3. If mixed punctuation is used, a comma follows the compli-mentary close.

4. If you are using the Simplified letter style, be sure to omit the complimentary close.

5. The following is a list of complimentary closes in order of decreasing formality:

Yours respectfully
Very respectfully yours
Respectfully yours

Yours truly
Very truly yours
Yours very truly

Sincerely yours
Sincerely

Cordially yours
Cordially

See pages 217–221 for complimentary closes used in writing to certain officials and dignitaries.

There are many styles for the signature of a business letter. **Signature** Usually a signature includes the penwritten signature of the person writing the letter and the typed name and title of the signer. The firm name is usually not included in the signature if a letterhead is used, nor does the title of the person signing the letter need to be repeated if the letterhead already gives that information. However, if the letter consists of two pages, include the firm name on the second page to make identification easier if the pages become separated.

Follow these suggestions for typing signatures:

1. The signature line begins a double space below the complimentary close. Regardless of the style, there should be at least three blank lines for the longhand signature of the person writing the letter (more, if the handwriting of the signer is large). The signature is usually blocked—but may also be indented—under the complimentary close.

2. *Ms., Mrs.,* and *Miss* are the only courtesy titles typed before names. Never put *Mr.* or any other title before a man's name in a signature line. Abbreviations of academic degrees and professional ratings are typed after the signer's name. They are not included in penwritten signatures.

Examples: Sincerely yours   Sincerely yours

John Harper   *Ann Martin*

John Harper, C. P. A.   Ann Martin, Ph. D.

3. An unmarried woman may write *Miss* in parentheses in her penwritten signature, or she may include it in the typed signature. The tendency is to omit *Miss* altogether unless her given name is one that might be mistaken for a masculine name (for example, Francis or Marion).

Examples: Cordially yours   Cordially yours

Mary Hastings   *(Miss) Mary Hastings*

Mary Hastings

4. A professional woman or a businesswoman who is married may include *Ms.* or *Mrs.* in parentheses before her penwritten signa-

ture, or her typed signature may include *Ms.* or *Mrs.* Her social name—her husband's name preceded by *Mrs.*—is usually not used in business.

Examples: Cordially yours   Cordially yours

Mary Hastings Lee   *(Mrs.) Mary Hastings Lee*

Mrs. Mary Hastings Lee

5. If no title precedes a woman's signature, *Miss* is assumed.

6. A secretary signing a letter for her employer should use one of these styles:

Cordially yours   Cordially yours

Mary Hastings   *David H. Hall*
                           m. h.

Secretary to Mr. Hall   David H. Hall

If the person signing the letter is not the secretary but is signing for someone else, one of these styles should be used:

Cordially yours   Cordially yours

Jane Farrell   *David H. Hall*
                   J.F.

For Mr. Hall   David H. Hall

Identification (or reference) initials   The identification initials are the dictator's initials followed by those of the typist. Some companies use only the initials of the typist. The initials are typed at the left margin and generally a double space below the last line of the letter. There are many styles for typing these initials. No one style is preferable unless an office wishes to make one uniform throughout the company.

Examples: DHW/MH   DHW/mh   DHW:mh   MH

Enclosure notation   If something is being enclosed in the envelope with the letter, note this by typing the word *Enclosure* one or two lines below the identification initials. This notation may be abbreviated *Enc.* or *Encl.,* and it may be plural if more than one item is being enclosed. Some typists indicate the number of enclosures after the word; some list the item or items being enclosed.

Examples: `Enclosures     Encs. 3     Enclosure:   Check`

Carbon-copy notation

The initials *cc* typed one or two lines below the identification initials (or below the enclosure notation, if any) mean that a carbon copy of the letter is being sent to the person or persons who are listed after *cc*. Because the copy is often a photocopy, some secretaries are using *c* only. A title (such as *Mr.*) should precede the name. Ordinarily the surname is enough identification for the carbon-copy notation. If it is not, include the complete name. Sometimes the address is given to assist the typist in sending the carbon copy or if necessary for filing. Place a colored check mark next to the name on the carbon copy before sending it to that person. This indicates that the person named was intended to receive the carbon, and it can take the place of a covering letter.

The initials *bcc,* meaning *blind carbon copy,* are used when the addressee is not to be informed that copies of the letter are being sent to anyone else. The *bcc* notation may also be typed in the upper left-hand corner of a carbon copy. Although the original should not carry this notation, be sure that all file copies do.

Examples: `cc Mr. Martin          bcc Mr. Williams`
`             Mrs. Ryan          cc: Mr. James Green`

Postscript

In business letters, postscripts are no longer used as afterthoughts; instead, they are used for emphasis. If it is not brief, a postscript may lose its effectiveness.

A postscript is typed a double space below the last line of the letter, and it is indented or blocked to agree with the style of the letter. The letters *P.S.* need not be included.

Envelope

The installation of Optical Character Readers and other mail-sorting machines in many post offices has, of course, affected the addressing of mail. So that machines will be able to read and sort the mail and thereby increase the speed of mail delivery, envelopes must be addressed so that they can be read by the machines.

Follow these suggestions for typing envelopes:

1. Envelopes must be addressed this way: All addresses are single-spaced and blocked; nothing is typed in the lower left corner; the official two-letter state abbreviations (see page 224) are used; the last line of the address contains three items—city, state, and ZIP Code.

2. Incoming mail is sorted by programming the machines to read the next to the bottom line of the address. This line contains the address where the mail is to be delivered (usually a street address or post office box number). If the mail is addressed to occupants of a multi-unit building, the number of the apartment, room, suite, or other unit appears after the street address and on the same line.

3. The Postal Service recommends that type fonts such as italic and script be avoided, that the typewriter keys be clean and the ribbon dark, and that the address be typed in a straight line and not on a slant. Envelopes should be rectangular in shape and the size no smaller than 3½ by 5 inches and no larger than 6⅛ by 11½ inches. Envelopes smaller than 3½ by 5 inches will be returned to the sender, and envelopes larger than 6⅛ by 11½ will require a surcharge.

4. Stationery should be white or pastel colored, since dark-colored stationery does not provide enough contrast for the machine to read the address.

5. The Postal Service has also recommended that envelopes be addressed in all capitals and without punctuation, but this computer style is not usual.

6. If window envelopes are used, make sure there is at least one-quarter inch between the address and the left, right, and bottom edges of the window, whatever the position of the insert.

7. An easy-to-remember rule for addressing envelopes is:
     Down 14 lines and over 4 inches for No. 10 envelopes
     Down 12 lines and over 2 inches for No. 6¾ envelopes
     (used for one-page letters).

If the address is long, it may be necessary to begin the first line further to the left. These margin allowances will keep the address within the area of the envelope that can be read by the Postal Service's scanner.

8. Type any instructions such as *Personal, Please Forward,* or *Attention* either below the return address or on the line after the addressee's name. Mailing instructions such as *Special Delivery* or *Registered* are typed below the stamp position, approximately nine or ten spaces from the top of the envelope.

9. When a plain envelope is used, type the sender's name and address in the upper left corner.

Letters of More Than One Page

If a letter requires more than one page, follow these suggestions:

1. Use a six-inch writing line for the letter.

2. Leave at least a one-inch margin at the bottom of the first page.

3. Type the second and succeeding pages on plain paper of a quality comparable to that of the letterhead.

4. Have at least two lines of a paragraph at the bottom of a page and at the top of the succeeding page.

5. On the second and succeeding pages, type a reference line or heading at least an inch from the top of the paper. This line should include three things: the name of the addressee, the page number, and the date. The heading may be blocked to the left on three lines, or it may be centered across the page on one line. Allow at least three blank lines above the body of the letter. This same heading can be used for a two-page memo.

Examples: Mr. William Scott
Page 2
February 14, 19---

or

Mr. William Scott   2   February 14, 19---

Folding and Inserting Letters

To fold a letter to fit the No. 6¾ envelope:

1. Fold the lower half of the letter to within a half inch of top; crease.

2. Fold from right to left a little more than a third of the width; crease.

3. Fold from left to right, leaving a half-inch margin at the right; crease.

4. Insert the last fold into the envelope first.

**No. 6¾
envelope**

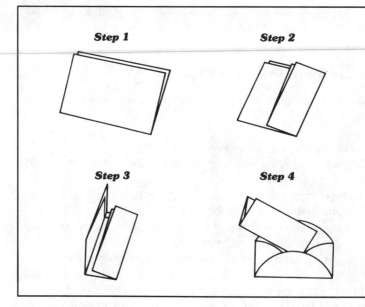

No. 10 Envelope

To fold a letter to fit the No. 10 envelope:

1. Fold the lower third of the letter; crease.
2. Fold from the top down, leaving a half-inch margin from the first fold; crease.
3. Insert the last fold into the envelope first.

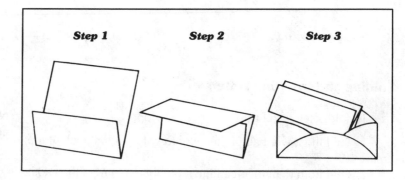

Window envelope

Letters to fit window envelopes are folded so that the inside address of the letter appears through the window and the envelope does not need to be addressed.

To fold a letter to fit a window envelope:

1. Fold the lower third of the letter; crease.
2. Fold the upper edge of the letter *back* to the first fold so that the inside address will be on the outside; crease.
3. Insert the letter so that the address appears in the window.

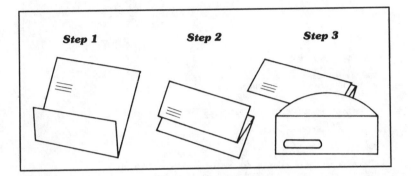

Step 1   **Step 2**   **Step 3**

Interoffice Letters

Letters within a firm are typed on interoffice memo forms that usually contain, in addition to the letterhead, four items in the heading: *To, From, Date,* and *Subject.* Personal titles (*Mr., Mrs., Ms., Miss*) are omitted in the heading. There is no salutation, complimentary close, or signature. The writing line is usually a long one— six inches. Triple space between the last line of the heading and the first line of the body. Identification initials and other notations are typed a double space below the body of the letter.

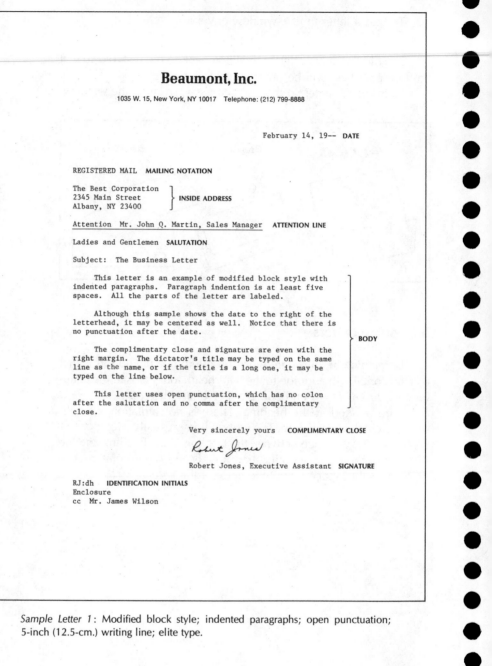

Beaumont, Inc.

1035 W. 15, New York, NY 10017   Telephone: (212) 799-8888

February 14, 19-- **DATE**

REGISTERED MAIL **MAILING NOTATION**

The Best Corporation
2345 Main Street   **INSIDE ADDRESS**
Albany, NY 23400

Attention Mr. John Q. Martin, Sales Manager   **ATTENTION LINE**

Ladies and Gentlemen **SALUTATION**

Subject: The Business Letter

    This letter is an example of modified block style with
indented paragraphs. Paragraph indention is at least five
spaces. All the parts of the letter are labeled.

    Although this sample shows the date to the right of the
letterhead, it may be centered as well. Notice that there is
no punctuation after the date.

    The complimentary close and signature are even with the
right margin. The dictator's title may be typed on the same
line as the name, or if the title is a long one, it may be
typed on the line below.

    This letter uses open punctuation, which has no colon
after the salutation and no comma after the complimentary
close.

BODY

      Very sincerely yours   **COMPLIMENTARY CLOSE**

Robert Jones, Executive Assistant **SIGNATURE**

RJ:dh   **IDENTIFICATION INITIALS**
Enclosure
cc Mr. James Wilson

Sample Letter 1: Modified block style; indented paragraphs; open punctuation; 5-inch (12.5-cm.) writing line; elite type.

DARWIN INSURANCE CO.

1928 Gloucester St., Boston, MA 02115 617/235-4179

November 14, 19--

CONFIDENTIAL

Miss Irene K. Masters
407 East 12 Street
Evanston, IL 62204

Dear Miss Masters

This is an example of a short letter typed on a
four-inch writing line. It is typed in modified
block style.

Because it is a short letter and written on a
full-sized letterhead, it has the shortest writing line that can be used. Contrast the placement and appearance of this letter with the one
that follows; that letter is the same size but
is written on a longer writing line.

Do you prefer the appearance of this letter?
Which letter is more nearly centered? Perhaps
it is more work to change margin widths for each
letter, but the appearance is, in most instances,
worth the extra effort.

Sincerely,

Dorothy Fowler
Dorothy Fowler
Administrative Secretary

DF/mt

Sample Letter 2: Short letter typed on a 4-inch (10-cm.) writing line; modified block
style; open punctuation; elite type. *Confidential* notation.

GIROUX PAPER SUPPLIES

Westfield Loop Road, Houston, TX 77006
Telephone: 713/671-9324

November 14, 19--

Miss Irene K. Masters
407 East 12 Street
Evanston, IL 62204

Dear Miss Masters

This is a short letter, typed on a five-inch writing line.
The five-inch line is used when all letters are typed with
the same line length, regardless of the number of words in
the body.

Because this style tends to make a letter look flat, it
is not as attractive as one with a variable line length.
Using the same line length for every business letter typed
does, however, save the secretary's time.

You or your employer will need to decide whether a more
attractive letter is worth the time required to type it.

Sincerely

Dorothy Fowler

Dorothy Fowler
Administrative Secretary

DF/ap

Sample Letter 3: Short letter typed on a 5-inch (12.5-cm.) writing line; modified
block style; open punctuation; elite type.

Nicotra Construction Co.   39 Indiana Blvd., Baltimore MD 21401   Telephone: (301) 533-3606

February 14, 19--

Crown Development Company
745 Seventh Avenue West
Seattle, WA 96200

Attention Mr. Fredericks

Ladies and Gentlemen

This is a full-block letter; every line of the letter is
begun at the left margin. Although it speeds the typing
of the letter to use full-block style, the letterhead needs
to be planned for it, or the result may be a letter that
does not have a balanced appearance. For example, a
letterhead with printing on the left side of the page
would present an awkward appearance if used with full-
block style. A full-block letter cannot be double spaced.

Notice that the attention line in this letter is underscored. Remember when using an attention line that the
salutation is always addressed to the firm, not to the
person whose name is in the attention line.

If several persons are to receive carbon copies, their
names are listed after the carbon-copy notation. They are
listed either by rank or in alphabetical order.

Yours very truly

Robert T. Walker

Robert T. Walker, Director

RTW/DW

cc Mr. Elliot
    Mr. Holmes
    Mr. Scott

Sample Letter 4: Full-block style; open punctuation; 6-inch (15-cm.) writing line;
pica type.

BOB'S RECORDS

17 Blankenship Circle, Richmond, VA 23227
Telephone: (804) 505-9133

Mr. Lee Walker, Manager   June 14, 19--
Wilson and Martin, Inc.
9748 Orange Way
Miami, FL 33101

Dear Lee:

           SUBJECT: THE SQUARE-BLOCK LETTER

This is a square-block letter. It is attractive and is a
space saver in that more words can be written on the page
with this style than with any other style.

Use a five- or six-inch writing line. Begin the first line
of the letter two or three lines above the first line of the
inside address of other letter styles.

The date is placed even with the right margin on the same
line as the name of the addressee; the identification initials are also placed even with the right margin on the
same line as the last line of the letter (or one line above
if the enclosure notation is necessary). Mixed punctuation
is used--a colon is placed after the salutation and a comma
after the complimentary close.

The attention and subject lines may be blocked or centered.

Sincerely,

James T. Sherman

James T. Sherman, Director   JTS:DW

P. S. Since the postscript no longer indicates something
added to the letter, it is now used for emphasis or to attract
attention.

Sample Letter 5: Square-block style; mixed punctuation; 5-inch (12.5-cm.) writing
line; elite type; postscript shown.

Galleria Shoes   1127 Glenbriar Ave., Tampa, FL 33608   Telephone: (813) 917-6788

February 14, 19--

Mr. Peter L. Rankin
490 Alder Street
Santa Fe, NM 87501

SIMPLIFIED LETTER STYLE

This is a letter style adopted by the Administrative Management Society (formerly the National Office Management Association) for use in business-letter writing.

It has these features:

1. All lines are blocked at the left margin.

2. The inside address is typed at least three blank lines below the date.

3. The salutation and complimentary close are omitted.

4. The subject line is typed in all caps a triple space below the inside address. Triple space from the subject line to the body of the letter.

5. Numbered items are blocked at the left margin, but unnumbered items are indented five spaces.

6. The writer's name and title are typed in all caps at least five spaces below the body.

7. Identification initials, consisting of the typist's initials only, are typed a double space below the writer's name. Enclosure or carbon-copy notations are typed below the initials.

This letter form does save space and time, and thus it helps cut correspondence costs.

Robert T. Randolph

ROBERT T. RANDOLPH - DIRECTOR

dw
Enclosure

Sample Letter 6: Simplified letter style; 6-inch (15-cm) writing line; elite type.

Gould Brothers, Inc.

Ames, IA · Lansing, MI · Topeka, KS

January 15, 19--

Mr. Benjamin R. Wilson
President, Wilson & Dawson
432 South High Street
Denver, CO 56270

Dear Mr. Wilson

                    Subject: The Two-Page Letter

A letter that has over 300 words will require two pages. Even shorter
letters may require two or more pages if there are quotations, tabulations, or enumerations. The size of type being used and the number
of paragraphs will also affect the length of the letter.

If the letter requires two pages, use a six-inch writing line and
margins of at least an inch at the bottom of the first page and at
the top of the second. Use a letterhead for the first page and plain
paper of comparable quality for the second and succeeding pages.

The reference line or heading is typed at the top of the second page.
It can be blocked at the left margin on three lines or spread across
the page on one line. It contains three things:

            1. The name of the addressee
            2. The page number
            3. The date

Triple space before going on to the body of the letter.

Enumerations can be made to stand out by indenting both the left and
right margins and numbering the items. Quoted material should be
indented.

Tabulated material should also be indented, as in this example:

This is a breakdown of letters mailed from our office for the past two
months:

	June	July
First Class	1,245	1,328
Airmail	1,516	1,429
Total	2,761	2,757

Sample Letter 7: Two-page letter; modified block style; block paragraphs; open
punctuation; 6-inch (15-cm.) writing line; elite type.

Mr. Benjamin R. Wilson   2   January 15, 19--

If the title of the addressee is included in the inside address, it can be placed after the addressee's name on the first line or before the firm name on the second line. It should be placed so that the lines of the inside address will be of approximately equal length. If the title or firm name is unusually long, it can be divided and carried over to the second line with an indention of two spaces.

Very sincerely yours,

Robert T. Walker

Robert T. Walker, Director

RTW/dw
bcc: Ms. Johnson

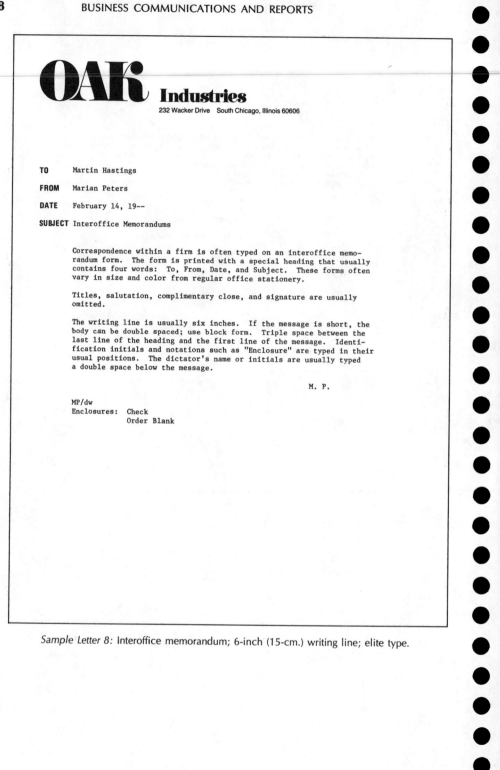

OAK Industries

232 Wacker Drive   South Chicago, Illinois 60606

TO   Martin Hastings

FROM   Marian Peters

DATE   February 14, 19--

SUBJECT Interoffice Memorandums

Correspondence within a firm is often typed on an interoffice memorandum form. The form is printed with a special heading that usually
contains four words: To, From, Date, and Subject. These forms often
vary in size and color from regular office stationery.

Titles, salutation, complimentary close, and signature are usually
omitted.

The writing line is usually six inches. If the message is short, the
body can be double spaced; use block form. Triple space between the
last line of the heading and the first line of the message. Identification initials and notations such as "Enclosure" are typed in their
usual positions. The dictator's name or initials are usually typed
a double space below the message.

                                              M. P.

MP/dw
Enclosures: Check
             Order Blank

Sample Letter 8: Interoffice memorandum; 6-inch (15-cm.) writing line; elite type.

MASS PRODUCTIONS

Kenneth W. Padgett
President   January 14, 19--

My dear Senator

This letter is typed on stationery that is smaller
(7 1/4 by 10 1/2 inches) than the usual letterhead.
It is called Monarch or executive-size stationery
and is used for personal or professional letters. It
requires a special-size envelope, the No. 7, which is
3 7/8 by 7 1/2 inches.

The length of writing line for this letterhead is
adjustable. Use a four-inch writing line if the
letter has fewer that 150 words; use a five-inch
writing line if the letter is over 150 words. If the
letter is over 250 words, it will require a second
page.

A letter with its inside address at the bottom is
more formal. When placed at the bottom, the address
is typed three or four spaces below the last line of
the letter. Identification initials and other
notations are omitted.

Very truly yours,

K. W. Padgett

President

The Honorable William Black
The United States Senate
Washington, DC 20510

2300 Mt. Vernon Parkway   Alexandria, Virginia 22304

Sample Letter 9: Modified block style on Monarch letterhead; open punctuation;
elite type; inside address at bottom of letter.

▼▼▼
WESTERN GRAPHICS

369 Fourth Avenue   San Diego, CA 92104

ART DEPARTMENT

August 14, 19--

Miss Susan Ramsey
246 North 45 Avenue
Boise, ID 83701

Dear Miss Ramsey:

This is a half-size letterhead; actually it
is half the size of a standard letterhead
turned the long way. It measures 5 1/2 by
8 1/2 inches and is called Baronial.

This letterhead is used for very short mes-
sages--fewer than 125 words. Use a four-
inch writing line. Type the date on the
ninth or tenth line from the top and begin
the inside address four lines below the date.

Sincerely,

Barbara A. Smith

Barbara A. Smith

DW

Sample Letter 10: Modified block style on half-size letterhead; mixed punctuation;
4-inch (10-cm.) writing line; elite type.

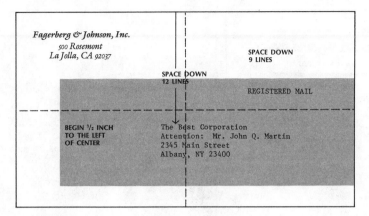

Sample Envelope 1: No. 6¾; mailing notation (attention line); read zone of postal scanner shaded.

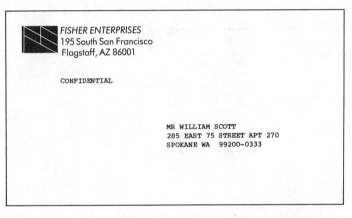

Sample Envelope 2: No 6¾; mailing notation ("Confidential"); address conforms to Postal Service recommendations and includes multi-unit building apartment number. It also includes the ZIP + 4 that the Postal Service plans to use, beginning October 1, 1983.

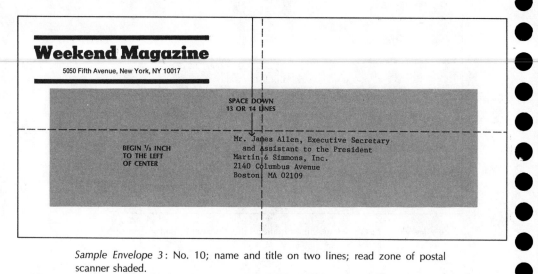

Weekend Magazine

5050 Fifth Avenue, New York, NY 10017

SPACE DOWN
13 OR 14 LINES

BEGIN ½ INCH
TO THE LEFT
OF CENTER

Mr. James Allen, Executive Secretary
and Assistant to the President
Martin & Simmons, Inc.
2140 Columbus Avenue
Boston, MA 02109

Sample Envelope 3: No. 10; name and title on two lines; read zone of postal scanner shaded.

Nicotra Construction Co.

39 Indiana Blvd., Baltimore MD 21401

HOLD FOR ARRIVAL

Mr. Lee Walker, Manager
Wilson & Martin, Inc.
9748 Orange Way
Miami, FL 33101

Sample Envelope 4: No. 10; mailing notation ("Hold for Arrival").

Cards

Typing cards can be difficult because they are stiff and small. For typing a few cards, use the card holders on the typewriter to hold the cards.

For jobs that involve a great deal of typing of cards, labels, or other small-sized pieces of paper, special typewriter platens can be interchanged with regular platens to prevent slippage. Cards and labels are also available in connected sheets that can be fed continuously into the typewriter and separated later.

If you need to type a number of cards, a simple aid can be made **How to make** from an ordinary 8½ by 11 sheet of typing paper. Fold a sheet of **a card holder** paper into a pleat or pocket, which becomes a holder for the card while it is being typed.

To do this:

1. Make a quarter-inch horizontal fold in the center of a sheet of paper. Don't make the pleat any deeper or else you will not be able to type on the last few lines of the card.

2. Tape the sides of the pleat to each other.

3. Roll the pleated page into the typewriter until the top of the pleat appears.

4. Place the card in the pleat and turn the platen backwards until the card is in the correct typing position.

5. If you are typing a number of cards, draw a vertical line on the left side of the paper as a guide for inserting cards. Do not remove the paper until you have finished typing all the cards.

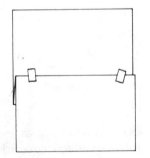 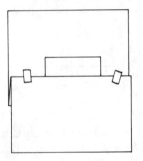

Samples of Card Holder

Government postal cards are 5½ by 3½ inches. Type the **Government** message lengthwise on the card, using a 4½-inch writing line. Type **postal cards** the date in the upper right corner. The return address may be typed above the date or in the upper left corner of the address side. Omit the inside address. If the message is long, the salutation and complimentary close may be omitted. Begin the address a triple space below the printed line on the address side. Begin typing a half inch to the left of center and follow the same procedure as for addressing envelopes.

Old Post Office
St. Louis, Missouri USA 13c

Historic Preservation

Mrs. William Harper
340 Crown Road
Portland, OR 92100

February 14, 19--

Dear Customer

Beginning Friday, April 10, Benson's is holding a
two-day sale of fur coats for all charge-account
customers. This sale will not be advertised. All
fur coats in regular stock will be reduced 20 percent for these two days, and you may use your
charge account for any purchase.

We hope to see you!

Marian Bell
Marian Bell
Manager, Fur Salon

Sample Government Postal Card: Shows both message and address.

In addition to single cards, the post office sells double cards and cards in sheets for use in printing. The post office will redeem cards that have been spoiled in typing or printing.

Chain feeding   Chain feeding speeds the process of addressing a number of cards or envelopes. There are two methods:

BACK FEEDING   1. Stack the cards or envelopes to the left of the typewriter, *face down,* flap toward you (in the case of envelopes).

2. Insert the first card or envelope into typing position in the typewriter.

3. Insert the second card or envelope between the first one and the *back* of the platen.

4. Address the first card or envelope.

5. Insert the third card or envelope as you did the second with your left hand while twirling the first out of the typewriter with your right hand. The second one will move into position for typing.

1. Stack the cards or envelopes to the left of the typewriter, *face up,* flap away from you (in the case of envelopes).

2. Insert the first card or envelope into the typewriter and address it. Roll it back until a half inch shows above the alignment scale.

3. Insert the second card or envelope between the first and the *front* of the platen.

4. Turn the platen back to remove the first card or envelope and to bring the second into writing position.

BUSINESS REPORTS

Writing Business Reports

Although report writing is a different process from letter writing, the principles of writing remain the same. The chief difference is in the presentation. Most business letters are written with the point of the letter presented in the opening, but most reports present the information and details first with the conclusions or recommendations presented at the end.

Reports are usually presented in one of four forms: memorandum, letter, short informal report (no more than ten pages), and long formal report. Most reports fall into one of the first three categories.

Forms of reports

The report in either memorandum or letter form is both short and informal; the letter form, since it goes outside the company, is usually a little more formal. Both are written in letter form with the point or conclusion that has been reached presented in the opening. The length of either of these reports is no more than three or four pages. Letterhead or memorandum stationery is used for the first page. The second and subsequent pages have headings that are the same as those of any two-page letter or memo (see page 47). Headings, subheadings, and visual aids can be used to make reading easier. A subject line is often useful.

The short informal report is the form that most reports take; certainly it is the form that the average office worker will use most often. A short report may include some or all of these parts:

1. a title page
2. a summary of findings with conclusions and recommendations

3. an authorization letter or a statement that the authorization was made informally
4. the purpose or problem of the report
5. a statement of findings, conclusions, and recommendations

Other items that might be added include graphic illustrations such as tables or charts and bibliographical information. Headings and other typographical display devices might be used to make the report easier to read. The report in its final form may be unbound or bound either at the top or side.

The long formal report is structured in a definite pattern, and it differs significantly from the other reports discussed. It is presented in more detailed form; that is, it is longer, more complex, and has more parts. Because of its length, it contains more reading aids in the form of headings, subheadings, graphs, charts, indices, and other visual aids. The writing style is usually more formal and impersonal than that of other business writing; it makes use of passive voice and third person and is written objectively. It should be typed or printed in uniform style. Often the formal report is prepared by specialists, either inside or outside of the company; and it is rarely the responsibility of the office worker or secretary.

Outline   After you have gathered and organized the material, the first step in writing the report is to prepare an outline. The outline can be arranged either by numbers and letters or by decimals. The number-letter arrangement is more familiar, but the decimal format allows for greater breakdown.

Suggestions for making and typing the outline:

1. Each heading or subheading must be broken into at least two items; there must be, for example, both *A* and *B* under *I*. There should not be more than five divisions.
2. Observe the rules of parallel or balanced structure when making an outline. This insures that items are expressed in the same form (infinitive phrase to infinitive phrase, for example) and that points show relationship to each other and are grouped according to their level of importance.
3. When typing second or subsequent pages of an outline:
    a. Follow the margin and tab stops used on the first page.
    b. Have a short page of typing rather than a long one.
    c. Try to complete sections on the same page, and do not type one line of a division at the bottom of one page or at the top of another.

4. To type a number-letter outline:
   a. Roman numeral *I* is typed at the left margin followed by a period and two spaces. Align subsequent Roman numerals by depressing the margin release key and backspacing the necessary number of spaces.

Example:

```
 I.   First major heading
II.   Second major heading
```

   b. The subheadings are aligned four spaces to the right of the previous heading. Set tab stops for each subheading. Follow each number or letter of a subheading by a period and two spaces.

Example:

```
I.  Major heading

    A.   Subheading

    B.   Subheading
         1. Subheading
         2. Subheading
```

   c. Double-space between Roman-numeral and capital-letter items; single-space between Arabic-numeral and lower-case letters.

Example:

```
I.  Major heading

    A.   Subheading--first degree
         1. Subheading--second degree
         2. Subheading--second degree
            a. Subheading--third degree
            b. Subheading--third degree
               (1) Subheading--fourth degree
               (2) Subheading--fourth degree

    B.   Subheading--first degree

II.  Major heading
```

    5. To type a decimal outline:
      a. The whole number of a major heading is typed at the left margin followed by a period and two spaces.
      b. Each first-degree subheading is aligned four spaces to the right of the major heading and is followed by two spaces. Each second-degree subheading is aligned to the right of the first-degree subheading (not the number) and is followed by one space.

Example:

```
1.   Major heading

     1.1   Subheading--first degree
           1.1.1 Subheading--second degree
```

      c. Double-space between major and first-degree subheadings; single-space between second-, third-, and fourth-degree subheadings.

Example:

```
1.   Major heading

     1.1   Subheading--first degree

     1.2   Subheading--first degree

           1.2.1 Subheading--second degree
           1.2.2 Subheading--second degree
                 Subheading--third degree
                 1.2.2.1 Subheading--third degree
                         1.2.2.2.1 Subheading--fourth
                                   degree
                         1.2.2.2.2 Subheading--fourth
                                   degree

2.   Major heading
```

Suggestions for writing reports:

1. After preparing an outline from the information you gathered, you are ready to begin the first draft of the report. Use a simple, straightforward writing style.

2. Keep the report impersonal—avoid the use of personal pronouns (even *you*), since it makes the report sound as if it were the

opinion of the writer rather than the presentation of objective data. Passive voice can be used in place of personal pronouns.

3. Write objectively—avoid words that tend to persuade or to give unsupported evaluations.

4. Write the entire first draft before you do any revising. You may need to do a rewriting of the first draft before the report is ready for its final typing. In the second writing concern yourself with style, clarity, and conciseness. At this time check mechanics—spelling, punctuation, grammar—and detail.

Manuscript and Report Typing

This section is primarily for use in the typing of office reports and manuscripts. Many publishers and colleges requiring theses for advanced degrees have specific instructions for preparation of manuscripts.

Suggestions for typing manuscripts and reports:

1. Use white paper of a good quality, usually measuring 8½ by 11 inches, and use a black ribbon. Pica rather than elite type is often preferred because it is easier to read and copies are more legible.

2. You will probably not make carbon copies but will photocopy the report when it is typed.

3. Margins for manuscripts are a minimum of one inch; wider margins may be used but not narrower ones. The top margin on the first page should be at least two inches. Type a short line if necessary but do not go beyond the set margins. If a manuscript is to be bound at either the top or the left side, allow an additional half inch for this.

4. Double-space the text of a manuscript; triple-space after titles. Indent paragraphs at least five spaces. Quoted matter of more than three lines is single-spaced and indented five spaces from both the left and right margins—or just from the left margin. If the quotation is a paragraph, the first line should be indented ten spaces from the left margin. Omissions in the quoted matter are indicated by using ellipses (see page 183).

5. Do not divide the last word on a page or break a paragraph so that only one line is at the bottom of a page or at the top of the following page.

6. Center the title over the manuscript; this means that if a half inch is allowed on the left side for binding, the title will be centered over the typing and not on the page.

7. Number with Arabic numbers all pages except the first. The numbers may be placed in the upper right corner or centered at the

bottom. Usually, if a manuscript is bound at the top, it is numbered at the bottom; if bound at the left or not bound, it is numbered at the top.

Footnotes   Footnotes give credit for quotations, explain terms in the text, and call attention to other parts of the manuscript.

The usual method is to place a footnote at the bottom of the page where the reference is made. A two-inch line separating footnotes from the text is typed with the underscore key one line below the last line of the text. Double-space after the line. Single-space footnotes but double-space between them.

Number consecutively with superior figures (typed slightly above the line of writing). A footnote must appear on the same page as the notation to which it refers. Therefore, plan the page so that there will be room for the footnotes.

Examples:

[1]Zinsser, William, On Writing Well. New York, Harper & Row, 1980, p. 35.
[2]Zinsser, p. 129.

Another method that is becoming popular is to place the citation of a source in the body of the report so that the reader is not interrupted by having to look down to the bottom of the page.

Example:

Safire points out (William Safire, On Language, New York, Avon, 1980, p. 19) that. . .

A second citation to the book is made this way:

(Safire, p. 22)

A short title should be added if more than one work by the same author is referred to in the report.

Still another method of citing sources of information is this: Number the listings in the bibliography at the end of the report. Refer at the point in the report where the citation occurs to the bibliography number, plus the page number of the reference being quoted. Example: *(8:10)*. Where you first use this form, be sure that you give an explanation in a footnote, for example: "8:10 means page 10 of Item 8 in the Bibliography."

The practice of using Latin terms and abbreviations in footnotes is disappearing. Instead of such Latin terms as *ibid., loc. cit., op. cit., passim, supra,* and *et al.,* English words and abbreviations are now being used. (See Appendix page 223 for a listing of abbreviations that you are likely to find in both footnotes and bibliographies.)

Bibliography

The bibliography appears either at the end of the manuscript or after each chapter. It identifies the source materials used by the author.

A bibliography should be arranged in alphabetical order and include this information:

1. Name of the author, surname first. If the source material has two or three authors, invert the name of the first author but list the names of additional authors in normal order. If there are more than three authors, give the first author's name followed by *and others* (not the Latin *et al.*).

2. Title of book or name of periodical in italics (underscored).

3. Title of magazine article in quotes.

4. Place of publication, name of publisher, and date of publication for books. You may give a shortened form of the publisher's name, so long as it is clear.

5. Volume number and page numbers for periodicals.

Styles and forms for bibliographies, like those for footnotes, vary greatly. The field in which you are writing can also determine the style of bibliographies and footnotes. For more detailed information, consult one of these publications:

Gibaldi, Joseph, and Walter S. Achert. *MLA Handbook for Writers of Research Papers, Theses, and Dissertations.* New York: Modern Language Assn., 1977.

Hodges, John C., and Mary E. Whitten. *Harbrace College Handbook.* 9th Ed. New York: Harcourt Brace Jovanovich, 1982.

Turabian, Kate L. *A Manual for Writers of Term Papers, Theses, and Dissertations.* 4th Ed. Chicago: University of Chicago Press, 1973.

Willis, Hulon. *Writing Term Papers.* New York: Harcourt Brace Jovanovich, 1977.

Below is a sample bibliography that has been adapted for use in business offices. Check other style manuals if you are preparing a bibliography in another area.

Example:

BIBLIOGRAPHY

BOOKS

Hanna, J. Marshall, Estelle L. Popham, and Rita S. Tilton. <u>Secretarial Procedures and Administration</u>. 7th ed. Cincinnati: South-Western, 1978.

Hodges, John C., and Mary E. Whitten. <u>Harbrace College Handbook</u>. 9th ed. New York: Harcourt Brace Jovanovich, 1982.

BULLETINS AND PAMPHLETS

<u>Report of the 74th General Motors Stockholders Meeting</u>. Detroit: General Motors Corporation, 1982.

<u>What Mailers Should Do to Get the Best Service</u>. U.S. Postal Service Publication 153. Washington: Government Printing Office, 1970.

ENCYCLOPEDIAS

"Eisenhower, Dwight David." <u>Who's Who in America</u>. 1966-67, XXXIV, 612.

"Palestine." <u>Encyclopaedia Britannica</u>. 1964. XVIII, pp. 117-42.

MAGAZINES AND NEWSPAPERS

Kunen, James S. "How Can You Defend Those People?" <u>Harper's</u>, 264, No. 1582, April 1982, pp. 80-91.

"Pollution Is Termed Long-Run Challenge," <u>The New York Times</u>, 19 December 1976, p. 29, col. 6.

UNPUBLISHED DISSERTATION

Wilson, Brian G. "Grounded Theories Related to the Skills, Knowledge, and Attitudes of Certified Administrative Managers," Arizona State University, 1981.

PERSONAL LETTER

Long, Samantha. Personal letter, 15 May 1982.

FILM

<u>The John Glenn Story</u>. Ames, IA: University of Iowa, Film No. S58619, 1974.

LECTURE

Bella Abzug. "An Evening with Bella Abzug." Lecture presented at the College of Marin, 16 March 1981.

PERSONAL INTERVIEW

Interview with Alan Cranston, United States Senator, Washington, 12 July 1983.

RECORDING OR TAPE

Shaw, Bernard. "Saint Joan" with Siobhan McKenna. RCA Victor recording, No. LOC-6133.

TELEVISION PROGRAM

"St. Augustine." <u>Third Testament Series</u>. Hosted by
Malcolm Muggeridge. San Francisco: KQED—TV, 2 Jan—
uary 1977.

Material to be presented in columns should be so arranged that it **Tabulation**
is attractive and easy to read. It may be necessary to make a rough **of charts**
draft, and it is certainly necessary to plan the typing very carefully. **and tables**

Although automatic typewriters have eliminated most of the
counting and backspacing for doing tabulation and have made it far
easier to revise a chart before the final typing, you will still need to do
some planning. For example, the machine needs to know how
many spaces between columns. If you are not using an automatic
typewriter, you will need to follow the instructions given here.

A simple tabulation may be set up by eye—that is, instead of   ESTIMATED
figuring exact placement, the typist estimates the margins, the   PLACEMENT
spacing between columns, and the number of lines to drop down
before beginning to type. However, if it is necessary to retype,
estimating can take more time than planning a tabulation; it would
then be preferable to use either the exact (or mathematic) plan or the
backspace plan.

Vertical placement

1. Determine the number of lines available for typing (six lines
to an inch; 66 lines on a standard page).

EXACT OR
MATHEMATIC
PLAN

2. Count the number of lines needed for the tabulation,
including the blank lines.

3. Subtract the number of lines needed for the tabulation
(including the blank lines) from the number of lines available. In
other words, subtract the result of step 2 from that of step 1.

4. Divide this figure by two. This will give you the number of
blank lines for the top and bottom margins.

5. If you wish the tabulation to be in reading or eye position
rather than in the exact center of the page, subtract three lines from
the figure found in step 4 in order to determine the top margin.

Horizontal placement

1. Determine the number of spaces in a line available for typing
(85 pica spaces, 102 elite on a standard page).

2. Count the longest item in each column; total the number of
spaces needed for all the columns.

3. Determine the number of blank spaces between the columns

either by selecting the number of spaces you wish to leave (six is often selected, so that the columns are about a half inch apart) or by adding two more (representing the right and left margins) to the number of columns and dividing the unused spaces among the columns and the margins.

4. From the center of the page, backspace half the total spaces to be used (the columns plus the space between the columns) and set the left margin at this point.

5. Set tab stops for each column; the first stop will be set the width of the first column plus the space following it. Repeat until all stops are set.

Vertical placement

BACKSPACE PLAN

The vertical placement is determined in the same way as was described in the exact or mathematic plan.

Horizontal placement

1. Select the longest item in each column.

2. Determine the number of blank spaces to be left between the columns.

3. From the center of the page, backspace once for every two spaces in the longest item in each column and once for every two spaces between the columns. Set left margin.

4. Space forward for each space in the first column plus the space following it. Set the first tab stop.

5. Repeat until all stops are set.

The main heading is centered and usually typed in all capital letters. Column headings are centered over the columns, and the first and important words are usually capitalized. These headings may be underscored.

WARNINGS:

1. *Clear all tab stops before beginning to set the stops for the tabulation.*
2. *Type tabulations line by line rather than column by column.*
3. *If lines are included in the tabulation, it is easier to rule vertically with a pen. The underscore can be used for horizontal lines; however, if both the horizontal and vertical lines are drawn with a pen, they will match.*
4. *To make a tabulation easier to read, use leaders (a line of periods) between the columns. Although leaders may be typed without*

spaces between them, the page is better looking if each period is followed by a space. Type the first leader two spaces after the last word of the first column. Strike the period and the space bar alternately. Leave three or four spaces between the last leader and the first word of the second column. To align periods down the columns, notice on the scale of the typewriter whether the first leader is typed on an odd or even number. On the following lines, begin the leaders on the same numbered space (that is, odd or even). The shortest line of leaders should contain at least three periods.

5. Proofread tabulations very carefully, particularly if any figures are involved. It might be better to proof with another person (one reading, one proofing) if there are many figures or unusual spellings to check.

Below is an example of a tabulation with rules, leaders, and headings.

EARNED DEGREES CONFERRED, BY LEVEL OF DEGREE:
1930 to 1978

Year	Total	Bachelor's or 1st Professional Degrees	Master's or 2d-Level Degrees	Doctor-ates
1930........	139,752	122,484	14,969	2,299
1940........	216,521	186,500	26,731	3,290
1950........	498,373	433,734	58,219	6,420
1955........	352,881	285,841	58,200	8,840
1960........	476,704	394,889	77,692	9,829
1961........	487,513	395,248	81,690	10,575
1962........	514,323	414,287	88,414	11,622
1963........	551,810	443,518	95,470	12,822
1964........	614,194	494,153	105,551	14,490
1965........	663,622	530,003	117,152	16,467
1966........	709,832	551,047	140,548	16,121
1967........	768,871	590,547	157,707	18,163
1968........	866,548	666,710	176,749	20,183
1969........	984,129	764,185	193,756	22,752
1970........	1,065,391	827,234	208,291	25,890
1978........	1,341,200	998,000	311,000	32,200

Source: Bureau of the Census, Statistical Abstract of the United States: 101st ed. Washington, D.C., 1980.

**Typing
symbols**

   If a machine is used for technical typing that requires special symbols, it is possible to order keys with these symbols to replace some of the infrequently used keys (#, @, for example). If a machine does not have these special keys, symbols can be made on the typewriter. To do so, follow these suggestions:

   Exclamation Point (!). Use the period and apostrophe. Type the period, backspace, and type the apostrophe.

   Equal Sign (=). Type the hyphen, backspace, turn the platen away from you slightly, and type another hyphen under the first.

   Plus Sign (+). Type the hyphen, backspace, and type an apostrophe or a diagonal over the hyphen.

   Multiplication Sign (x). Use the small x.

   Minus Sign (–). Use the hyphen.

   Division Sign (÷). Type the hyphen, backspace, and type the colon.

   Pound Sterling Sign (£). Type a capital *L*, backspace, and type a small *f* or a hyphen over it.

   Inches, Seconds, Ditto Signs ("). Use quotation marks.

   Feet ('). Use the apostrophe.

   Superior or Inferior Symbols (chemical symbols or degrees—H_2O, $75°$). These are typed either above or below the line of writing. Use the variable line spacer. If the symbol is to be raised (called "superior"), roll the platen toward you a half space, type the symbol, and return to the normal line of writing. If the symbol is below the line of writing (called "inferior"), roll the platen away from you a half space, type the symbol, and return to the normal line of writing.

   "Care of" Symbol (c/o). Type a small c, a diagonal, and a small o.

   Brackets (工). For the left bracket, type the diagonal, backspace, type the underscore, roll back one line, and type the underscore. For the right bracket, type the diagonal, backspace twice, type the underscore, roll back one line, and type the underscore.

   If a symbol cannot be made on the typewriter, leave space and insert the symbol with a pen. Use black ink to match the color of the typewriter ribbon.

3. Methods of Communicating

Communication, whether spoken or written, is the process that keeps business functioning. Three methods of communicating— the telephone, the telegraph, and the mails—have, in a relatively short period of time, expanded their capabilities dramatically and are continuing to do so. Today's telephone, once providing only voice communication, can now handle video, graphics, and data communications as well. The telegraph and telephone companies work together with the United States Postal Service in wire and wireless communicating, providing services such as Mailgram and E-COM mail. The new methods of transmitting sound and writing are called telecommunications; they involve voice communications, the sending of written and visual communications by wire and wireless methods, and computer-linked data communications. Such communicating is done quickly, often in a matter of seconds.

Some of the electronic communication methods are teletypewriters that transmit written material to machines in other offices, facsimile units that send original copy (written, drawn, or typed), closed-circuit television systems that add a visual element to voice transmission, and data communication systems that use data processing equipment to send information to faraway locations.

As a secretary, you need to know what the different methods of communications are, which are available to your company, what each can offer, and when each can best be used. There are many factors to consider, including speed of delivery, whether a message needs to be in writing, whether proof of delivery or reply is necessary, and cost.

POSTAL INFORMATION

One of the secretary's responsibilities may be that of handling both incoming and outgoing mail, so it is important that the secretary know about classes of mail and services provided by the United States Postal Service. Rates change frequently, but classes of mail and available services remain much the same.

77

Automation of mail sorting is being done in many post offices by computers called Optical Character Readers (OCR), as well as by other mechanical sorting devices. They can sort outgoing mail—by "reading" the bottom line of the address—and incoming mail—by "reading" the next to the bottom line of the address. To enable the machines to sort the mail, the Postal Service has requested that envelopes conform to certain size limitations and that envelope addresses be typed in a certain manner. (See pages 45–47.)

Classes of Mail

All pieces of mail accepted for delivery[1] by the United States Postal Service fall in one of these classes:

First class   First-class mail, which is sent by the fastest transportation possible, includes:

1. letters
2. postal and post cards
3. business-reply mail
4. priority mail (any mailable matter weighing between 12 ounces and 70 pounds, with a maximum size of 100 inches in length and girth combined), to be marked "Priority Mail" on all sides of the package or envelope by using special stickers or envelopes
5. all matter wholly or partly in writing, whether sealed or unsealed, except manuscripts for books, periodical articles and music, manuscript copy accompanying proofsheets or corrected proofsheets of the same, and the writing authorized by law on matter of other classes
6. all matter sealed or closed against inspection

Rates are based on each ounce or fraction of an ounce to any place in the United States, its territories, and its possessions and to Armed Forces outside the United States when addressed to an APO or FPO.

---

[1] There are restrictions on material that can be mailed—for example, intoxicating beverages, explosives, radioactive materials, and lottery tickets are some of the items that cannot be mailed. If there is any question in this regard, be sure to consult the local post office or company mail room.

WARNING:

A letter should be weighed if there are enclosures that could make the letter heavier than the one-ounce maximum. Scales are available for this purpose. A letter sent without adequate postage will be returned to the sender undelivered.

Second class

Second-class mail includes newspapers, magazines, and other periodicals containing notice of entry as second-class matter.

This class may be either single-copy mailings by the general public or bulk mailings by publishers. For bulk mailings (identical pieces of third-class matter in bulk lots of not less than 50 pounds or 200 pieces), it is necessary to consult the local post office for rates and permits. This mail must be sorted into bundles by ZIP Code. Rates are determined by weight and mailing distance. There is no weight limit.

Third class

Third-class mail includes mailable matter not included in first or second class and not weighing over 16 ounces. These may be:

1. circulars, books, catalogs, and other printed matter
2. merchandise
3. seeds, bulbs, cuttings, roots, and plants
4. hotel keys and identification devices that carry instructions for return and a statement guaranteeing payment of postage due

Rates are determined by weight and mailing distance. There are separate rates for some nonprofit organizations. Bulk mailing permits for third-class mail are available through the local post office. This mail, too, must be sorted into bundles by ZIP Code.

Fourth class (parcel post)

Fourth-class mail (mainly domestic parcel post) includes merchandise, printed matter, mailable live animals, and all other mailable matter not included as first-, second-, or third-class mail. Each parcel must weigh 16 ounces or over. Packages mailed between larger post offices (first-class) in the continental United States are limited to 40 pounds in weight and to 84 inches in length and girth combined. Parcels up to 70 pounds and 100 inches can be mailed to and from smaller post offices and any post office in Hawaii and Alaska. Consult the post office about special mailing rates for books, records, and materials for the blind.

For faster delivery of parcels over long distances, use Special Handling, Priority Mail (formerly air parcel post), or Express Mail. Rates are determined by weight and mailing distance. Consult your local post office for size and weight restrictions.

**International
mail**
International mail is intended for delivery outside the United States and its territories and possessions. Letters, post cards, printed matter, and most packages can be mailed to foreign countries. Letters and post cards are usually sent airmail to speed delivery. Brief messages can be sent at lower rates by using Aerogrammes, which are prestamped sheets of stationery that fold into the shape of an envelope and which can be purchased at any post office. Check with your local post office for regulations and restrictions, as well as international mail postal rates.

Special Mail Services

By payment of fees in addition to the regular postage, a number of special services are available through the local post office. Mark the envelope or wrapper with the type of special service being used. Place a notation of the service near the stamp position so that it is immediately noticeable. The special mail services include those discussed below. Consult the post office about the availability of any service at the destination post office.

**Special
delivery**
All classes of mail can be sent by special delivery. Rates are based upon weight and class of mail. Special-delivery mail is given immediate delivery at its destination, within certain distance and time limitations.

**Special
handling**
Third- and fourth-class mail is handled and delivered as quickly as possible when this service is used. It does not involve special delivery.

**Registered
mail**
This service adds protection for valuable and important mail and gives evidence of delivery. It is the safest way to send valuables. The liability of the Postal Service for the safe delivery of registered mail is limited to the declared value that the sender places on it, up to a maximum of $10,000.

**Return
receipt
requested**
For an additional fee the sender can request a return receipt, signed by the receiver of the mail (not necessarily the addressee), showing that the mail was safely delivered. Restricted delivery, also available at an additional fee, will limit delivery of the mail to the addressee.

Insured mail
Third- or fourth-class mail or airmail containing third- or fourth-class matter can be insured against loss or damage up to $200. For an additional fee a return receipt can be requested for a parcel

insured for more than $15. Another fee will restrict delivery of the mail to the addressee.

Parcels containing items for sale that have not been ordered by the receiver, parcels containing items so fragile as to make their safe delivery doubtful, and parcels not adequately prepared for mailing cannot be insured.

C.O.D.

First-, third-, and fourth-class mail can be sent C.O.D. (*collect on delivery*), which means that the buyer need not pay for the merchandise until receiving it and the sender is assured of payment. The sender pays the usual postage on the mail plus a C.O.D. fee, which also includes insurance. The total of the C.O.D. charges is added to the amount collected by the post office before the mail is delivered to the addressee; the amount collected by the post office is then paid to the sender. The addressee is not permitted to examine the contents before accepting the mail. The maximum amount that may be collected on one parcel is $300.

This service cannot be used (1) for sending articles to addressees who have not ordered the contents of the parcel, (2) for collection-agency purposes, (3) for returning merchandise considered unsatisfactory by the addressee, or (4) for parcels sent to APO's or FPO's.

Certified mail

Any matter on which first-class postage has been paid may be certified to provide proof of mailing and a record of delivery for the sender.

Return receipt, restricted delivery, and special delivery are also available when additional fees are paid.

Certificate of mailing

A certificate of mailing furnishes evidence of mailing only. No receipt is obtained from the addressee upon delivery.

Mailgram service

A Mailgram is a combination of a telegram and a letter. The message is given to Western Union and is then relayed to the post office of its destination and delivered the following day by regular letter carrier. The cost is approximately half that of a regular interstate telegram.

Express Mail service

Express Mail service provides businesses with high-speed air delivery of letters and parcels between major cities. If a firm wishes, postal employees will pick up a shipment, take it to the airport, and deliver it upon its arrival. There are other options, including one that allows the business to deliver the shipment to the airport and the addressee to pick it up at the airport after it has come in. Overnight delivery of letters and parcels is guaranteed.

E-COM   Recently the Postal Service initiated Electronic Computer Orig-
service   inated Mail Service (E-COM). It is a computer-originated service
transmitted via telecommunications companies (such as TRT Telecommunications Corp., ITT World Communications, and Net-
word). It permits volume mailers to send computer-generated messages of up to two pages in groups of 200 for delivery within two
days. E-COM provides paper-copy conversion, placement in envelopes, and delivery as first-class mail. Customer billings, announce-
ments, advertising, and fund-raising letters are examples of mail
suitable for E-COM use. The price of the service includes paper, ink,
printing, envelope, postage, and the labor for preparing messages.

WARNINGS:

1. *If speed of delivery is important to the sender, it would be well to
   check with the local post office or company mail room to determine when the addressee can be expected to receive the mail. If
   information is involved, another method of communicating—by
   telephone or telegraph or mailgram—may be more efficient. If
   an item must be mailed—a contract, check, or package, for example—using first-class mail or one of the special services may
   help speed its delivery.*
2. *Do not use registered mail to provide proof of delivery; instead
   use certified mail.*

Nonmail Services

Services not connected with delivery of the mail are also
provided by the Post Office Department. These include the following:

Money   Money orders provide a method of sending money. The
orders   maximum amount of a postal money order is $300. If a person wishes
to send more than $300, more than one money order can be pur-
chased.

Nonpostal   Nonpostal stamps and bonds include internal revenue stamps
stamps and   for documents, migratory bird-hunting stamps, and United States
bonds   savings stamps and bonds.

Passport   Recently ninety-one post offices in Massachusetts, New York,
applications California, and Minnesota were authorized to become passport
application centers. They do not issue final passports; they accept

applications that formerly had to be processed by regular State Department passport offices.

The Postal Manual

For more complete postal information, consult *The Postal Manual*. This book contains complete information on all aspects of regulations and instructions governing the various postal services and is kept up-to-date by periodic supplements. (See the list of reference sources, page 229, for information about where it can be purchased.) Your local post office can be consulted for assistance with specific questions. If a problem cannot be solved locally, the Postal Service Consumer Advocate in Washington, D.C., is available.

ZIP Codes

The ZIP Code (Zoning Improvement Program) presently used is a five-digit code system devised to identify by number geographic localities of all United States Post Offices. The Postal Service plans to implement this system with ZIP + 4, a nine-digit system that, even though it increases the number of ZIP Codes from 40,000 to 20 million, would cut labor costs. This will be a voluntary program with October 1, 1983, as the date that ZIP + 4 will go into effect. There is a *National ZIP Code Directory* that lists all ZIP Codes. See the list of reference sources, page 228, to learn where this publication can be obtained.

Postage Meters

Many business offices prefer using postage meters to buying stamps and putting them on envelopes by hand; in fact, over a third of all mail is put through meters. This machine is taken to any post office, where postage is prepaid and a locked meter is set. Meters can also be reset by a computerized telephone system. The user dials an 800 number, then gives information on the meter setting by punching digits on a push-button phone. The machine seals the envelopes and prints the correct postage on the envelope (or on tapes for packages). The amount used is subtracted in the meter of the machine from the total prepaid at the post office.

Because metered mail does not have to be canceled and postmarked, it can be processed more quickly than stamped mail. This is especially true of metered mail that is so addressed that it can be read by the OCR and that is deposited at a post office rather than in a mailbox.

TELEGRAPH INFORMATION

Although telegraphic services provide faster communication than the mails, such services are becoming more expensive and offering less. If a written message is not needed, the telephone is quicker and cheaper. If an oral message will not do, there are less expensive alternatives to the full-rate telegram: (1) the overnight telegram for longer messages (a minimum of 100 words); (2) special-delivery letters (but delivery may be slower than you wish); (3) the Mailgram, a combination of telegraphic and postal services.

Telegraph agencies, in addition to covering all phases of sending business and social messages, are used to transmit money, to serve national advertising locally (*Operator 25 service*), to offer message services, and to provide gift services (flowers, dolls, and candy). Special types of service that involve such automated equipment as private-wire systems, two-way teletypewriters, cathode-ray tube (CRT) devices, Telex, minicomputers, and other special equipment are available to any firm whose volume of business warrants such additional facilities.

Domestic Service

Telegram. A full-rate, fast service based on a fifteen-word minimum with additional charges for longer messages. It is accepted at any time and takes precedence over all other types of messages.

Overnight Telegram. A deferred service based on a 100-word minimum, with charges for additional words at the rate of 1 to 1½ cents per word. It is sent up to midnight for delivery the following morning.

Mailgram. The Mailgram combines the services of both the telegraph company and the Postal Service. The message, based on a 100-word minimum, can be sent by calling Western Union's toll-free 800 number (or by a business' teletype or computer terminal or facsimile machine). The message is then sent to the nearest post office that is equipped with telegraphic receiving equipment; it will be delivered to the addressee in the first mail of the following day.

You can also include a Business Reply Mailgram with the Mailgram so that the recipient can reply easily, or you can send the message by Certified Mailgram, which gives you a receipt with the addressee's signature, thus providing proof of mailing and receipt. The cost of a mailgram is about half that of an overnight telegram.

International Service

Full Rate (FR).   A full-rate, fast service based on a minimum of seven words. It can be sent in code or in any language expressed in Roman letters.

Ship Radiogram.   For messages to and from ships at sea.

Chargeable Words

The cost of telegrams and cablegrams is based on a count of the chargeable words.

1. The inside address and signature (including the sender's title and the name of department or firm) are sent free.   **Domestic telegrams**

2. Common punctuation marks (comma, period, colon, semicolon, question mark, apostrophe, parentheses, dash, and quotation marks) are sent free. Paragraphs will be transmitted in paragraph form without extra charge.

3. Any standard dictionary word in the English, German, French, Italian, Dutch, Portuguese, Spanish, and Latin languages is counted as one word.

4. Each initial separated by spaces is counted as a word; initials written together are counted at the rate of one word for each five letters. *A. L. Jones* would be counted as three words, but *AL Jones* would be counted as two.

5. A common abbreviation typed without spaces (such as *C.O.D.* or *F.O.B.*) is counted as one word.

6. Hyphenated, dictionary compounds are counted as one word, but hyphenated words not found in the dictionary are counted as separate words. *Webster's New International Dictionary* is used to determine hyphenation.

7. Groups of figures, letters, or mixed figures and letters are counted as one word for each five characters.

8. Each word in a geographic name is counted. *New Jersey* is counted as two words.

9. Contractions are counted as separate words and should not be used.

International messages

1. Each word in the address and signature is chargeable. Because of this, many firms use one-word code addresses.

2. Each dictionary word is counted at the rate of fifteen letters to a word.

3. Each punctuation mark is counted.

4. Code or cipher words are counted at the rate of five characters per word.

Typing Telegrams

Type telegrams on the forms furnished by the telegraph company, making at least one carbon. Type either in all caps or in lower case, capitalizing when necessary. Mark an X in the box in the printed heading if the message is being sent by overnight service and indicate the method of sending the service—paid, collect, or to whom charged.

western union							Telegram
MSG. NO.	NO. OF MSGS. PD.-COLL.	PD.-COLL.	CASH NO.	ACCOUNTING INFORMATION	DATE	FILING TIME	SENT TIME
				Davis & Hall, Inc.	4/14/--	A.M. P.M.	A.M. P.M.

Send the following message, subject to the terms on back hereof, which are hereby agreed to   ☐ OVER NIGHT TELEGRAM
UNLESS BOX ABOVE IS CHECKED THIS MESSAGE WILL BE SENT AS A TELEGRAM

TO John Williamson, Davis & Hall, Inc.

ADDRESS & TELEPHONE NO. 1450 S. W. Broadway, 234-1000

CITY – STATE & ZIP CODE Portland, OR 91220

Send immediately special delivery any files
pertaining to Standard Insurance Company account.
                    Robert T. Weston, President

SENDER'S TEL. NO. (503) 456-1200 **NAME & ADDRESS** Davis & Hall, Inc.
(Area Code)   (Zip Code)
                    850 Market Street, San Francisco, CA 94100

W.U. 5210 (3/73)

Sample Telegram

Complete the top of the form by typing the date and the addressee's name and address on the lines provided. Check to be sure that the address is correct and as complete as possible so that the addressee may be located quickly. Omit *Mr.* in the inside address but include *Miss, Ms.,* or *Mrs.*

Begin the message a double space below the address. Double-space short and single-space long messages. The length of the writing line will vary with the message length. Do not divide words at the ends of lines.

Type the sender's name and title or name of department or firm a double space below the message. Below the message space type the sender's telephone number and name and address.

If the sender wishes a report of delivery, write "Report Delivery" immediately following the addressee's name. These words, which are charged for, are sent to the destination, and a report (also charged for) is telegraphed back stating to whom and when the telegram was delivered.

WARNINGS:

1. *To insure that the message is not sent late or garbled in the process of being recorded, try to deliver the typed message to the nearest Western Union office instead of phoning it in. Be sure that the recipient's address, ZIP Code, and telephone number are included correctly.*
2. *If you must telephone (you'll be charged an additional fee), spell out all difficult or easily misunderstood words —and insist that the message be read back to you.*
3. *Because Western Union does not deliver around the clock, time your messages so that they can be transmitted within delivery hours.*
4. *Under Federal Communications Commission regulations, if a telegram is not delivered within five hours, the sender is entitled to a full refund; therefore, ask your local Western Union office when you may expect the message to be delivered. If you find that a message did not reach the recipient or was delayed beyond the five-hour limit, request a refund in writing. This does not apply to Mailgrams, for which there are no delivery speed standards.*
5. *Western Union does not guarantee the accuracy of its messages, and few operators automatically read back the message. For an additional fee you can get a copy of your message; however, this assures you only that the operator took down the message correctly, not that the recipient received it that way.*
6. *If you receive a telegram late or in garbled condition, let the sender know. This is the only way that the sender can straighten out the message and discover whether a refund is justified.*

TELEPHONE INFORMATION

Because the telephone is such a vital part of business, it is difficult to imagine that, like the typewriter—another indispensable tool of business—it has been in existence barely one hundred years. In order to use the telephone effectively, the secretary must know how to handle both incoming and outgoing calls and be aware of all the services that are available through the telephone.

Your voice is the first thing that a caller hears, and your company is immediately judged by what you say and how you say it. Assume that any call is important; therefore, your voice must sound friendly and pleasant. Use simple, straightforward language—avoid technical terms or slang. Speak clearly and distinctly at your normal speed and speak directly into the telephone. Vary your tone of voice to avoid sounding monotonous, but also avoid extremes of loudness or softness.

Incoming Calls

Make a point of answering the telephone on the first ring. Identify yourself either with your name or with your name and the name of the department; never say just "hello" or "yes." As soon as you learn the caller's name, use the name in the conversation.

A very important telephone technique is learning to be a good listener. Give full attention to your caller by concentrating on what is being said and ignoring distracting noises in the office. Listen carefully so that repeating will not be necessary; however, do take accurate messages and don't hesitate to ask how to spell a name or to repeat a number for verification.

If the call is for someone else, be tactful about the information that is given. Such an explanation as "He's out on a coffee break" may give the wrong impression.

Sometimes a caller is reluctant to give a name or leave a message; if that happens, indirect approaches may produce results. Such answers as "Mr. Kelly is out of the office. This is his secretary; may I help you?" or, "May I have Mr. Kelly call you when he returns?" are not direct questions asking who is calling or what is wanted; therefore, the caller should not be offended.

Leaving the line   If you must leave the line, telling the caller, "Hold, please," or, "Just a second," gives that person no information. Give the caller a chance to respond; it is annoying when the call is long distance or an emergency to be told abruptly to "hold" rather than be asked if he or she will do so. If you know that you will be away from the line for longer than a minute (even 30 seconds seems a long time when you are waiting), ask if you can call back. When you return to the line, use a suitable phrase such as, "Thank you for waiting," and if possible use the caller's name.

When you take messages, be sure to write down the date, time, name and identity of the caller, and telephone number (get the area code if it is a long-distance message). In any event, get all of the details. Repeat messages and check all spellings and figures. Most offices have special pads for phone messages. They are available in stationery shops if your firm does not have printed forms of its own.

Taking messages

If you cannot handle the call or answer the caller's questions, explain that you would like to transfer the call to someone who can be of help. If the caller is willing to have the call transferred, signal the switchboard operator and stay on the line until the operator answers; then ask that the call be transferred. If the caller is not willing to have the call transferred, ask if you can call back when you have the required information.

Transferring calls

Before the call is completed, review any details and check any needed information. Remember the amenities: Say "thank you," "please," and, if needed, "I'm sorry." If you hang up first, do it gently so that the caller's ears are not jarred.

Closing the call

Outgoing Calls

Whether you are calling for yourself or for your employer, make sure that you have the right number. Allow adequate time for the person being called to answer; let the phone ring seven to ten times (at least a minute). When the phone is answered, identify yourself immediately (unless, of course, a switchboard operator answers; then ask for the person or extension number that you wish). In identifying yourself, use not only your name but also the name of the firm you represent and indicate something about the nature of the call you are making.

Telephone Lists

A directory of telephone numbers called frequently by you and your employer should be organized alphabetically. Use a system to which additions and deletions can be quickly made without getting the list out of alphabetic order. One possibility is a card file; another is the rotary wheel file; still another is a directory in which the names are typed on tabs, slipped into slots, and changed by removing or adding tabs to the directory pages. A short list can be kept in a small directory, such as a loose-leaf notebook for easy addition or removal of pages.

Do remember to include area codes for those numbers outside of your immediate area. Frequently called long-distance numbers can be identified by making a special mark or writing them in a different color. To avoid calling a number before an office is open or after it has closed, note the time difference between your area and that of the long-distance number by writing the number of hours of difference after the phone number. (You might also want to record whether you can call station-to-station rather than person-to-person.)

In addition to firm names, your list should also include the names and extension numbers of those persons with whom you have talked before or who you know handle certain matters.

Keep, in addition to local telephone directories, up-to-date out-of-town directories. Ask the telephone company for directories for any cities to which you make frequent calls.

Telephone Services

There are a number of services offered to telephone subscribers, including directory assistance (both local and long distance) and assistance in placing long-distance, conference, mobile, and over-seas calls. Information concerning yellow-page advertising, special services, and equipment is available by calling your local telephone company's business office. The telephone directory, too, includes information about using telephone equipment and services. Consult with representatives of the phone company for assistance with any specific telephone problems.

International calls are becoming increasingly easy to make, for in many instances it is possible to dial direct—International Direct Distance Dialing (IDDD). Telephone directories and operators can provide additional information.

Wide Area Telecommunications Service (WATS) is a bulk-use tariff available to large users of telephone service. It provides for both inward and outward calls. The inward toll-free calls ("800" numbers) allow the public to call companies who subscribe to the service. Outward WATS service lets the customer place unlimited calls in the allotted purchased time.

Some directories for "800" WATS numbers are printed outside

of the telephone company. However, many "800" numbers are of short duration (for a special advertising campaign, for example) so directories are difficult to keep up-to-date. It is possible to call the long distance operator (800-555-1212) to get the numbers of those businesses and people who subscribe to "800" services.

HINTS:

1. Always ask the name of the person with whom you are talking. If it is necessary to call again, you can save time by talking with that same person.

2. Keep a map of your geographical area near the telephone. If an out-of-town caller needs directions, you can give directions easily and accurately. The map will also help you if you need to find a street or address that is unfamiliar to you.

3. If you make promises to call back with more information, do so—even if only to say that getting the information is taking longer than you had expected. Don't break a promise to call again or to return a call.

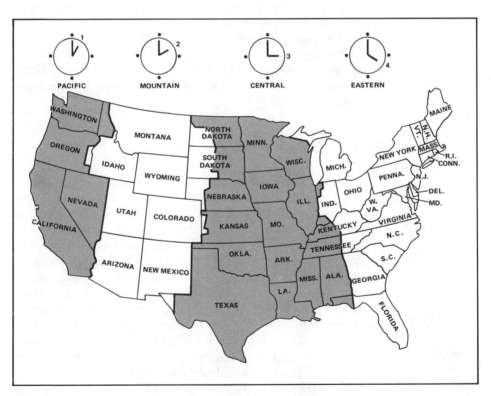

Time-Zone Map of the United States

4. Plan your call *before* you make it. This not only will prevent your forgetting important information and having to call back, but it will help you make your call brief but effective.

5. Should you have a special telephone equipment need, such as an automatic dialer or hands-free telephone, consult with the telephone company. New equipment is constantly being added.

MEETING CALLERS

How you handle the people who come into the office has a definite influence on the attitudes such visitors develop toward the company. Even the unwelcome visitor or the one your employer does not wish to see should be treated courteously.

The size of your office will determine your responsibilities in dealing with office callers. In the small office you may be the first one whom the visitor sees; in the larger office the visitor probably will be met first by a receptionist. In any event, the secretary learns first how the employer wants visitors handled. Some executives want to see everyone who calls, while others see callers on an appointment basis only. Most, however, will tend to be flexible, depending on their commitments for a given day. Some callers are on a special privilege basis—such as personal friends, relatives, or top executives within the company—and usually go into your employer's office unannounced.

Greeting Callers

Whatever the status of the caller, whenever he or she arrives, give the caller your immediate and undivided attention. Your greeting and response to the caller should be friendly. Listen attentively and find out who the person is, the name of the company represented, and the purpose of the visit. If the caller has been in before, try to remember and use names. If the visitor has made an appointment, help him or her feel at ease until your employer is available. If you can determine that someone other than your employer should handle the matter, refer the caller to the proper person; then phone the person who should handle the matter and find out if it is possible for the caller to be seen. If the caller does not have an appointment, ask the purpose of the visit. Know your employer's preferences in seeing visitors; if in doubt about a specific visitor, ask your employer. When you have made sure your employer does not wish to see a caller, turn the visitor away tactfully. Suggest that the caller write a note to your employer telling the reason for the meeting and asking that an appointment be scheduled.

Announcing Callers

Announce all visitors to your employer either on the intercom system or by escorting the visitor into the office. Use the visitor's name so that your employer knows whom to expect. If it is necessary to introduce the caller to your employer, be sure that both the caller and your boss hear and understand each other's names. In making introductions, men are presented to women—unless the man is much older or is an important person. If those being introduced are of the same sex, the younger person is introduced to the older. If there is no difference in sex, age, or importance, either person may be introduced to the other. If possible, tell your employer a little about the visitor so that a conversation can be started easily.

Interrupting Callers

If the caller seems to be staying too long (and you have checked with your employer and know such action is approved), interrupt the visit. This can be done by a telephone call or a quiet reminder to your employer that another appointment will arrive shortly. If your employer has a tight schedule, a comment as the caller goes into the office that there is another appointment in fifteen minutes should aid in keeping the call within time limits.

When Callers Leave

At the end of the visit, there may be things that you will need to do for the caller, such as schedule another appointment, make note of anything that should be sent, or follow up on getting needed information. If there is nothing that you need to do and if appropriate, offer to give the visitor whatever assistance you can, such as providing directions or calling a taxi; then say goodbye pleasantly.

4. Making Travel Arrangements

Sooner or later most employers make business trips. The trip may be a short one within the United States requiring only a few days, or it may be an international trip extending over several weeks. Some or perhaps all of the details of the travel are almost certain to involve you in your job as secretary.

Large companies often have travel or traffic departments that handle reservations and give travel information. If your company has such a department, all you need do is supply the details of your employer's proposed trip; the travel department will work out suggested itineraries and possible alternate plans. If your company has no such department, then you will probably handle most of the details personally. A competent travel agency can be most helpful, but selecting the right one can be difficult. Often an error is not discovered until the traveler is many miles from home. Travel agencies do not ordinarily charge a customer fees (with the exception of telephone or telegraph charges that may be necessary when time is short). Instead, travel agency fees are generally paid by the transportation lines, hotels, and other agencies.

ORGANIZING A BUSINESS TRIP

Initial Planning

When your employer plans a trip, you will need answers to the following questions before the trip can be planned:

1. When does your employer plan to leave, arrive at various stops, and return?

2. Where is your employer going? What places and what people will your employer need to see? Are hotel accommodations available convenient to these places and people?

3. Does your employer have preferences as to hotels or airlines?

4. What kinds of accommodations does your employer prefer? Does the company have limits on employees traveling first-class and a maximum on amounts that can be spent on hotel accommodations? (Perhaps your employer's executive status automatically determines first-class accommodations all of the way.)

5. Will a rental car be needed at any of the various stops? If so, does your employer have preferences as to makes of cars or car rental agencies? Will supplemental information be needed—road maps, lodging guides, or lists of recommended restaurants?

6. Determine the amount of money that will be needed for expenses. How does your employer prefer to handle these expenses? Are credit cards current? Schedule time for your employer to pick up traveler's checks in person.

Supplied with these facts, you can begin gathering information. If you are dealing with an agency, get to know one of the representatives and consult the same agent each time. The same is true if you are going direct to the airlines—dealing regularly with the same agent will save time and be helpful should you need special assistance. Remember, too, that services and regulations of the airlines are constantly changing. Such items as baggage allowances and check-in times can and do vary, so be sure to check them for every new trip.

If you are working on your own, begin with a work sheet and a file. Start by filling in the times and dates of your employer's trip and any other facts that you know. Then as reservations are confirmed, complete the rest of the itinerary. File letters of confirmation, copies of letters that you write, tickets, and other papers pertaining to the trip. When all of the arrangements are completed and approved by your employer, type the itinerary in its final form.

Travel by Air

Although most people prefer to travel by air because of the comparative shortness of the travel time, there are disadvantages to consider, including the time involved in getting from the center of a city to an airport, the possibility of canceled flights, and the adjustment of time from one part of the country to another (three hours from the East to the West Coast and even more on international flights). However, the advantages do outweigh the disadvantages, and most business trips today are made by air.

Generally, two flight classes are available: first-class and tourist (or coach). In addition, there are shuttle flights between two cities (such as New York and Washington) that do not require reservations.

The airlines offer special travel rates for such things as trips made in the middle of the week or at specific periods of time, and for additional members of the same family traveling together. Business people are usually more concerned with tailoring travel time to fit their schedules than with saving a few dollars by traveling at inconvenient hours.

Keep copies of up-to-date airline timetables in your files. (Remember, though, that airlines do frequently change flight times; check with airline ticket offices for last-minute changes.) If you ask them to do so, airlines will put you on mailing lists to receive schedules as they are revised. If the people in your office travel a great deal, your company may wish to subscribe to an airline guide such as *Official Airline Guide*, which alphabetically lists American and Canadian cities along with the airlines serving those cities and the schedules of those airlines. This guide also includes information about international flights, airport facilities, distances from airports to cities, transportation to and from airports, and car rentals. It is also available in various editions (world-wide and North American editions are examples) and a pocket-sized form.

For flight information, the easiest and quickest source is the airline ticket office. Although you can get information by phone, if the trip involves several stops, it may be better for you to visit the airline office and deal with one representative. A single agent working for one line can make all the reservations for you even if several airlines are involved. Availability of space can be checked electronically, which means that space can be reserved quickly. Once space is confirmed, tickets are issued. They can be picked up in person at the airline office, mailed to the business office, or held at the ticket office or airport. Payment can be by cash or check or charged to a credit card, including those issued by the airlines.

Airline reservations may be canceled or changed by the passenger, but there are usually certain time limits that have to be observed. An airline will notify passengers by phone if flights are changed or canceled.

Transportation available to and from the airport includes private taxis, car rentals, airport buses, and chartered limousines; in the larger cities helicopter service is provided. The airline or travel agent can give you detailed information about these services and, if necessary, make reservations.

Car Rentals

Car rentals are available at practically all airports and in almost every city and town. Rentals can be made in advance; if at all possible, they should be. Travel agents, airline agents, and local offices of rental agencies can make the reservations.

On arrival at the car delivery point, the person renting the car merely goes to the agency where the reservation is being held, presents a valid driver's license, and makes the financial arrangements for the rental. (Credit cards are a more satisfactory method of payment than cash.) It is possible to rent a car in one city and turn it in in another.

If your employer plans to rent a car, obtain road maps for both the city and the surrounding area. Automobile clubs, oil companies, and car rental agencies will supply them. At the same time, compile information on motels and restaurants in the area. Such information is available from automobile clubs and in local guidebooks.

Other Travel

Should your employer decide to travel by train or bus, check with the local offices of these companies for information. Check carefully the kinds of accommodations available: most domestic railroads today offer limited service—both in transportation and accommodations; as for travel by bus, the travel time involved might be so long that a car rental would prove more satisfactory.

Hotel and Motel Reservations

If you are making hotel or motel reservations, find out whether your employer has any preferences. Accommodations can be checked in such guidebooks as *Hotel and Motel Red Book* (published annually by the American Hotel Association Directory Corporation, 888 Seventh Avenue, New York, NY 10019), *Hotel & Travel Index* (published quarterly by Ziff-Davis Publishing Co., One Park Avenue, New York, NY 10016), and in the specific area directories published by the American Automobile Association and distributed to its members. These guides list the number of rooms, rates, types of accommodations, and locations of the hotels or motels.

Reservations can be made in a number of ways: If you have the time, you can write to the hotels for reservations. If a hotel is a member of a chain, you can phone the local hotel that belongs to the chain and make reservations in member hotels in other cities. If time is important, reservations can be made by telephone. (Check the telephone directory to see if the hotel has a toll-free telephone number.) Travel agencies and airline offices will make hotel reservations for their customers.

However the reservations are made, you need to supply the hotel or motel with certain information: the date of your employer's arrival and the expected arrival time (so that a room can be made ready for an early arrival or held for a late one); the kind of accommodations desired—such as a bedroom or suite, double or twin beds; the approximate rate for the room; the number of persons to be accommodated; and the length of time the room will be required.

Financial Arrangements for Travel

It may be your responsibility to arrange for your employer to have ample money for the trip. Aside from cash, there are three ways of supplying funds for travel: traveler's checks, letters of credit, and credit cards.

Traveler's checks   If your employer plans to carry traveler's checks, he or she will have to buy them in person because the checks must be signed when purchased in the presence of the issuing agent. Banks, savings and loan associations, American Express offices, and Western Union offices sell traveler's checks; they come in denominations of $10, $20, $50, and $100 and cost $1 per $100 to buy. Each check is numbered. After the checks have been issued, their numbers should immediately be recorded in duplicate, with one record kept by you and one carried by your employer. A traveler's check is cashed when it is signed in the presence of the person accepting it.

Letters of credit   If extensive travel is involved, a letter of credit can be issued by a bank, stating that the holder (your employer) is entitled to draw funds from the issuing bank up to a maximum amount. The holder of the letter of credit presents the letter to designated banks in certain cities and as amounts are withdrawn, they are listed on the letter of credit.

Credit cards   Credit cards are another means of supplying funds for travel. Cards are issued by organizations such as American Express, Diner's Club, MasterCard, and the Bank of America (VISA), and can be used for hotel accommodations, meals, car rentals, and other business expenses. Airline, telephone, railroad, and gasoline company credit cards are also available. You should keep a register of the numbers of credit cards that your employer has so that any loss of cards can be reported promptly. (Most companies issuing credit cards have toll-free numbers that can be called to report losses.) Renewals of the cards are handled by the companies issuing the cards.

International Travel

If a business trip involves international travel, the first thing your employer will usually need is a valid passport. (A passport is not required for a United States citizen to visit Canada, Mexico, Bermuda, or the West Indies.) Application for a passport should be made three or four weeks before departure. Forms can be obtained from passport agencies in Boston, Chicago, Honolulu, Los Angeles, Miami, New Orleans, New York, Philadelphia, San Francisco, Seattle, and Washington, as well as from clerks of various courts and from many United States post offices. A first-time applicant for a passport must present *in person* at any passport agency: (1) proof of United States citizenship (a birth certificate or naturalization papers are best), (2) some means of establishing identity (proof of naturalization, a driver's license, or similar identification), (3) two signed duplicate photographs taken within the past two years, and (4) the passport fee. Renewal of a passport that is no more than eight years old can be handled by mail by requesting a special form from one of the passport agencies. All passports are valid for five years.

In addition to the passport, a visa—an entry permit granted by a foreign government—may be required. Airline or travel agents can tell you which countries require visas, and they can usually obtain visas for their customers.

For reentry into the United States, it may be necessary to show proof that a traveler has received a smallpox vaccination within the past three years. In addition, some countries in which certain diseases are prevalent require inoculations against those diseases. A record of vaccinations and inoculations should be kept on an International Certificate of Vaccination.

Foreign travel for business purposes will undoubtedly be by air, if for no other reason than it is the fastest way to go. A disadvantage of air travel over long distances, however, is that of time differentials. For example, a Los Angeles executive arriving in London at 10 a.m. is also arriving at 2 a.m. *Los Angeles time*, a difference of eight hours. Plan itineraries with this in mind; don't schedule an important business meeting only a few hours after your employer's arrival following a long-distance trip by air. Another factor to remember is that overseas timetables are printed in 24-hour time. To convert, add 12 hours to any p.m. time—for example, 1 p.m. is 1300.

Hotel reservations in a foreign city can be made direct or

through a travel agency or airline. Some of the big American hotel chains are international (Hilton, for example) and can also make reservations for you at any of their foreign branches. It is increasingly important for travelers in foreign countries to reserve accommodations in advance.

Car rentals are available in most major foreign cities. Arrangements should be made in advance and can be made through international car rental agencies (such as Hertz) or through travel or airline agents. A car can be picked up at one airport or city and left at another if arranged for in advance. If a driver wishes, an International Driving Permit can be acquired from the American Automobile Touring Alliance; usually, though, a valid driver's license is all that is necessary.

Travel Checklist

Before your employer leaves, there are a number of final responsibilities that you will have:

1. Confirm all appointments and write the letters that are necessary.

2. Check your employer's appointment calendar to be sure that any appointments scheduled while he or she is away are either rescheduled or transferred to someone else.

3. In your employer's absence, find out what to do with incoming mail and who is responsible for his or her duties.

4. Send ahead any materials (particularly bulky or awkward ones) that your employer is not carrying. If the material is to be returned to you, include packing supplies and addressed labels.

5. Ask if there are any personal things that you are to do while your employer is away—for example, send salary checks to the bank or remind members of the family to pay bills.

Be sure that your employer has:

1. Copies of the itinerary

2. Travel tickets with confirmation of flight reservations and information about check-in times

3. Confirmations of hotel reservations

4. Details and forms for car rental arrangements, along with maps, restaurant and hotel guides and information, a valid driver's license, automobile club membership card

5. Travel documents (passport, visas, International Certificate of Vaccination)

6. Travel funds (preferably in traveler's checks, with a separate listing of check numbers), credit cards, blank personal checks

7. Any necessary files or papers, including copies of correspondence and background information on people to be seen, with all files separated into folders or manila envelopes

8. Listing of names, addresses, and telephone numbers of people in the area or areas to be visited

9. A supply of business cards

10. Letterhead stationery, envelopes, and addressed envelopes for mail to you, people in the company, and family members.

11. Forms so that a record of expenses can be kept easily.

THE ITINERARY

The final itinerary is so complete that the traveler will know at all times exactly where and when to go and all of the details of appointments. Make as many copies of the itinerary as will be necessary: for your employer, for other people within the company, for members of the employer's family, and for yourself.

Here is a sample:

```
           ITINERARY FOR DAVID H. WALKER
                 May 1 -- 5, 19--
           New York --- Washington, DC
```

SUNDAY, May 1 -- San Francisco to New York

```
            Check-in time:  11:15
12 noon  Leave San Francisco International Airport, TWA
(PDT)    Airlines, Flight #85, F/C, dinner served, nonstop.
         Tickets in TWA Airlines envelope.

8 p.m.   Arrive John F. Kennedy Airport, New York. Take
(EDT)    taxi to hotel.
         Hotel: The Regency, Park Avenue at 61 Street, New
                York  10021
                Phone:  (212) 759-4100
                Confirmation in Confirmations folder in
                briefcase.
```

MONDAY, May 2

```
10 a.m.  Interview in your room with James Coe for position
         in Advertising Department; resume and job specifi-
         cations in briefcase.
```

1 p.m.   Luncheon with June Lake and Hugh Warren of Adver-
         tising Department. Meet at offices at 475 Madison
         Avenue. Discussion of advertising of new electric
         portable typewriter. Folder on West Coast adver-
         tising plans in briefcase.

7 p.m.   Dinner at hotel (make reservations in morning)
         Guests: Mr. and Mrs. Donald Hastings (wife's first
                 name: Virginia)

TUESDAY, May 3 -- New York to Washington

10 a.m. Leave Penn Station on Metroliner (buy ticket at
         station)

1 p.m.   Arrive Washington.
         Pick up Hertz car. Reservations and map of Wash-
         ington in folder.
         Hotel: The Madison, 15 and M Streets, N.W., Wash-
                ington 20005
                Phone: (202) 838-3110
                Confirmation in Confirmations folder in
                briefcase.

4 p.m.   Drive to Arlington for meeting with Ross Hale
         about specifications for new government contract.
         Folder with information in briefcase.

8 p.m.   Dinner with Lee and Kate Martinson, 2540 0 Street,
         N.W.
         Call if you will be late: 837-4162.

WEDNESDAY, May 4 -- Convention of Office Equipment
Manufacturers, Madison Hotel

10 a.m. Convention opens

1 p.m.   Luncheon meeting in Gold Room. Ticket in
         Convention folder in briefcase.

7 p.m.   Banquet in Empire Room. Ticket in Convention
         folder in briefcase.

THURSDAY, May 5 — Washington to San Francisco

        Allow time to turn in rental car at airport and check in by 11.

12 noon   Leave Dulles Airport, TWA Airlines, Flight #75,
(EDT)   F/C, dinner served, nonstop. Tickets in TWA Airlines envelope.

2 p.m.   Arrive San Francisco International Airport.
(PDT)

5. The Sentence

A sentence is a group of related words that make a complete thought. This unit may be a question, a command, an exclamation, or a statement. Because forming good sentences is the heart of communicating effectively, it is important to understand what *constitutes* a sentence. The functions of the individual words in the sentence are discussed in Chapter 6, "The Parts of Speech."

SENTENCE STRUCTURE

Subject/Verb/Predicate

The framework of the sentence is made up of the *subject* and the *verb*. The subject of the sentence is the person or object that the sentence is talking about. It may be one word (the *simple subject*), or it may be the simple subject and any words that describe it (the *complete subject*). The subject may be the person speaking (*I*), the person spoken to (*you*), or the person or thing spoken of (*he, she, it*).

Usually there is an *object* or a *complement* after the verb, as well as *modifiers*. The verb together with its modifiers and object or complement is called the *predicate*.

Sentence Order

The natural order of a sentence is: subject/verb/complement or direct object. The order may be inverted so that the verb precedes the subject. (Questions, exclamations, and emphatic statements often appear in inverted order.)

Examples:

Marian	typed	the letter.	
subject	*verb*	*direct object*	} *natural order*
My employer	is	Mr. Grant.	
subject	*verb*	*complement*	

104

Whom	did	you	see?	inverted order
object	*verb*	*subject*	*verb*	

Clauses

A group of words containing a subject and a predicate is called a *clause.* An *independent (main) clause* makes sense standing by itself; a *dependent (subordinate) clause* cannot stand by itself because it depends on some other part of the sentence to make sense. Classified as dependent clauses are (1) the *adjective clause,* modifying a noun or pronoun; (2) the *adverb clause,* modifying the verb or indicating time, place, manner, cause, condition, degree, or comparison; and (3) the *noun clause,* used in any way that a noun may be used. Dependent clauses are introduced by subordinate conjunctions (see page 168). Adjective clauses are usually introduced by *that, which,* or a form of *who;* adverb clauses, by any of the many subordinate conjunctions such as *when, if, since, before, after,* and *because;* and noun clauses, by *that* and sometimes by *what, whatever, why, when,* or a form of *who.*

Examples: My employer has offices in the Broadway Building.
independent clause
My employer, who is a well-known attorney, has offices in the Broadway Building. *dependent adjective clause*
If you have any further information, please let me know immediately. *dependent adverb clause*
I said that my employer has an office in the Broadway Building. *dependent noun clause*
Whatever he can do will be helpful. *dependent noun clause*

Phrases

A group of related words that does not have a subject and a predicate is called a *phrase.* There are six kinds of phrases:

1. *Prepositional* preposition plus an object

Example: The eraser was under the typewriter.

2. *Infinitive* infinitive plus an object

Example: I wanted to <u>read my mail</u>.

   3. *Participial* participle plus an object

Example: He found the child <u>running down the street</u>.

   4. *Gerund* gerund plus an object

Example: <u>Reading the mail</u> required two hours.

   5. *Verb* complete verb

Example: I <u>should have read</u> the assignment.

   6. *Absolute* words modifying a sentence or clause as a whole but not linked to it by a conjunction or a relative pronoun

Example: <u>As a matter of fact</u>, I should have mailed the letter earlier.

KINDS OF SENTENCES

Simple

A *simple* sentence consists of one independent clause. It may comprise only two words: *Secretaries type.* Or it can include many words: *Secretaries in our office take dictation and do a lot of typing.* The latter example contains a compound verb, but it has only one clause.

Complex

   A *complex* sentence contains one independent clause and one or more dependent clauses.

Example: Secretaries who work in our office take dictation.

Compound

   A *compound* sentence has two or more independent clauses.

Example: Secretaries in our office take dictation, and they do a lot of
typing.

Compound-Complex

A *compound-complex* sentence contains two or more independent clauses plus one or more dependent clauses.

Example: Secretaries who work in our office take dictation, and they
do a lot of typing.

SENTENCE FAULTS

Three problems connected with writing sentences are creating a
sentence fragment, a comma splice, or a fused (run-together) sentence.

Fragment

A sentence fragment is a part of a sentence. The fragment may
be a phrase or a subordinate clause, neither of which can stand
alone as a sentence. Check any sentence that has beginning capitalization and end punctuation to see that it contains a subject and a
verb and that it stands by itself as a complete thought.

Examples: *avoid:* To finish the typing. *phrase fragment*
use: Will you have time to finish the typing?
avoid: Without making a copy for the files. *phrase fragment*
use: She mailed the letter without making a copy for
the files.
avoid: When Mr. Ryan called. *subordinate clause fragment*
use: Joyce did not know when Mr. Ryan called.

Comma Splice

Independent clauses can be simple sentences; two of them
(other sentence elements may also be included) can be joined to
form compound or compound-complex sentences. If the clauses

are separated by a comma when a semicolon or period should be used, a comma splice is created. See page 174 for punctuation of a compound sentence.

Examples: *avoid:* Polly is Mrs. Hall's secretary, occasionally she works for Mr. Peterson as well. *No conjunction connecting independent clauses; use either a period or a semicolon to separate.*

use: Polly is Mrs. Hall's secretary; occasionally she works for Mr. Peterson as well.

avoid: Polly would like to become an administrative assistant, however, she will have to wait for an opening. *Conjunctive adverb connecting; use semicolon to separate.*

use: Polly would like to become an administrative assistant; however, she will have to wait for an opening.

Fused Sentence

A fused (run-together) sentence consists of two sentences joined together without separating punctuation and without a capital letter beginning the second sentence.

Examples: *avoid:* After finishing the report, Polly made an extra copy for her supervisor that is what she had been instructed to do.

use: After finishing the report, Polly made an extra copy for her supervisor. That is what she had been instructed to do.

avoid: She planned the typing very carefully this helped reduce the chance of making errors.

use: She planned the typing very carefully. This helped reduce the chance of making errors.

6. The Parts of Speech

Any word in any sentence can be classified as one of the eight parts of speech. Classifying words, understanding their use in sentences, and recognizing their relation to one another is the study of grammar. Classifying words as parts of speech helps you to identify their functions in sentences so that you can further your understanding and use of them.

The traditional classification identifies eight parts of speech.

1. *Noun*   names a thing, person, place, quality, idea, or action
2. *Pronoun*   replaces a noun
3. *Verb*   expresses action or state of being
4. *Adjective*   modifies a noun or pronoun
5. *Adverb*   modifies a verb, adjective, or another adverb
6. *Preposition*   connects a noun or pronoun to the rest of the sentence
7. *Conjunction*   connects words or groups of words
8. *Interjection*   expresses strong emotion in the form of an exclamation

These eight definitions tell you that words in a sentence have these functions: naming, asserting, modifying, connecting, and exclaiming. Nouns and pronouns name; verbs assert; adjectives and adverbs modify; prepositions and conjunctions connect; and interjections[1] exclaim.

Any word can be classified as one of the eight parts of speech. However, many words have more than one classification; for example, *run, set,* and *stand* are both verbs and nouns, and *but* can be both a conjunction and a preposition.

Dependent clauses are labeled as adjective, adverb, or noun clauses. Prepositional phrases may also be used as adjectives or adverbs. Therefore, how a word, phrase, or clause is *used* in a particular sentence determines its classification as a part of speech.

[1] Although an interjection is mentioned here as one of the eight parts of speech, it will not be discussed further because its use in a sentence is obvious.

CHART OF PARTS OF SPEECH, PHRASES, AND DEPENDENT CLAUSES

USE	PARTS OF SPEECH (WORDS)	PHRASES	SUBORDINATE CLAUSES
Name	noun pronoun *gerund *infinitive	prepositional *gerund *infinitive	noun
Show Action or Being	verb	verb	
Modify	adjective adverb *participle *infinitive	prepositional *participial *infinitive	adjective adverb
Connect	conjunction preposition	**phrasal preposition	

* The verbals—infinitives, gerunds, and participles—are not usually classified as separate parts of speech. Verbals are defined as verb forms used as adjectives, adverbs, or nouns. This chart is a breakdown of these verbals to show their uses in sentences.

** A phrasal preposition is two or more words used as a preposition. Examples: *because of, in spite of, according to.*

NOUNS AND PRONOUNS

Because nouns and pronouns are so closely related, they are easier to understand if they are considered together. There will be times when they will need to be considered separately, but they will always be labeled so that there will be no confusion.

A noun is a name. A pronoun stands for a noun.

A noun can be defined as the name of a thing (*book*), person (*woman*), place (*city*), quality (*happiness*), idea (*socialism*), or action (*swimming*). Therefore, the name of *anything* classifies a word as a noun.

The word *pronoun* defines itself. It merely adds the prefix *pro,* meaning "for," to the word *noun.* The literal meaning, then, is "for a noun," which is exactly what it does mean: a pronoun is a word used for, or in place of, a noun.

If pronouns did not exist, it would mean that every time you talked about any noun you would have to use the name of that noun.

For example, you could not say "Mr. Brown is in his office doing his work." You would have to say "Mr. Brown is in Mr. Brown's office doing Mr. Brown's work." Therefore, any pronoun must refer specifically to the noun for which it stands; that noun is called the *antecedent*. Pronouns *must* agree with their antecedents in number, gender, and person.

Classes of Nouns

A *common* noun refers to all members of a group—persons, places, or things.   **Common**

Examples: businessman   car   street   refrigerator
building   city   park   summer

A *proper* noun designates a particular person, place, or thing. A proper noun is *always* capitalized.   **Proper**

Examples: Charles Lee   Chrysler   Fifth Avenue   Exxon
Flatiron Building   New York   Central Park   August

A *collective* noun refers to a group or collection of persons or things.   **Collective**

Examples: jury   crowd   committee   faculty
audience   company   regiment   data

A *concrete* noun designates a particular person or thing that can be sensed—seen, heard, touched, smelled, or tasted.   **Concrete**

Examples: desk   man   smoke   coffee
river   book   office   elevator

An *abstract* noun names a quality, state, or idea.   **Abstract**

Examples: responsibility   loyalty   democracy
treachery   honesty   utopia

A compound noun consists of two or more words, usually a noun plus qualifying words. They can be written as one word, two or more words, or hyphenated. For more complete rules and examples, see the section on one-word, two-word, and hyphenated forms, pages 205–206.   **Compound nouns**

Examples: businessman   self-control   father-in-law
            airmail   down payment   New Jersey

Kinds of Pronouns

Personal   A *personal* pronoun, as the name indicates, refers to a person—the person speaking, the person spoken about, or the person spoken to. The personal pronouns are *I, you, he, she, it, we,* and *they.* The chart on pages 115–116 gives the declension of pronouns.

Relative   A *relative* pronoun joins a dependent adjective clause (relative clause) to the antecedent of that relative pronoun. The chief relative pronouns are *who* (*whom* or *whose*), *which,* and *that. What, whoever, whomever, whatever,* and occasionally *as* are other less frequently used relative pronouns.

Be aware of these points:

1. These pronouns can be either singular or plural. Their number is determined by their antecedents.

Example: I bought a pen that writes very good shorthand notes.
           sing.

2. Place a relative clause (introduced by the relative pronoun) immediately after the noun or pronoun it modifies.

Example: *avoid:* The man is dead who wrote the book.
           use: The man who wrote the book is dead.

3. *Who* can change its form to *whom* or *whose* to indicate a change in case, but it remains a relative pronoun.

Examples: My employer, *whom* you met in the elevator, will leave Friday for Chicago.
My sister, *whose* job takes her to many foreign countries, is now in Egypt.

4. Relative clauses can be restrictive or nonrestrictive. Nonrestrictive relative clauses (that is, those not necessary for the sentence to make sense but which add information) are usually introduced by *which;* restrictive clauses (those necessary for the sentence to make sense) are usually introduced by *that.* The nonrestrictive clauses are set off by commas, but restrictive clauses are not. *Who* can introduce either restrictive or nonrestrictive clauses.

Examples: Mary's typewriter, which needs frequent repair, was purchased in 1975. *nonrestrictive*

The typewriter that is used for typing reports is in need of repair. *restrictive*

The antecedents of *who* should be persons; of *which,* animals, things, or situations; of *that,* persons or things.

Sometimes the relative pronoun that introduces a restrictive clause is omitted, especially if the first word of the clause is a proper noun or a pronoun.

Examples: The time (that) I remember most distinctly is the summer (that) I held my first job. *Both relative pronouns could be omitted.*

The company president is a person (whom) everyone likes. *The relative pronoun whom could be omitted.*

The company president is someone who is well-liked. *The pronoun could not be omitted.*

It was the company president (whom) John met. *The relative pronoun whom could be omitted.*

Indefinite pronouns (sometimes called *adjective pronouns*) do not name any particular individual or thing. **Indefinite**

Examples: someone, somebody, either, each, neither, anyone, nobody, no one, another, one, everyone, both

The pronouns or nouns referring to these indefinite pronouns must agree with them in number.

Example: *avoid:* Will everyone please turn in their papers. *Everyone is singular; therefore, the pronoun referring to it must be singular.*

use: Will everyone please turn in his or her paper.

This distinction is usually violated in informal usage and in speech. You are much more likely to hear "If anyone calls, tell *them* I'll return at three" than "If anyone calls, tell *him* or *her* I'll return at three." These indefinite pronouns can also be treated as collectives; in this case the pronouns referring to them are plural.

Example: Everyone approved of Mr. Scott's speech, and they applauded vigorously when he concluded.

The chart on pages 115–116 tells which indefinite pronouns are singular and which are plural.

Reciprocal   *Each other* and *one another* are *reciprocal* pronouns. Though *each other* refers correctly to two and *one another* to more than two, *each other* may be used informally for any number.

Examples: Margaret and Jean wrote to <u>each other</u> for many years.
The members of the organization saw <u>one another</u> at their convention.
Kate told me that the people in the word processing center compete with <u>each other</u> for the easy jobs. *informal*

Demonstrative   *Demonstrative* pronouns point out. They include *this* (plural, *these*) and *that* (plural, *those*). *This* (*these*) is used to point out items close at hand; it limits. *That* (*those*) is used to point out items further away in either time or distance. They may also be used as demonstrative adjectives.

Examples: <u>This</u> is a good book. *pronoun*
<u>This</u> book is a good one. *adjective*
<u>These</u> books are good ones. *adjective*
<u>Those</u> who travel to Europe will need passports. *pronoun*

Interrogative   The *interrogative* pronouns are *who, which,* and *what* when they are used in asking questions.

Examples: <u>Who</u> is calling?
<u>What</u> is that?
<u>Which</u> of the two books is yours?

Reflexive   *Reflexive* pronouns are formed by adding the suffixes *self* (singular) or *selves* (plural) to the personal pronouns *my, our, your, him, them, her,* and *it*. Reflexive pronouns are used for two purposes: for *emphasis* (in this case they are also called intensive pronouns) and for *reflecting* the action of the verb toward a pronoun already used—usually the subject. If the pronoun is used as an intensive, it is considered to be in apposition to the noun.

Examples: The chairman <u>himself</u> typed the letter. *emphatic*
I saw <u>myself</u> in the mirror. *reflexive*
Jane cut <u>herself</u> on the paper cutter. *reflexive*

WARNING:

Do not use reflexive pronouns in place of personal pronouns.

Examples: *avoid:* He gave the books to Helen and myself.
    use: He gave the books to Helen and me.
    avoid: Mr. Smith and myself will attend the meeting.
    use: Mr. Smith and I will attend the meeting.

The chart that follows includes all the pronouns and tells whether each is singular or plural. Keep in mind that how a pronoun is *used* in a sentence determines what kind of pronoun it is. *Who*, for example, can be relative or interrogative, depending on its use in the sentence.

CHART OF PRONOUNS

1. PERSONAL PRONOUNS

CASE:	NOMINATIVE		OBJECTIVE		POSSESSIVE	
PERSON	**SING.**	**PL.**	**SING.**	**PL.**	**SING.**	**PL.**
1st	I	we	me	us	my, mine	our, ours
2d	you	you	you	you	your, yours	your, yours
3d	he, she, it	they	him, her, it	them	his, her, hers, its	their, theirs

2. RELATIVE PRONOUNS (singular or plural, as determined by antecedent)

NOMINATIVE	OBJECTIVE	POSSESSIVE
that	that	(of) that
who	whom	whose
which	which	(of) which, whose
what	what	

3. INDEFINITE PRONOUNS (always in 3d person)

SING.		SING. OR PL.	PL.
another	much	all	both
anybody	nobody	any	few
anyone	no one	either (*usually sing.*)	many
anything	nothing	neither (*usually sing.*)	others
each	one	more	several
each one	somebody	most	
everybody	someone	none	
everyone	something	other	
everything		some (*usually pl.*)	
		such	

4. RECIPROCAL PRONOUNS

each other (refers to two)
one another (refers to more than two)

5. DEMONSTRATIVE PRONOUNS

SING.	PL.
this	these
that	those

6. INTERROGATIVE PRONOUNS (singular or plural, as determined by antecedent)

NOMINATIVE	OBJECTIVE	POSSESSIVE
who	whom	whose
which	which	(of) which
what	what	

7. REFLEXIVE (or INTENSIVE) PRONOUNS

PERSON	SING.	PL.
1st	myself	ourselves
2d	yourself	yourselves
3d	himself, herself, itself, oneself	themselves

Properties of Nouns and Pronouns

Nouns and pronouns are given certain form changes to indicate number, gender, person, and case.

Because nouns and pronouns are so similar, the properties of nouns and pronouns are discussed together.

Number

Pronouns   The plurals of personal, demonstrative, and reflexive pronouns have been given previously. Relative and interrogative pronouns are singular or plural in agreement with their antecedents; and indefinite pronouns are usually singular. For more detailed information, see the chart on pages 115–116.

Nouns   To form the plurals of singular nouns, ordinarily s is added to the singular form.

Examples: typewriter/typewriters
typist/typists
student/students
house/houses

If the singular form of a noun ends in *ch, sh, s, x,* or *z,* add *es.* ENDING IN
CH, SH, S, X, Z

Examples: lunch/lunches   church/churches
rush/rushes   blush/blushes
boss/bosses   miss/misses
tax/taxes   blintz/blintzes

If the singular form of a noun ends in *y* and the *y* is preceded by a ENDING IN Y
consonant, change the *y* to *i* and add *es.*

Examples: company/companies   baby/babies
secretary/secretaries   copy/copies

If the singular form of a noun ends in *y* and the *y* is preceded by a
vowel, add *s.*

Examples: attorney/attorneys   journey/journeys

Exceptions: obloquy/obloquies   colloquy/colloquies
soliloquy/soliloquies

To form the plural of *all* proper nouns ending in *y,* add *s.*

Examples: Harry/Harrys   Jerry/Jerrys
Mary/Marys   Rodney/Rodneys

If the singular form of a noun ends in *o* and the *o* is preceded by a ENDING IN O
vowel, add *s.*

Examples: radio/radios   studio/studios
folio/folios   cameo/cameos

If the singular form of a noun ends in *o* and the *o* is preceded by a
consonant, add *es.*

Examples: potato/potatoes   tomato/tomatoes
veto/vetoes

A number of singular nouns ending in *o* can form their plurals by adding either *s* or *es*.

Examples: banjo/*pref.* banjos   motto/*pref.* mottoes
cargo/*pref.* cargoes   grotto/*pref.* grottoes

If the singular noun ending in *o* is a proper name, add *s* only.

Example: Otto/Ottos

<u>**WARNING:**</u>

There are many exceptions to the rules for forming the plurals of nouns ending in o; check the dictionary if you have the slightest doubt.

Examples: alto/altos   soprano/sopranos
dynamo/dynamos   credo/credos
quarto/quartos

IRREGULAR   Many singular nouns form their plurals by changing a vowel or
PLURALS   vowels within the word.

Examples: man/men   mouse/mice   woman/women
tooth/teeth   goose/geese   foot/feet

Three singular nouns form their plurals by adding *ren* or *en*, and one of them changes its vowel as well.

Examples: child/children   brother/brethren   ox/oxen

ENDING IN <u>F</u>   Many singular nouns ending in *f* or *fe* change the *f* or *fe* to *v* and
OR <u>FE</u>   add *es*.

Examples: calf/calves   half/halves
leaf/leaves   self/selves
wife/wives   knife/knives

Exceptions: belief/beliefs   chief/chiefs
grief/griefs   proof/proofs
safe/safes   beef/beefs (*pref.*) *or* beeves

The plurals of letters, numbers, symbols, signs, and words regarded as words are formed by adding an apostrophe and *s*. *This is the only time an apostrophe is used to form a plural.*

Examples: C.O.D.'s
the why's and wherefore's
&'s
7's

Hyphenated compound nouns and compound nouns made up of two or more words form their plurals by making the significant word plural.

Examples: mother-in-law/mothers-in-law
product manager/product managers
court martial/*either* courts martial *or* court martials
deputy sheriff/deputy sheriffs
post office/post offices

A compound noun written as one word forms its plural at the end of the word.

Examples: spoonful/spoonfuls
footnote/footnotes
stepson/stepsons

The plurals of proper nouns are formed in the same way that common noun plurals are formed: Add *s* unless the name ends in *ch, sh, s, x,* or *z*; then add *es*.

Examples: Smith/Smiths   Finch/Finches
Fox/Foxes   Jones/Joneses

When there is a courtesy title of address (*Mr., Mrs., Miss, Ms.*) with the proper noun, either the proper noun or the title may be made plural. Do not make *both* the title and proper noun plural. *Messieurs* (abbreviated *Messrs.*) and *Mesdames* (*Mmes.*) are the French plurals that we use as the plurals of *Mr.* and *Mrs. Misses* is the plural of *Miss. Mses.* (or *Mss.*) is the plural of *Ms.*

Because a plural title sounds very formal, it is better to avoid using it in business. Use the plural name form when referring to two or more persons with the same name; repeat the title with each name when referring to persons with different names.

Examples: *avoid:* Messrs. Wilson and Mason
           use: Mr. Wilson and Mr. Mason
         avoid: Mmes. Carl Wilson and Ralph Mason
           use: Mrs. Carl Wilson and Mrs. Ralph Mason
         avoid: Misses Jean and Carol Wilson
           use: Miss Jean and Miss Carol Wilson
         avoid: the Misses Wilson
           use: the Miss Wilsons

SAME
SINGULAR AND
PLURAL FORM

Certain nouns are the same in both the singular and plural forms.

Examples: Chinese   moose   gross
          salmon   deer   fish (*or* fishes *if designating*
          series   sheep   *more than one species*)

ALWAYS
PLURAL

Certain nouns are always plural.

Examples: goods   scissors   headquarters
          auspices   proceeds   trousers
          billiards means (*income*)   morals
          species   earnings

ALWAYS
SINGULAR

Certain nouns are always singular.

Examples: news   whereabouts   music

ENDINGS IN
ICS

Some nouns that end in *ics* are singular when referring to a body of knowledge (a subject-matter field) and plural when referring to individual facts.

Examples: electronics   statistics   economics
          athletics   civics   mathematics

Statistics <u>is</u> taught at most colleges.
Statistics <u>are</u> known to be wrong.
Athletics <u>is</u> not enjoyed by all students.
Athletics <u>are</u> provided for varying degrees of ability.

FOREIGN
WORDS

Foreign nouns in use in the English language may either retain the foreign plurals or have English plurals. In some cases, a foreign noun may have both an English and a foreign plural.

Examples:

Foreign nouns ending in sis:

basis/bases	thesis/theses	parenthesis/parentheses
analysis/analyses	crisis/crises	synopsis/synopses
ellipsis/ellipses		

Foreign nouns ending in a:

alumna/alumnae (*fem.*)   antenna/antennas *or* antennae
formula/formulas *or* formulae

Foreign nouns ending in um:

medium/mediums *or* media   datum/data (*see page 131*)
ultimatum/ultimatums *or* ultimata agendum/agendums *or* agenda[1]

Foreign nouns ending in x:

appendix/appendixes *or* appendices (*technical*)
index/indexes *or* indices (*technical*)

Foreign nouns ending in us:

alumnus/alumni (*masc.*)   radius/radii *or* radiuses
stimulus/stimuli   syllabus/syllabi *or* syllabuses
terminus/termini *or* terminuses

These foreign nouns now form plurals by adding *s* or *es,* as the case may be:

area	campus	diploma	memorandum	plateau
bureau	circus	era	museum	quota

Collective nouns (for example, *jury, committee, company, family, corps, army*) are considered singular if the collective noun acts as a unit, plural if the members of the collective noun are acting separately.   COLLECTIVE NOUNS

Examples: The committee is meeting in Room 90. *The noun* committee *is singular because it is acting as a unit.*
The committee are unable to agree. *The noun* committee *is plural because the members of the committee are not acting as a unit.*

---

[1] An *agendum* is something to be done. *Agenda* may be used to mean a list of agendums and is then singular. In this sense, the plural of *agenda* becomes *agendas.*
Examples: The agenda has been prepared for the next meeting.
There have been no agendas for any of the meetings.

Gender

Gender as applied to the English language is the indication of sex distinction or the absence of such a distinction. The three genders are *masculine, feminine,* and *neuter.* Except for pronouns such as *he, she,* and it, and for nouns that change the ending to show sex distinction (actor/actress; host/hostess), gender is indicated by the meaning of the word (aunt/uncle; boy/girl). Nouns that refer to inanimate objects and singular collective nouns are considered to be in the neuter gender.

Examples: Every student must close *his or her* book.
The company has a parking lot for *its* employees.

Person

There are three *persons* in grammar. *First person (I, we)* denotes the speaker; *second person (you),* the person spoken to; and *third person (he, she, it, they),* the person spoken of. Pronouns have all three persons; nouns are regarded as third person.

Case

Case is the form of a noun or pronoun indicating its relationship to other words in the sentence. There are three cases: *nominative* (also called *subjective*); *objective* (also called *accusative*); and *possessive* (also called *genitive*). The forms for the nominative and objective cases of nouns are the same. Pronouns, however, often change form to indicate case; in fact, some personal, relative, and interrogative pronouns change their forms in all three cases.

Nominative and objective cases   The case of a noun or pronoun is determined by the *use* of the noun or pronoun in the sentence. Both the nominative and objective cases have many uses and are often confused. Therefore, their uses will be listed and considered together before the possessive case is discussed.

SUBJECT OF A SENTENCE (NOMINATIVE)   As the name implies, the *subject* of a sentence is the person or the object that the sentence is about. The subject may be a noun or pronoun with or without qualifying elements, two or more nouns or pronouns (it is then compound), or a clause.

Examples: John is late for the meeting. *a noun as a subject*
　　　　　 Helen and John will be late for the meeting. *two nouns*
　　　　　　　 as a compound subject
　　　　　 Mary and I are going to work on Saturday. *a noun and*
　　　　　　　 pronoun as a compound subject
　　　　　 The old, weather-stained building is being torn down. *a*
　　　　　　　 noun plus qualifying words as a subject
　　　　　 That I would work on Saturday was obvious. *a noun*
　　　　　　　 clause as a subject

　　　A word (or word group) is a *predicate nominative* if it meets two   PREDICATE
conditions: It must follow a form of the verb *be*, and it must "rename"   NOMINATIVE
the subject. It can be a word, a phrase, or a clause, and it can be   (NOMINATIVE)
compound. The predicate nominative is also called *subjective
complement, predicate complement,* and *predicate word.*
　　　A form of the verb *be* may be any of a number of forms; it is
conjugated and all of the forms are given on page 145. However,
remember that the verb is followed by the nominative case if it is any
one of the following forms of *be*:

am	was	has been
is	were	have been
are	be	had been

Examples: It is Betty. *a noun as a predicate nominative*
　　　　　 She is a very efficient secretary. *a noun plus qualifying*
　　　　　　　 words as a predicate nominative
　　　　　 The callers were David and Bill. *two nouns as a*
　　　　　　　 compound predicate nominative
　　　　　 The message was that he would be late. *a noun clause as*
　　　　　　　 a predicate nominative
　　　　　 The girls who are working late are Joan and she. *a noun*
　　　　　　　 and pronoun as a compound predicate nominative

　　　A noun or pronoun that is connected to the sentence by a   OBJECT OF A
preposition is the *object* of that preposition. The object of a   PREPOSITION
preposition may be compound.   (OBJECTIVE)

Examples: This story is about Queen Elizabeth.

　　　　　 I waited for Barbara and Shirley.　⎫ *compound*
　　　　　 Give the message to Mr. Smith or his ⎬ *object of*
　　　　　　　 secretary.　　　　　　　　　　⎭ *the
　　　　　　　　　　　　　　　　　　　　　　 preposition*

DIRECT OBJECT OF A VERB (OBJECTIVE)
A noun or pronoun that receives the action of the verb is the *direct object*. It will answer *whom* or *what* about the verb. It, too, can be compound.

Examples: I wrote <u>a letter</u>. *Wrote what? A letter.*
I saw <u>him</u>. *Saw whom? Him.*
I read <u>a book and a magazine</u>. *compound*
Virginia made <u>four copies of the letter</u>.

SUBJECT OR OBJECT OF ANY INFINITIVE (OBJECTIVE)
An infinitive is a verb form plus *to* and is used as a noun, adjective, or adverb—not as a verb. The person or thing that the infinitive is about is the *subject;* the noun or pronoun receiving the action of the infinitive is the *object.*

Examples: I wanted <u>Vera</u> to read the <u>book</u>. *Vera is the subject of the infinitive* to read; book *is the object.*
We asked <u>Mr. Smith</u> to help in the matter. *Mr. Smith is the subject of* to help; *there is no object.*

COMPLEMENT OF THE INFINITIVE <u>TO BE</u> (NOMINATIVE AND OBJECTIVE)
To be cannot take an object, but it can have a noun or pronoun that completes its meaning.

Examples: I was thought to be <u>Margaret</u>.
We thought Mr. Davis to be <u>you</u>.

The rule for determining the case of the complement of the infinitive *to be* is as follows: The complement agrees in case with the subject of the infinitive. To apply this rule, follow these steps:

1. Remember that the subject of *any* infinitive is in the objective case.
2. Determine whether the *to be* has its own subject; if it does, both the subject and the complement must be in the objective case.
3. If the *to be* does not have its own subject, the complement must then agree in case with the subject of the sentence—which is in the nominative case—and must therefore be nominative.

Examples: I thought John to be <u>him</u>. John *is the subject of* to be *and is in the objective case, so the complement* him *is also in the objective case.*
I was thought to be <u>he</u>. *To be does not have its own subject, so the complement agrees with the subject of the sentence—I—and is in the nominative case.*
I did not want the guilty one to be <u>him</u>.

I thought the president to be <u>him</u>.
Mary thought you to be <u>her</u>.
Mary was thought to be <u>she</u> who typed the letters.

With verbs that ask or give, there is often an *indirect object* that names the receiver.

Examples: He gave <u>Mary</u> the book.
He told <u>her</u> the message.

A noun or pronoun placed next to another noun or pronoun so that the second explains by completing or supplementing the first is an *appositive* or is in *apposition*.

Examples: Mr. Smith, <u>the president of the company</u>, is out of town.
My uncle, <u>Dr. William Armstrong</u>, is a well-known lawyer.

The noun or pronoun that is in apposition has the same case as the noun or pronoun for which it stands.

Examples: We, <u>Miss Lynn and I</u>, will do the typing. *nominative case*
I, <u>William Smith</u>, swear this to be true. *nominative case*
Mr. Hill asked us, <u>Miss Lynn and me</u>, to do the typing. *objective case*
I gave the message to him, <u>William Smith</u>. *objective case*

<u>WARNINGS</u>:

1. *When a noun is in apposition to a pronoun, the pronoun usage still determines the case.*

Examples: <u>We girls</u> ate lunch in the park.
Lunch was served in the park for <u>us girls</u>.

2. *Notice that one-word appositives are not set off by commas.*

Examples: My cousin <u>Bill</u> attends college in New York.
I know that my sister <u>Ann</u> is in New York.

A noun or pronoun used to address a person (or object) in speaking or writing is a *direct address*. It is also called *nominative of address*.

Examples: <u>Julie</u>, will you type this letter?

May we hear from you, <u>Mr. Wilson</u>, in regard to this matter.

If you know how a pronoun is used in a sentence, using the correct case form becomes a matter of following rules. The uses for nominative and objective cases are listed below.

The *nominative case* is used as:

1. Subject of a sentence or clause
2. Predicate nominative
3. Complement of the infinitive *to be* when that infinitive does not have its own subject
4. Direct address
5. Appositive when the noun or pronoun the appositive stands for is in the nominative case

The *objective case* is used as:

1. Direct object of a verb
2. Object of a preposition
3. Subject or object of any infinitive
4. Complement of the infinitive *to be* when that infinitive has its own subject
5. Indirect object
6. Appositive when the noun or pronoun the appositive stands for is in the objective case

WARNINGS:

1. *Errors in nominative and objective case often occur when the pronoun is part of a compound. To avoid such errors, mentally eliminate the other member (or members) of the compound.*

Examples: Give the message to Betty and _____ (he *or* him?). *If you leave out* Betty and, *the sentence becomes:* Give the message to <u>he</u> *or* <u>him</u>. *Now the choice of pronoun is easy:* Give the message to <u>him</u>.

Ask <u>Ted and him</u> to do the work.

Tell either <u>Mr. Smith or him</u> that I shall be late.

Either <u>you or I</u> must work on Saturday.

2. *If the pronoun following* than *or* as *in a statement of comparison is part of an understood clause, test whether or not you have used the correct case form by mentally completing the clause.*

Examples: Judy types faster than I (do).
We received the news as soon as they (did).
I would rather work with Bill than (with) her.

If there is any chance that the meaning might not be clear, complete the clause, as shown by the underlined words.

Examples: I have known Margaret as long as Mary <u>has</u>.
I have known Margaret as long as <u>I have known</u> Mary.

The *possessive case* (also called *genitive*) is used when a noun or pronoun shows ownership. Nouns and pronouns *do not* form their possessives in the same way. **Possessive case**

Possession by nouns may be indicated in two ways: (1) the addition of an apostrophe or (2) the use of an *of* phrase (for example, *Henry's car* or *that car of Henry's*). The second example is a "double" possessive (the *of* and the *'s* both show possession) and is usually considered to be informal. POSSESSIVE NOUNS

If the noun that is to become possessive ends in *s*, add an apostrophe only. If it does not end in *s*, add an apostrophe and *s*. BASIC RULE

Examples:

Nouns not ending in s:

child/child's   children/children's   company/company's
Mr. Smith/Mr. Smith's   lady/lady's   men/men's

Nouns ending in s:

companies/companies'   attorneys/attorneys'   boys/boys'
mothers/mothers'   ladies/ladies'   employers/employers'

Authorities differ on the forming of possessives for singular nouns ending in *s* or an s-sound, such as *actress, hostess,* and *boss.* As a general rule, add the apostrophe only (basic rule), unless the noun is a one-syllable word; then add *'s*. Remember, though, that you can add only the apostrophe in all instances. SINGULAR NOUNS ENDING IN <u>S</u>

Examples: hostess'   actress'   Frances'   boss's (or boss')

WARNING:

Whether a noun is singular or plural has nothing to do with how its possessive is formed. It is the ending of the word that is the determining factor.

Examples: woman/woman's   girl/girl's   boss/boss's or boss'
women/women's   girl/girl's   bosses/bosses'

COMPOUND
NOUNS

To form the possessive of a compound noun, add the apostrophe or 's to the last word only.

Examples: father-in-law's   businessman's
commander in chief's   policyholders'

JOINT
OWNERSHIP

Joint ownership is shown by making only the last noun possessive. Making each noun possessive indicates separate ownership of two or more items. If this is the intended meaning, whatever is owned must also be plural.

Examples: John and Bob's typewriter *two persons owning one typewriter*
John's and Bob's typewriters *two persons, each owning at least one typewriter*
Helen and Kay's mother *sisters*
Helen's and Kay's mothers *two persons with different mothers*

APPOSITIVE
EXPRESSIONS

In such appositive expressions as *Paul, the tailor,* make the last word possessive.

Examples: Paul, the tailor's, shop is on Elm Street.
It was Mary, my secretary's, voice that I heard on the phone.

The examples above show how awkward these expressions are. If you prefer, change to an *of* phrase.

Examples: The shop of Paul, the tailor, is on Elm Street.
It was the voice of Mary, my secretary, that I heard on the phone.

OWNERSHIP
BY AN
INANIMATE
OBJECT

Generally, the *of* phrase is used to show ownership by an inanimate object. It is possible to use *the typewriter's cover,* but *the cover of the typewriter* sounds less awkward. (Since the *of* phrase is longer, there are instances when it is more formal.)

Examples: the chimney of the house
the drawer of the desk

There is an idiomatic use of the possessive in expressions involving time or amounts; for example, *one week's vacation* (a vacation of one week); *two months' sick leave* (sick leave of two months); *fifteen minutes' intermission* (intermission of fifteen minutes). The possessive is also used in expressions employing personification, such as *for mercy's sake, season's greetings.*

EXPRESSIONS OF TIME OR AMOUNT AND OF PERSONI- FICATION

Notice that the apostrophe is not used in names of many organizations—*Veterans Administration, United States Post Office, Doctors Hospital.* Since use of the plural noun is increasing, check letterheads and other official forms to determine the usage in each case.

NAMES OF ORGANIZA- TIONS

The forms of personal pronouns change to indicate the possessive case. The chart of pronouns (pages 115–116) shows the correct forms for the possessive case. Notice that more than one form is given for many of the personal pronouns—*my/mine; your/yours.* In many instances, one pronoun is used when it is placed *before* the object it possesses and another is used when the pronoun is written *after* the object it possesses (*my book* but *the book is mine; her dress* but *the dress is hers*).

POSSESSIVE PRONOUNS

The possessives of indefinite and reciprocal pronouns are formed in the same way as the possessives of nouns.

Examples: one's place   anyone's coat   each other's work
someone's book   somebody's pen

Who is the only relative or interrogative pronoun that changes its form to indicate the possessive case; thus, *who/whose.* Reflexive and intensive pronouns do not show possession.

The possessive case before a gerund is discussed in the section on verbals (pages 148–152).

WARNING:

An apostrophe in a personal pronoun indicates a contraction. Never use an apostrophe in a personal pronoun to show possessive case.

Examples: Whose book are you using?
Who's using the electric typewriter?
The magazine was delivered with its cover torn.
It's too late to start the work.

Noun clauses   Noun clauses function as nouns and can therefore be used as subjects, objects, complements, and appositives. They are, however, most frequently used as direct objects. Although usually introduced by that, they can also be introduced by *what, where, who, whoever, whether, why, when,* and *whatever.*

Examples: He said <u>that the meeting would take most of the day.</u> *noun clauses used as direct object*
  I wondered <u>where he had gone.</u>
  I could not understand <u>what he said.</u>

  Give the magazine to <u>whoever wants it.</u> *a noun clause as object of a preposition*

<u>WARNING:</u>

Avoid using long noun clauses beginning with that *as subjects because they sound awkward.*

Examples: *avoid:* <u>That the painting was not a genuine Picasso</u> did not occur to him.
    use: It did not occur to him that <u>the painting was not a genuine Picasso.</u>
    use: <u>Where the treasure is hidden</u> will probably never be known.

Agreement

Agreement in a sentence occurs in two ways: (1) a pronoun must agree with its antecedent (the word for which the pronoun stands) in number, gender, and person; (2) the verb of a sentence must agree in person and number with its subject. Agreement, then, means that the parts of the sentence go together—that is, the subject and the verb (the backbone of the sentence) are a unit and pronouns match their antecedents. The following rules should help in avoiding agreement errors.

Collective   When a collective noun is the subject (or antecedent) of a
nouns   sentence or clause, the noun may be singular or plural, depending upon how it is used. If the collective noun acts as a unit, it is singular; if the members making up the collective noun are acting individually, it is plural.

Examples: The committee is holding its meeting in Room 90. *The committee is acting as a unit; therefore, it is singular.*

Since it is the singular subject of the sentence, the verb is singular. The pronoun its is also singular to agree with its antecedent, committee.

The committee are unable to reach a decision. *The members of the committee are not functioning as a unit, so the verb must be plural to agree with its plural subject,* committee.

Both *data* and *number* are collective nouns. Although *data* is the plural form of *datum*, it can be used in both a singular and a plural sense. When it refers to a mass of facts that form a unit, it is singular. *Number* is singular when preceded by *the* and plural when preceded by *a*.   DATA, NUMBER

Examples: The data have been examined by many persons.
This data is of no importance to his study.
The number of accidents is small.
A number of accidents were reported recently.

Indefinite pronouns (*somebody, anyone,* etc.) are usually considered to be singular. Check the chart on pages 115–116 to find which are singular and which are plural. If an indefinite pronoun is used as the subject of the sentence, the verb and any pronouns referring to the indefinite pronoun must agree in number.   **Indefinite pronouns**

The indefinite pronoun is no longer considered masculine; until a pronoun that does not express gender is coined, use *he or she (him or her, his or her).*

Examples: Everyone must close his or her book.
The average consumer thinks that he or she should be
protected from unscrupulous merchants.

Since the plurals of foreign nouns are not usually formed by adding *s*, they are often difficult to recognize. They must, of course, take a plural verb.   **Plurals of foreign nouns**

Examples: Bacteria are found in drinking water.
The analyses are proving him to be wrong.
The alumnae of Barnard are meeting at two.

It is sometimes difficult to determine the subject of a sentence when phrases come between the subject and the verb or when the subject follows the verb. In a sentence beginning *There is* or *There are* (called *anticipatory subjects*), the subject follows the verb and determines whether the verb is singular or plural. (Frequent use of this construction in writing results in a lack of emphasis.)   **Recognizing the subject of the sentence**

Examples: <u>One</u> of the men is dictating the report now. *The subject is underscored.*
<u>Tony</u>, in addition to Tom and Bill, is failing the course.
In my office is the <u>report</u> for the convention.
There are many <u>people</u> at the meeting. *Notice that the sentence would be stronger if it read:* Many people are at the meeting.

Subject as part of something   When the subject of the sentence is part of something, the number of the verb is determined by what the subject is part of. If it is a part of something that is plural, use a plural verb; if it is a part of something that is singular, use a singular verb.

Examples: Half of the book is missing. *but* Half of the books are missing.

Compound subject   If the subject is compound—two nouns or pronouns joined by *and*—it is considered to be plural. The verb and any pronouns referring to the subject will, therefore, be plural.

Examples: The book and the magazine are on my desk.
Elizabeth and Joan are finishing the work.
You and I are supposed to do the filing.

COMPOUND SUBJECT CONSIDERED AS A UNIT   There are two exceptions to this rule: (1) If the subject joined by *and* is considered to be the same person or thing, the subject is singular.

Examples: Ham and eggs is my usual breakfast.
The secretary and treasurer is Mr. Smith. *If there are two persons serving in the two positions, the article* the *is placed before* treasurer: The secretary and the treasurer are Mr. Smith and Mr. Wilson.

COMPOUND SUBJECT PRECEDED BY <u>EACH</u>, <u>EVERY</u>, OR <u>MANY A</u>   (2) If the subject joined by *and* is preceded by *each, every,* or *many a,* it is singular.

Examples: Each boy and girl is expected to complete the lesson.
Every man and woman has the right to vote.

COMPOUND SUBJECT JOINED BY <u>OR</u> OR <u>NOR</u>   If the compound subject is joined by *or* or *nor,* the verb agrees with the part of the compound nearer it. (In informal usage, though, a plural verb is often used.) If the subject is two singular nouns joined by *or* or *nor,* a pronoun referring to the subject will also be singular.

Examples: Neither the boys nor Bill was on time. *Verb agrees with Bill.*

Neither Bill nor the boys were on time. *Verb agrees with boys.*

Either Bill or Dave will give you his golf clubs.

<u>WARNING:</u>

Be sure to select the correct antecedent for the pronoun, particularly if it is a relative pronoun. Usually the noun or pronoun immediately preceding the relative pronoun is the antecedent.

Examples: I gave the report to one of the men who are dictating. *The relative pronoun* who *refers to* men, *not to* one.

One of the men is dictating the report now. *This sentence is an entirely different construction. Ask this question: In each sentence, how many are dictating?*

I gave the report to the man who is dictating.

It is I who am the new president.

It is he, not she, who is the new president.

Who/Whom

Although use of *whom* in informal speech and writing tends to be neglected (except when *whom* immediately follows a preposition), in formal writing and speech it is necessary to use *who* and *whom* correctly.

Who and *whom* have two pronoun uses: interrogative (used in asking questions) and relative (used in relating a clause to an antecedent). *Who* is the nominative case form; *whom,* the objective; and *whose,* the possessive.
<small>USES AND FORMS OF <u>WHO</u>/<u>WHOM</u></small>

The case form does not change when *who* and *whom* are compounded with *ever.* When trying to determine which form to use, mentally substitute *the person who* for *whoever* and *the person whom* for *whomever.*
<small><u>WHOEVER</u>/ <u>WHOMEVER</u></small>

Example: Give the message to <u>whoever/whomever</u> answers the phone. *Substitute* <u>the person who</u> *and the correct answer is* <u>whoever</u>.

WHO
INTRODUCING
A NOUN
CLAUSE

Who or a form of *who* (usually *whoever* or *whomever*) can introduce a noun clause. Where this occurs, the noun clause—not just *who* or its form—is used as a noun. The case of the *who* form will be determined by the use of *who* in the clause, not by the use of the noun clause in the sentence.

Examples: No one knew who had unlocked the safe. *The noun clause is used as the direct object, but* who *is the subject of the noun clause.*
Mr. Jay wanted to know who was calling. *The noun clause is used as the object of the infinitive, but* who *is the subject of the noun clause.*

SENTENCE
ORDER OF
WHO/WHOM

Often, *who* and *whom* are not in the natural sentence order of subject, verb, and object or complement. In fact, this is the *only* time when the direct object can be the first word in the sentence.

Examples: Whom would you choose for president? *The natural order is:* You would choose whom for president?
Who shall I say is calling? *The natural order is:* I shall say who is calling.
I do not know the man whom you called. Whom *is a direct object coming before the subject.*
Mary is one of those persons who know everybody.
Mary is one of those persons whom everyone knows.

HE/HIM FOR
WHO/WHOM

A good device is to substitute *he* for *who* and *him* for *whom* when trying to decide whether to use nominative or objective case. Take this sentence for an example: *Who/Whom did you say is calling?* Change the sentence to natural order and substitute *he/him*. Now the sentence is: *You did say he/him is calling.* The correct choice is *he,* since it is the subject of *is calling.* Use *who* in place of *he*, and the sentence reads correctly: *Who did you say is calling?*

WITH PAREN-
THETICAL
EXPRESSIONS

Do not be confused by a parenthetical or interrupting expression (such as *I believe* or *he says*) within a *who/whom* clause. The expression will not affect the case of the pronoun.

Examples: Jane is a person who I believe will soon be promoted. *Take out* I believe. *It is easy to see now that* who *is the subject of the clause.*
He is the person who I think should do the job.
The girl is someone who it is believed is a talented musician.

Do not confuse the contraction *who's* (*who is*) with the
possessive pronoun *whose.*

Examples: Whose car is parked across the street?
Who's going to do the work?

VERBS

A verb expresses action, condition, or state of being.

A verb says something about the subject: It may tell what the subject is doing, or it may describe the subject. To realize the importance of a verb, read some sentences and omit the verbs. The sentences will make no sense.

Example: Sam _____ in the pool. *What happened to Sam? He swam? jumped? looked? ran? Add the verb and the action takes place: Sam <u>swam</u> in the pool.*

Verb Characteristics

A verb can be a word or a phrase. A *verb phrase* consists of more   **Verb phrases**
than one word—the main or principal verb and one or more auxiliary or helping verbs.

The auxiliary verbs are: *is, was, were, am, are, be, being, been, do, does, did, shall, will, should, would, may, might, must, can, could, has, have, had.* The auxiliary verb (or verbs) is always first, followed by the main verb; but sometimes the components of verb phrases are separated by other words, usually adverbs.

Examples: John is <u>leaving</u> the company. *Verb phrase:* <u>is</u> (*auxiliary*)
<u>leaving</u> (*main*)
Jean <u>should have been studying</u> English. *Verb phrase:* <u>should have been</u> (*auxiliaries*) <u>studying</u> (*main*)
Kay <u>does</u> not <u>understand</u> French. *Verb phrase separated by* not

WARNING:

Some verbs can be either main or auxiliary verbs. When alone, they are main verbs; when followed by another verb, they are auxiliaries.

Examples: I <u>have</u> a lot of time to complete the work.
I <u>have talked</u> with Mr. Smith on several occasions.
I <u>did</u> the filing on Friday.
I <u>did talk</u> with Mr. Smith on several occasions.

Compound verbs   The main verb can consist of two or more verbs joined by conjunctions.

Examples: Jack <u>sorted</u> and <u>distributed</u> the mail.   *two main verbs joined by* and
He neither <u>saw</u> nor <u>heard</u> anything unusual that evening.

Transitive and intransitive verbs   If there is a word in the sentence that answers *whom* or *what* about the verb, the verb is transitive because it requires an object to complete its meaning. The word *transitive* actually means "between one condition and another." Therefore, in grammar a transitive verb is between the subject and the object, and it passes the action to the object. An intransitive verb does *not* take an object. It describes the subject or expresses a condition or state of being, that is, it says something about the subject. Whenever a form of *be* is the main verb, the verb is intransitive. Some other commonly used intransitive verbs are: *become, seem, grow, appear, look, feel, smell, taste, remain, sound, stay.*

Examples: I saw Kate.   *Ask yourself:* I saw <u>whom</u>? <u>Kate</u> *is the answer. The verb is transitive.*
I typed the letters this morning. *Ask yourself:* I typed <u>what</u>? <u>Letters</u> *is the answer. The verb is transitive.*
I typed this morning. *Now there is no answer to* I typed <u>what</u>; *the verb is intransitive.*

COMPLETE AND LINKING INTRANSITIVE VERBS   An intransitive verb may be *complete,* or it may need a predicate nominative or predicate adjective to complete it. It is then called a *linking* (or *copulative*) verb. A predicate adjective is an adjective that comes after the verb and describes the subject.

Examples: He sat by the window.   *complete*
He is a teacher.   *Predicate nominative completes verb.*
He is busy.   *Predicate adjective completes verb.*

Regular and irregular verbs   Verbs are classified as regular or irregular by the way they form their past tenses and past participles.
The principal parts of *any* verb are: *present tense, past tense,* and *past* (or *perfect*) participle.

Regular verbs form their past tenses and past participles by adding *d* or *ed* to the present tense, as in *walk, walked, walked.* Irregular verbs, however, follow no set rules when forming their past tenses and past participles; for example, *do, did, done.* Consult the dictionary if you have any doubt about the principal parts of a verb.

FORMING PRINCIPLE PARTS

WARNING:

When the past participle is used as part of a verb phrase, it will always need an auxiliary; it cannot be used alone as a verb. (You cannot say I done the typing. *You must say* I have done the typing.)

To form the third-person singular present tense and any past tense or past participle forms of verbs ending in *y*, follow the rule for forming the plurals of nouns ending in *y* (page 117): If the *y* is preceded by a vowel, add *s* (or *ed*) to the word; if the *y* is preceded by a consonant, change the *y* to *i* and add *es* (or *ed*).

VERBS ENDING IN Y

Say, pay, and *lay* are exceptions and do not form their past tenses or past participles according to this rule.

		3D SINGULAR PRESENT	PAST TENSE AND PAST PARTICIPLE
Examples:	cry	cries	cried
	study	studies	studied
	try	tries	tried
	stay	stays	stayed
	carry	carries	carried
	play	plays	played
Exceptions:	say	says	said
	pay	pays	paid
	lay	lays	laid

The following list shows most of the irregular verbs. Notice the variety of ways in which these verbs form their past tenses and past participles.

TROUBLESOME IRREGULAR VERBS

PRESENT	PAST	PAST PARTICIPLE
be	was	been
bear	bore	born (to give birth to), borne (all other senses)
begin	began	begun
bite	bit	bitten, bit (in passive)
blow	blew	blown
break	broke	broken

PRESENT	PAST	PAST PARTICIPLE
bring	brought	brought
burst	burst	burst
catch	caught	caught
choose	chose	chosen
come	came	come
dig	dug	dug
dive[1]	dived, dove (informal)	dived, dove (informal)
do	did	done
draw	drew	drawn
dream[1]	dreamed, dreamt	dreamed, dreamt
drink	drank	drunk
drive	drove	driven
eat	ate	eaten
fall	fell	fallen
fly	flew	flown
forget	forgot	forgotten
freeze	froze	frozen
get	got	got, gotten
give	gave	given
go	went	gone
grow	grew	grown
hang (to take a life)	hanged	hanged
hang (to suspend)	hung	hung
know	knew	known
lay[2]	laid	laid
lead	led	led
lend	lent	lent
lie[3]	lay	lain
light	lighted, lit	lighted, lit
lose	lost	lost
pay[2]	paid	paid
prove	proved	proved (pref.), proven
ride	rode	ridden
ring	rang	rung
rise	rose	risen
run	ran	run
say[2]	said	said
see	saw	seen
set[4]	set	set
shake	shook	shaken
shine	shone, shined	shone, shined

[1] Included as an irregular verb because of the second (irregular) form of the past tense and past participle.

[2] Spelling only is irregular.

[3] The regular verb *lie* means "to tell a falsehood." It forms its principal parts regularly: *lie, lied, lied.*

[4] *Set* is either transitive or intransitive. The transitive verb means "to place"; the intransitive verb means "to become firm" or "to pass below the horizon" (when referring to a heavenly body).

[continued on next page]

PRESENT	PAST	PAST PARTICIPLE
show	showed	showed, shown
sing	sang, sung	sung
sink	sank (pref.), sunk	sunk, sunken
sit	sat	sat
slide	slid	slid, slidden
speak	spoke	spoken
spring	sprang, sprung	sprung
stand	stood	stood
steal	stole	stolen
swim	swam	swum
take	took	taken
tear	tore	torn
throw	threw	thrown
wake[5]	waked, woke	waked, woke
wear	wore	worn
weave	wove, weaved	woven
wring	wrung	wrung
write	wrote	written

[5] Both *wake* and *awake* have so many forms that a dictionary should be consulted.

Tense

Verbs change form to indicate tense. *Tense* refers to the form of a verb used to express distinctions of time. But sometimes it is not necessary to use the actual tense because context makes it obvious. For example, both future tense and future time are used in the sentence *I shall leave tomorrow.* However, future time (but not future tense) is expressed in the sentence *I leave tomorrow;* the tense of the verb is present, but the time is future because of the adverb *tomorrow.*

There are six tense forms for verbs. The *primary* tenses include the present, past, and future tenses; the *perfect* tenses include the present perfect, past perfect, and future perfect tenses.

1. The *present* tense indicates action taking place *now.* It also indicates general or permanent truths or habitual action.

PRIMARY TENSES: PRESENT, PAST, FUTURE

Examples: Mr. Smith <u>is eating</u>. *action taking place now*
Honesty <u>is</u> the best policy. *permanent truth*
Our office <u>opens</u> at eight o'clock. *habitual action*

<u>WARNING:</u>

The form of the verb changes in the present and perfect tenses when the subject is in the third person singular. In the present tense third person singular, s is added to all verbs. In the present perfect tense, the auxiliary changes from have *to* has. Any third-person present tense verb will end in *s.*

Examples: is, has, walks, goes, lies, writes

2. The *past* tense indicates action that has already taken place.

Examples: I <u>worked</u> on the report last week.
Mr. Smith <u>was</u> in his office all morning.
The play <u>began</u> at eight o'clock.

3. The *future* tense indicates action that will take place in the future. It is formed by putting *shall* or *will* before the present tense. (*Shall* and *will* are discussed on page 147 in the section on auxiliaries.)

Examples: I <u>shall work</u> on the report next week.
He <u>will take</u> care of the matter soon.
Ruth <u>will leave</u> next week for New York.

PERFECT
TENSES:
PRESENT
PERFECT,
PAST
PERFECT,
FUTURE
PERFECT

The *perfect* tenses indicate action or state of being that is completed.

4. The *present perfect* tense indicates action begun in the past and completed in the present. It can also indicate habitual or repeated past action. The present perfect tense is formed by placing *has* or *have* before the past participle.

Examples: I <u>have finished</u> the report that I began typing yesterday.
I <u>have used</u> the copier many times. *repeated past action*
Mr. Smith <u>has completed</u> the work on the report.

5. The *past perfect* tense indicates action begun in the past and completed before a stated time in the past. It is formed by placing *had* before the past participle.

Examples: I <u>had left</u> my desk when Emily called.
John <u>had completed</u> the report before Mr. Smith asked for it.

6. The *future perfect* tense indicates action that will be completed before a stated future time. It is formed by placing *shall have* or *will have* before the past participle.

Examples: I <u>shall have completed</u> my typing before next Friday.
John <u>will have completed</u> the report before it is due.

The *progressive* form of a verb tends to emphasize the actual activity and to show action over a space of time. In the active voice it is formed by combining the appropriate tense form of *be* with the present participle. In the passive voice it contains the auxiliary *being*. (*Voice* is discussed on pages 142–143.)

PROGRESSIVE FORM

Examples: I <u>was reading</u> a magazine when you called. *past progressive, active voice*

John thought he <u>was being followed</u>. *past progressive, passive voice*

To make a verb more emphatic, add *do, does,* or *did* to the present tense form. Emphatic verbs may be present or past tense.

EMPHATIC FORM

Examples: I <u>do read</u> the letter before I file it. *present tense*

Mary <u>does type</u> accurately. *present tense*

Helen <u>did write</u> the letter. *past tense*

Verbs should show proper time relation to one another. If a sentence contains dependent clauses or verbal phrases (see page 148), their tenses should agree with the time of the main verb. Generally, use the tense form that indicates the proper time order.

SEQUENCE OF TENSES

Examples: I typed the letter that he had written. *The writing preceded the typing.*

I am glad that I finished the work. *I am glad <u>after</u> the work was finished.*

If the dependent clause states a general truth, express that general truth in the present tense.

Examples: He said that 32° Fahrenheit is freezing.

He stated that the cost of living is rising.

If the verbs are of the same time, be sure to use the same tense.

Examples: He ran down the street and caught the bus.

He read the letters and signed all of them.

Use the perfect infinitive (for example, *to have read*) when you want to show action completed before the time of the main verb and occasionally to indicate something contrary to fact.

Examples: I am glad to have finished the typing. *The typing was finished before the being glad.*

He expected to have read the report before the meeting. *contrary to fact*

Active and passive voice   *Voice* is the verb characteristic used to show whether the subject is acting or receiving the action. When the subject is doing, being, or becoming something, the verb is in the *active voice*. When the subject is the receiver of the action, the verb is in the *passive voice*.

FORM OF THE PASSIVE-VOICE VERB   The verb in the passive voice is always a phrase—some form of the verb *be* plus the past participle, such as *was seen, am told, has been heard*. All passive-voice verbs are transitive, with the subject taking the place of the direct object. An intransitive verb cannot be used in the passive voice because it takes no direct object.

Examples: Stories about his conduct <u>were circulated</u>. *transitive; passive*
Janet <u>was seen</u> at the ball game. *transitive; passive*
His voice <u>could be heard</u> above all others. *transitive; passive*
He <u>has been seen</u> there many times. *transitive; passive*
Water <u>flows</u> downhill. *intransitive; active*
I <u>read</u> until midnight. *intransitive; active*

USING ACTIVE AND PASSIVE VOICE   Because it uses fewer words than the passive voice, the active voice is considered more direct and forceful. The following example illustrates this.

Example: I saw Jerry at the library. *active*
Jerry was seen by me at the library. *passive*

When writing a story or describing something, use the active voice. Ideas or concepts can often be better expressed by using the passive voice. Use of the passive voice is also a means of increasing or decreasing emphasis.

Examples: Lies were told about him. *Who told the lies is either unknown or unimportant.*
They told lies about him.
The difficult problem was solved by a ten-year-old boy. *The emphasis is placed on the ten-year-old boy.*

The passive voice may also be used if the writer wishes to avoid beginning a sentence with *I*.

Example: I accepted the position as secretary in 1982.
The position as secretary was accepted by me in 1982.

The desire to make a certain noun the subject of a sentence can determine the voice to be used.

Examples: Elizabeth I was considered to be one of England's most important queens.
Historians consider Elizabeth I to be one of England's most important queens.
In the first example the emphasis is upon Elizabeth; *in the second, upon* historians.

Mood (or *mode*) is the form of a verb that indicates the manner of action expressed by that verb. There are three moods: *indicative, imperative,* and *subjunctive.*

Mood

The *indicative* mood states a fact or asks a question.

INDICATIVE MOOD

Examples: It is raining.
I forgot to mail a letter.
Who is calling?

The *imperative* mood gives a command or makes a request.

IMPERATIVE MOOD

Examples: Shut the window.
Will you please shut the window.

The *subjunctive* mood expresses a wish, a possibility, or a doubt. It differs from the indicative in certain forms of the verb *be* (for example, *if it be true*) and in the first and third person singular. The subjunctive mood is usually introduced by such conjunctions as *if, unless, whether, though,* and *that.*

SUBJUNCTIVE MOOD

Examples: If I were you, I would not take the job.
If this were true, I would resign immediately.
That may be the case, but I do not believe it.

The use of the subjunctive instead of the indicative is often a matter of choice. Except in formal language, such as that used in resolutions, demands, rules, and so on, the subjunctive mood is disappearing from the English language. Notice, though, that it is used in certain idioms such as *God bless you, Heaven forbid,* and *be that as it may.*

Troublesome Verbs

Three pairs of troublesome verbs are listed below with their principal parts. With the exceptions of *lay* and *raise,* they are irregular verbs.

TRANSITIVE	INTRANSITIVE
lay/laid/laid	lie/lay/lain
set/set/set	sit/sat/sat
raise/raised/raised	rise/rose/risen

lay/lie;
set/sit;
raise/rise

First, notice which verbs are intransitive and which are transitive. Since the action of a transitive verb must be received by something or someone, the subject or object answers *what* or *whom* about a transitive verb. If the subject receives the action, the verb is in the passive voice and one of the transitive verbs must be used. (Remember that *only* transitive verbs are used in the passive voice.) An intransitive verb describes or says something about the subject. If you select the verb on the basis of whether a transitive or intransitive verb is necessary, you should have little difficulty in using these verbs correctly.

Second, consult the conjugations for the correct tense form. (*Be, lie,* and *lay* are conjugated on pages 145–146.)

Examples:

Transitive verbs
I laid the <u>papers</u> on the desk. *takes object*
I set my <u>watch</u> at ten o'clock. *takes object*
I raised my <u>hand</u>. *takes object*
Now I lay <u>me</u> down to sleep. *takes object*
The rains raised the <u>waters</u> of the lake. *takes object*
He raised <u>$5,000</u> for the campaign. *takes object*
The <u>book</u> was laid on the desk. *passive voice: Subject receives the action.*

Intransitive verbs
The <u>dog</u> lies by the fire. *describing subject*
The <u>check</u> lay on the desk for several days. *describing subject*
The <u>ship</u> is lying in the harbor. *describing subject*
The <u>house</u> sits on a hill. *describing subject*
<u>Production costs</u> are rising rapidly. *describing subject*
<u>Mr. Smith</u> was sitting by the window. *describing subject*
Lie down, Rover. *Verb tells understood subject* <u>you</u> *what to do.*

WARNINGS:

1. The present tense of the transitive verb lay *is the same form as the past tense of the intransitive verb* lie.
2. Check the spellings of laid *and* lying.
3. Set *can be intransitive in certain instances.*

Examples: The sun sets in the west.
This concrete sets overnight.

The charts that follow show the conjugations (the forms the verb **Be, lay, lie** takes to show person, number, voice, and tense) of three troublesome verbs—*be, lay,* and *lie*. The conjugations are those used in the indicative mood, which is the mood used to state a fact or to ask a question. (See page 143.)

BE			
PRESENT		**PRESENT PERFECT**	
I am	We are	I have been	We have been
You are	You are	You have been	You have been
He is	They are	He has been	They have been
PAST		**PAST PERFECT**	
I was	We were	I had been	We had been
You were	You were	You had been	You had been
He was	They were	He had been	They had been
FUTURE		**FUTURE PERFECT**	
I shall be	We shall be	I shall have been	We shall have been
You will be	You will be	You will have been	You will have been
He will be	They will be	He will have been	They will have been

1. The present tense singular has four forms: *be, am, is, are.* The person or mood determines which one is used.

2. *Be* is always intransitive. This means that it will be followed by a predicate nominative or adjective, never by an object.

3. *Be* can be used as an auxiliary and as a main verb. When used as an auxiliary, it makes the tense progressive or the voice passive.

4. Form the progressive tenses by adding *being* (the present participle) to the simple tenses; for example, the present progressive first person singular is *I am being.*

LAY			
PRESENT		**PRESENT PERFECT**	
I lay	We lay	I have laid	We have laid
You lay	You lay	You have laid	You have laid
He lays	They lay	He has laid	They have laid
PAST		**PAST PERFECT**	
I laid	We laid	I had laid	We had laid
You laid	You laid	You had laid	You had laid
He laid	They laid	He had laid	They had laid
FUTURE		**FUTURE PERFECT**	
I shall lay	We shall lay	I shall have laid	We shall have laid
You will lay	You will lay	You will have laid	You will have laid
He will lay	They will lay	He will have laid	They will have laid

1. Form the progressive tenses by adding *laying* (the present participle) to the simple tenses; for example, the present progressive first person singular is *I am laying*.

2. Form the present emphatic by putting *do* before the simple present; form the past emphatic by putting *did* before the simple present; for example, *I do lay, I did lay*.

LIE			
PRESENT		**PRESENT PERFECT**	
I lie	We lie	I have lain	We have lain
You lie	You lie	You have lain	You have lain
He lies	They lie	He has lain	They have lain
PAST		**PAST PERFECT**	
I lay	We lay	I had lain	We had lain
You lay	You lay	You had lain	You had lain
He lay	They lay	He had lain	They had lain
FUTURE		**FUTURE PERFECT**	
I shall lie	We shall lie	I shall have lain	We shall have lain
You will lie	You will lie	You will have lain	You will have lain
He will lie	They will lie	He will have lain	They will have lain

1. Form the progressive tenses by adding *lying* (the present participle) to the simple tenses; for example, the present progressive first person singular is *I am lying*.

2. Form the present emphatic by adding *do* to the simple present; form the past emphatic by adding *did* to the simple present; for example, *I do lie, I did lie*.

The Use of Certain Auxiliaries

Shall and *will* are the auxiliaries used to show future tense. Grammatically, it has been traditional when expressing simple future time to use *shall* with the first person and *will* with the second and third persons. To express determination or promise, the order is reversed: use *will* with the first person and *shall* with the second and third person. (These distinctions are no longer generally observed.)   SHALL/WILL

Should and *would* have traditionally followed the same rules as *shall* and *will* with this exception (which is still observed): Use *would* in all persons to show habitual action or a condition and *should* in all persons to show obligation.   SHOULD/ WOULD

In formal usage *can* or *could* shows ability (to do something) and *may* or *might* indicates possibility or permission. In writing, this distinction should be observed. However, in informal usage *can* is increasingly substituted for *may* to express permission. (*Can I leave early? You can if you wish.*)   CAN/COULD; MAY/MIGHT

Although *may* and *might* are alike in meaning—they both express possibility or permission—they do differ in intensity; that is, *may* is stronger than *might*. For example, *I may take the job* expresses a stronger possibility than *I might take the job*. In modern usage they are considered to be subjunctive verbs, and both are used in expressing present and future time.

Examples: I shall call you soon. *simple future: 1st person*
He will be in tomorrow. *simple future: 3d person*
I will finish on time. *determination: 1st person*
He would walk to work. *habitual action*
I should do my homework. *obligation*
May I use your pen? *permission*
Can you lift this desk? *ability*

Contractions

Verb contractions (such as *can't, won't, don't, haven't*) are usually considered informal and are therefore used in spoken language more frequently than in written language. Be careful to spell contractions correctly by placing an apostrophe where the letter or letters have been omitted.

Examples: don't (*for* do not) *Place the apostrophe where the o is omitted.*

haven't (*for* <u>have not</u>) *Place the apostrophe where the* o *is omitted.*

can't (*for* <u>cannot</u>) *Place the apostrophe where the* no *is omitted.*

Verbals

A verbal is a verb form used as one of three parts of speech—an adjective, a noun, or an adverb. Since verbals are not used as verbs, they cannot exert action or being but can only express it. The three forms of a verbal are participle, gerund, and infinitive.

Participle   A participle is identified in two ways: by its form and by its use in the sentence. A participle ends in either *ing* (present participle) or *d* or *ed* (past participle). However, irregular verbs do not follow any set pattern in forming their past participles. The perfect participle combines the auxiliary *having* with the past participle.

A participle is always used as an adjective. The participle has the power to take a noun or a pronoun object or an adverbial modifier. With any of these elements, it forms a *participial phrase.*

Examples: The <u>singing</u> bird has many brilliant feathers. *present participle*

The work, <u>having no defects</u>, was approved by Mr. Evans. *participial phrase with noun object*

<u>Aided by his crutch</u>, the man was able to walk some distance. *past participial phrase of a regular verb*

The report, <u>written in great detail</u>, was inaccurate. *past participial phrase of an irregular verb*

<u>Having seen the thief</u>, the boy gave chase. *perfect participle*

<u>**WARNING:**</u>

Participial phrases are either restrictive or nonrestrictive (essential or nonessential). Nonrestrictive phrases are set off by commas.

Examples: An apple <u>containing worms</u> is worthless. *restrictive*

Our cement, <u>made from a special formula</u>, dries quickly. *nonrestrictive*

DANGLING PARTICIPLES   If there is no noun that a participle can reasonably modify or if the participial phrase is placed some distance from the noun it modifies, the participle is said to be *dangling.*

Examples: *avoid:* Driving along the freeway, numerous accidents
were seen. *no noun or pronoun that the phrase
can modify*
use: Driving along the freeway, I saw numerous accidents.
avoid: Lying on the table, Max saw the missing file. *participial phrase placed too far from the noun that
it modifies*
use: Max saw the missing file lying on the table.

Do not confuse the participial phrase that modifies one word   ABSOLUTE
with the participial phrase that relates to the whole sentence;   PHRASES
participles do not dangle when they are used as absolute phrases or
when they introduce or refer to a general truth.

Examples: Beginning January 1, prices on our products will be
increased 5 percent.
Speaking only for myself, this plan does not seem
feasible.

A gerund is *easy* to identify, for it always ends in *ing* and is   **Gerund**
always used as a noun. A gerund may have a subject, an object, an
adjective complement, or an adverb modifier. When accompanied
by any of these elements, it forms a gerund phrase. A gerund phrase
or gerund can be used any way that a noun is used—as subject or
object of a verb, object of a preposition, in apposition, and so on.

Examples: Correcting the papers was not easy. *subject*
George disliked correcting the papers. *direct object*
Our biggest task is correcting the papers. *predicate
nominative*
Thank you for correcting the papers. *object of a
preposition*
We finished a difficult task, correcting the papers.
apposition

If a phrase containing a gerund is used to modify, the relation-   DANGLING
ship of the phrase to the word it modifies should be easy to identify. If   GERUND
it is not, the phrase containing the gerund is a dangling modifier.

Examples: *avoid:* After working for four hours, the problem was still
not solved.
use: After working for four hours, I was still unable to
solve the problem.

avoid: In answering the letter, nothing was said about shipping the order.

use: In answering the letter, Mr. Smith said nothing about shipping the order.

POSSESSIVE
CASE BEFORE A
GERUND

Generally, use the possessive case before a gerund and the objective case before a participle. (There are times when the choice of the possessive or nonpossessive form becomes difficult and when you must decide by the sound of the phrase. In other words, do not use an awkward sounding possessive.) When in doubt whether the possessive or the objective case should precede an *ing* word, make this test: If a noun can be substituted for the *ing* word, use the possessive case; if a clause must be substituted for the *ing* word, use the objective case.

Examples: avoid: He thought something's being done was better than nothing's being done.

use: He thought doing something was better than doing nothing.

I watched him typing the report. *I watched him as he was typing the report.*

I saw his typing of the report. *I saw his copy of the report.*

Do you object to his going to Hawaii? *Do you object to his trip to Hawaii?*

The company objected to the manager's hiring someone else. *The company objected to the manager's employment of someone else.*

These points may help in making it easier to decide which form to use:

If the noun or pronoun before the *ing* word is a personal pronoun or a proper noun, use the possessive form; if a plural noun, use the nonpossessive form.

Examples: Our smoking in the office is prohibited.

We are pleased by Jack's handling of the problem.

The store manager did not like customers coming in by the side door.

If the noun or pronoun before the *ing* word is abstract or is modified by other words, use the nonpossessive form.

Examples: There is danger of the idea being forgotten.
Do you object to the president of the company signing the contract?

When the noun or pronoun before the *ing* word is emphasized, use the nonpossessive form.

Example: I could not imagine the company president resisting arrest.

Gerunds should not be preceded by *the* nor completed by an *of* phrase. The phrase will be made less awkward by omitting these two words. OMITTING THE AND OF IN GERUND PHRASES

Example: *avoid:* In the awarding of the government contract, the official violated two regulations.
use: In awarding the government contract, the official violated two regulations.

The infinitive is formed by the present tense of a verb plus *to*; for example, *to read, to leave, to learn*. When accompanied by a subject, a noun or adjective complement, or an adverb modifier, it forms an infinitive phrase. An infinitive may be an adjective, an adverb, or a noun, according to its construction in the sentence. The perfect infinitive is formed by *to* plus *have* and the past participle; for example, *to have gone, to have read, to have seen*. **Infinitive**

Examples: He made an effort to leave the company. *adjective*
This book is designed to help you. *adverb*
To do the job is not easy. *noun subject*
They tried to do the job. *direct object*
He could do nothing except (to) leave the job. *object of a preposition*
Our purpose is to do the job. *predicate nominative*
Seeing the expert (to) do the work was a privilege. *object of a verbal*
Our aim, to do the job, was realized. *apposition*

Sometimes the infinitive does not have *to* included with it.

Examples: He dared (to) leave.
Our mechanic can make the part (to) fit.
We saw them (to) leave the building.

DANGLING
INFINITIVES

Because an infinitive, like a participle, can be used as an adjective, it too can be dangling if there is no noun for it to modify. The infinitive like the participle can be an absolute phrase; if this occurs, it is not dangling.

Examples: *avoid:* To use our product properly, the directions must be followed exactly.

     use: To use our product properly, the customer must follow the directions exactly.

     avoid: To reach the top shelf, the ladder must be used.

     use: To reach the top shelf, Mary had to use a ladder.

     absolute: To come to the point, this is not a final decision.

SPLIT
INFINITIVES

An infinitive is split by placing an adverb between the *to* and the rest of the infinitive, as in *to quickly complete.* A split infinitive is acceptable if it is not awkward. For example, consider how to add *quickly* to this sentence: *Mr. Evans wanted to complete the work on the new government contract.*

1. Place *quickly* before the infinitive: Mr. Evans wanted *quickly* to complete the work on the new government contract. *Quickly* can now modify either the verb or the infinitive.

2. Place *quickly* after the infinitive: Mr. Evans wanted to complete *quickly* the work on the new government contract. Now *quickly* is awkward, because it comes between the infinitive and its object.

3. Place *quickly* at the end of the sentence: Mr. Evans wanted to complete the work on the new government contract *quickly.* Now it is too far from the infinitive it is modifying.

4. Split the infinitive: Mr. Evans wanted to *quickly* complete the work on the new government contract. This sounds better than any of the other constructions.

On the other hand, consider this split infinitive: *The legislator plans to relentlessly push for the passage of the bill.* This is awkward; it would be better to say: *The legislator plans to push relentlessly for the passage of the bill.*

COMPLEMENT
OF THE
INFINITIVE
TO BE

Review the section about the proper case of the complement of the infinitive *to be* (pages 124–125). Remember that the complement of the infinitive *to be* can be either nominative or objective.

Examples: From the description of the man, we thought Mr. Black to be <u>him</u>.

From the description of the man, Mr. Black appeared to be <u>he.</u>

They elected him (to be) <u>president.</u>

ADJECTIVES

Adjectives describe, restrict, or limit nouns or pronouns.

An adjective cannot be identified by its form; usage alone determines whether or not a word is an adjective. Words that are ordinarily nouns can be used as adjectives—for example, *work* in *worksheet*. Participles, which are verb forms, are always adjectives. Some words are used as both adjectives and adverbs. Therefore, even the dictionary may not be helpful. The only test is the function of the word in the sentence. If it describes, restricts, or limits a noun or pronoun, it is an adjective.

When selecting adjectives, choose those that add precision or vividness to your writing or speech. Avoid overuse of such general adjectives as *good, wonderful, fine, nice,* and *bad* by finding specific ones. For example, instead of saying *It is a fine day,* try substituting an adjective such as *sparkling* for *fine.* Many adjectives, although exact, are so overworked—particularly with certain nouns—that they have become trite and are no longer effective; for example, *big blue eyes, tired old world.*

Adjectives can be words, phrases, or clauses, but they will always describe nouns or pronouns.

Comparing Adjectives

The adjective form found in the dictionary is the simple or positive form (such as *high, old, new*). This form changes to show a greater or lesser degree of the characteristic that the adjective expresses. These changes are called *degrees of comparison.*

There are three degrees of comparison: *positive, comparative,* and *superlative.* The comparative is used to compare two items; the superlative, three or more items. The superlative can also be used as a form of emphasis.

THREE DEGREES OF COMPARISON

Examples: This is the better plan of the two. *comparative—comparing two*
This is the best plan of all. *superlative—comparing more than two*
We had the best time at Mary's party. *superlative—for emphasis*

THREE WAYS
OF FORMING
THE
COMPARATIVE
AND
SUPERLATIVE
There are three ways of forming the comparative and superlative from the positive:

1. *Regular:* Add *er* to the positive to form the comparative; add *est* to the positive to form the superlative.

Examples:

Positive	Comparative	Superlative
new	newer	newest
fine	finer	finest
old	older	oldest
young	younger	youngest
few	fewer	fewest

<u>WARNINGS:</u>

a. *In words with a short vowel followed by a single consonant, double the consonant when adding* er *or* est.

Examples:

thin	thinner	thinnest
fat	fatter	fattest

b. *In words ending in* y, *usually change the* y *to* i *before* er *or* est.

Example: dry   drier   driest

2. *Irregular:* The comparative and superlative are formed by changes in the words themselves.

Examples:

good/well	better	best
many/much	more	most
bad	worse	worst
little	less/lesser	least

(*When* little *means "small in size," it can be compared regularly:* little, littler, littlest.)

3. *Adjectives of more than three syllables:* Most adjectives of three or more syllables—and many of two—form the comparative and superlative by adding *more* or *most* (or *less* or *least*) to the positive. Even some one-syllable adjectives can be compared this way. In addition, there may actually be two ways of comparing the same adjective: Some authorities think that adding *er* or *est* to the adjective stresses the *quality of the adjective* and that adding *more* or *most* stresses the *degree of comparison.*

Examples:

delicate	more delicate	most delicate
efficient	less efficient	least efficient

He has been kinder about the matter than anyone else in
the firm.
He has been most kind about the matter.

WARNING:

Few/fewer/fewest *refer to number and things that can be counted
item by item. Less/lesser (both are comparative degrees of little) /least
refer to amount or quantity. Less usually refers to size or quantity* (less
money, less opportunity); *lesser, to value or significance* (a lesser
power, a lesser degree). *Lesser is a formal word that is not often used,
particularly in business writing.*

Examples: Fewer people came to the meeting than were expected.
There was less complaining about working late than I
expected.
His dishonesty seemed a lesser fault than his disloyalty.

Some adjectives—such as *dead, empty, correct, unique, per-*
fect, black—are considered to be absolute, representing the highest
degree of a quality, and cannot be compared. Therefore, instead of
saying, *Joe had a most unique idea for the annual sale,* say, *Joe had a
unique idea for the annual sale.*
In common usage, however, such adjectives are sometimes
compared. Even the Preamble to the Constitution uses the expression
"to form a more perfect Union." If these adjectives are used in a
general or figurative and not an absolute sense, they may be
compared.

COMPARISON
OF ABSOLUTE
ADJECTIVES

When comparing an object with the rest of its class (or a person
with the rest of his or her group), be sure to use *other* in the
comparative.

COMPARISON
OF AN OBJECT
WITHIN ITS
CLASS

Examples: *avoid:* Our school is larger than any school in the area.
Our school *is not separated from the group to
which it belongs; it is thus being compared to
itself as well as the other schools.*
use: Our school is larger than any other school in the
area.
Our store sold less furniture than any other store
in the city.
Joe had a higher score on the test than any other
student in the class.

If you are using the superlative, this does not apply.

Examples: Of all the schools in the area, ours is the largest.
Joe had the highest score on the test of any student in the class.

Compound Adjectives

A compound adjective is made up of two or more descriptive words, usually connected by hyphens, serving as a single adjective. Although a compound adjective is always hyphenated when it precedes the noun it modifies, it may or may not be hyphenated when it follows the noun. It is possible, therefore, to hyphenate a compound adjective regardless of its position in the sentence.

Examples: Bonnie wrote an up-to-the-minute report.
Bonnie wrote a report that was all-inclusive.
He finally paid his past-due account.
He finally paid his account that was past due.
He conducted a follow-up study of customer complaints.

In a series of adjectives modifying the same noun, hyphens followed by a space are used to carry the modifier over to the noun. These are called *suspending hyphens*.

Examples: Will your employer build a three- or a four-bedroom house?
Will this be a two- or a three-page letter?

Special Adjectives

Proper adjectives   Proper adjectives are derived from proper nouns and are, therefore, generally capitalized—for example, *English, American, Indian, Martian*. Over the years some proper adjectives have ceased to be capitalized, such as *macadamized, india ink, paris green, french-fried*.

Predicate adjectives   Predicate adjectives come after linking verbs and describe the subject. (Never use an adverb after a linking verb.)

Examples: Judy is happy.
The rose smells sweet.
The rug feels soft.
avoid: I feel badly.
use: I feel bad.

In the discussion of demonstrative pronouns on page 114, the following adjectives were mentioned: *this, that, these, those. This* and *that* are singular and are followed by singular nouns; *these* and *those* are plural and are followed by plural nouns. Do not use *them* as an adjective; it is always a personal pronoun. *Them books* is incorrect.

Demonstrative adjectives

Examples: this kind/these kinds
that book/those books

Adjective Clauses

Adjective clauses, like all adjectives, modify nouns and pronouns. These clauses are usually introduced by relative pronouns (see pages 112–113), which are often the subjects or objects in the adjective clauses. (Other words, such as *when, why,* and *where,* can also introduce adjective clauses.) If the relative pronoun introducing the adjective clause is not the subject of that clause, it may be omitted. Adjective clauses are classified as restrictive (necessary for meaning) and nonrestrictive (unnecessary for meaning).

In most instances adjective clauses follow the words they modify. If these clauses are not placed next to the words modified, they are misplaced.

MISPLACED
MODIFIERS

Examples: My desk, which was covered with papers and unfinished work, was not a welcome sight. *nonrestrictive adjective clause modifying* desk *and introduced by* which, *the subject of the clause*
There was no time when I could finish the work. *restrictive adjective clause introduced by* when *and modifying* time
All employees who are sixty-five must retire. *restrictive adjective clause modifying* employees *and introduced by* who, *which is the subject of the clause*
Mr. Smith, whom you have never met, will be our new president. *adjective clause modifying* Mr. Smith *and introduced by* whom, *which is the direct object of the clause*
He is the one (whom) I admire most. *relative pronoun omitted from adjective clause*

avoid: At the meeting the board members elected new officers, who voted by secret ballot. *misplaced adjective clause*

use: At the meeting the board members, <u>who voted</u> <u>by secret ballot</u>, elected new officers.

Articles

The three articles *a, an,* and *the* are considered to be adjectives. *A* and *an* are indefinite; they indicate any one person or thing—*a boy, a chair. The* is definite; it specifies the person or thing—*the boy, the chair.*

A/AN   Use *a* before a word beginning with a consonant sound, before a word beginning with an *h* that is pronounced, and before a word beginning with a *u* that is pronounced with a *y*-sound first (*unique, unit*). Use *an* before words beginning with a vowel sound.

Examples: a hill, *but* an hour
 a use, *but* an unusual event

REPEATING   Repeat the article before each of two connected nouns or
ARTICLES   adjectives to refer to two different persons or things. When two or more adjectives modify the same noun, use the article before the first adjective only.

Examples: an accountant and a secretary *two persons*
 an accountant and secretary *one person (Avoid by using a hyphen:* accountant-secretary.)
 A bacon and tomato sandwich *one sandwich*
 A bacon and a tomato sandwich *two sandwiches*

When two related nouns signify an object considered to be a unit, use the article before the first noun only. Such a noun requires a singular verb (see page 132).

Examples: The ham and eggs was served cold.
 He swallowed the toast and jelly without chewing it.

When the article is repeated before nouns in a series, emphasis is given to the distinctness of the nouns.

Examples: The beauty, the serenity, and the magnificence of the mountains inspired all who saw them.
 The beauty, serenity, and magnificence of the mountains inspired all who saw them.

The article *the* is used before a noun that signifies a whole class or category rather than a member of that class or category.

Examples: <u>The</u> eagle is an American symbol.
<u>The</u> public has a right to know the truth.

Do not use *a* or *an* before a noun following these expressions: *kind of, manner of, sort of, style of,* and *type of.*

Examples: *avoid:* What sort of a person is David?
use: What sort of person is David?
avoid: What kind of a car is that?
use: What kind of car is that?

ADVERBS

Adverbs qualify, modify, or limit the meaning of verbs, adjectives, or other adverbs.

Adverbs may be words, phrases (prepositional and infinitive), or clauses. They tell manner (how), time (when), place (where), degree (how much), cause (why), and condition.

Examples: The old man walked <u>slowly</u> and <u>carefully</u>. *modifying a verb*
The <u>very</u> old man walked slowly. *modifying an adjective*
The old man walked <u>too</u> slowly. *modifying another adverb*
Joe came <u>to repair the television set</u>. *infinitive phrase used as an adverb*
<u>When Mary finished her work</u>, she left for the meeting. *adverb clause*

Single-word adverbs modifying other single words should be placed next to the words modified. Adverb phrases and clauses usually precede or follow the main clause of the sentence.

Examples: It is a <u>most</u> disagreeable job.
<u>After the meeting</u> he spoke to me.
I <u>also</u> dusted the desk. *Someone else dusted it, too.*
I dusted the desk <u>also</u>. *as well as other furniture*

Comparing Adverbs

Like adjectives, most adverbs can be compared. They, too, have three degrees of comparison: *positive, comparative,* and *superlative.*

THREE WAYS
OF FORMING
THE
COMPARATIVE
AND
SUPERLATIVE

There are three ways of forming the comparative and superlative from the positive:

1. *Regular:* Add *er* to the positive to form the comparative; add *est* to the positive to form the superlative.

Examples: *Positive*   *Comparative*   *Superlative*
              soon   sooner   soonest
              fast   faster   fastest

2. *Irregular:* The comparative and superlative are formed by changes in the words themselves.

Examples: much   more   most
              well   better   best

3. *Adverbs that end in* ly: Add *more* or *most* (or *less* or *least*) to the positive.

Examples: slowly   more slowly   most slowly
              easily   less easily   least easily
              quickly   more quickly   most quickly

<u>**WARNING:**</u>

Follow the phrase no sooner *by* than, *not by* when.

Example: I had no sooner left than she called.

Conjunctive Adverbs

In addition to being simple modifiers, adverbs may be conjunctive; that is, they may connect two independent clauses to make a compound sentence. Some of the common conjunctive adverbs are: *moreover, in fact, however, nevertheless, so, thus, consequently, accordingly, therefore, besides, also, furthermore, likewise, otherwise, still, yet.*

The usual punctuation in such sentences is a semicolon before the conjunctive adverb. If the conjunctive adverb is *so* or *yet,* then a comma is sufficient.

Examples: I cannot finish the homework; however, I expect to finish it by Saturday.

I changed the typewriter ribbon; nevertheless, the type is still too light.

Mr. Hall did not return to the office, so I signed the letters for him.

Double Negatives

Two negative statements in the same clause or sentence should not be used to express a single negative. (The adverbs *hardly* and *scarcely* are considered to be negatives.)

Examples: *avoid:* I didn't see him nowhere.

use: I didn't see him anywhere.

avoid: He couldn't hardly read Mr. Lee's handwriting.

use: He could hardly read Mr. Lee's handwriting.

avoid: The fog was so thick we couldn't scarcely see a thing.

use: The fog was so thick we could scarcely see a thing.

The double negative is used in certain instances, as in the examples below.

Examples: It is not illegal to park overnight on the street.

This is not an impossible situation.

Confusing Adverbs with Adjectives

It is easy to confuse adjectives with adverbs. This confusion can be avoided if you master the following rules:

1. Use predicate adjectives, not adverbs, after linking verbs.

Examples: The girl looks pretty. *not* prettily

The apple tastes sour. *not* sourly

The perfume smells strong. *not* strongly

2. Don't use the adjective *awful* for such adverbs as *very, really,* and *extremely.*

Examples: It is <u>very</u> late. *not* awful
He was <u>extremely</u> ill. *not* awful

3. Use *bad* as an adjective; use *badly* as an adverb.

Examples: He feels <u>bad</u> about the error. *adjective*
She types <u>badly.</u> *adverb*

4. Use *good* as an adjective; use *well* as either an adjective or an adverb, depending on the sentence meaning. In speaking of one's health or appearance, *well* is an adjective; in other cases, it is an adverb.

Examples: The cake tastes <u>good.</u> *adjective*
He doesn't sing very <u>well.</u> *adverb*
Do you feel <u>well</u>? *adjective*

5. Don't use the adjectives *sure* and *real* for the adverbs *surely* and *really.*

Examples: *avoid:* I am <u>real</u> glad.
use: I am <u>really</u> (*or* very) glad.
avoid: It is <u>sure</u> cold.
use: It is <u>surely</u> (*or* very) cold.

6. *Different* is an adjective; *differently,* an adverb.

Examples: I wish I had a <u>different</u> pen. *adjective*
She should have signed the letter <u>differently.</u> *adverb*

7. Don't use the adjective *some* for the adverbs *rather* and *somewhat.*

Examples: *avoid:* He is <u>some</u> better.
use: He is <u>somewhat</u> better.
avoid: She is <u>some</u> older than Bill.
use: She is <u>somewhat</u> older than Bill.

8. Don't hyphenate an adverb ending in *ly* followed by an adjective.

Examples: *avoid:* A newly-formed plan was put before the president.

        use: A newly formed plan was put before the president.

    avoid: A poorly-paid job is a discouraging one.

        use: A poorly paid job is a discouraging one.

Adverb Clauses

An adverb clause is a dependent clause that modifies a verb, an adjective, another adverb, a verbal, or the rest of the sentence in which it appears. It can also express a relationship of time (when), place (where), cause (why), manner (how), condition, or concession.

Many subordinate conjunctions are used to introduce adverb clauses. Here are some that are more frequently used:

when	after	as	unless
because	until	as if	before
since	while	so	so that
if	though	though	whether

Examples: If he does not pay the bill, his credit standing will be affected.

When I answered the phone, no one was on the line.

Our company could not fill the order because the employees were on strike.

PREPOSITIONS

A preposition connects a noun or pronoun (the object of the preposition) to some other word in the sentence.

Prepositions may be single words or they may be groups of words (called *phrasal prepositions*). The nine most common—*at, by, for, from, in, of, on, to, with*—account for 92 percent of all prepositions used. Examples of phrasal prepositions are: *because of, in spite of, out of, instead of, according to.* It generally sounds better to use a single-word preposition rather than a phrase; for example, *inasmuch as* can be replaced by *since, prior to* by *before, subsequent to* by *after, in regard to* by *about.*

Object of the Preposition

The noun or pronoun joined to the rest of the sentence by the preposition is the *object of the preposition*. Since a word, phrase, or clause may be used as a noun, the object of the preposition can be any one of these. The object of the preposition may also be compound.

Examples: The package was addressed to her. *word used as object of the preposition*
I found my pen in my coat pocket. *phrase used as object of the preposition*
I listened to what was said. *clause used as object of the preposition*
I made the notation on the original and the carbon copy. *compound object of the preposition*

Prepositional Phrases

The preposition, its object, and any modifiers constitute a *prepositional phrase*. Prepositional phrases usually modify; that is, they are used as adjectives or adverbs. They should be placed in the sentence so that the word or phrase modified is clearly indicated. If this is not done, the modifier will be misplaced. Adjective prepositional phrases are nearly always placed after the nouns they modify. Adverb prepositional phrases are usually placed after intransitive verbs or after direct objects of a transitive verb, or they may be placed at the beginning of a sentence.

Examples: A file is a receptacle for storing papers. *prepositional phrase used as an adjective*
She read on the train. *prepositional phrase used as an adverb and placed after intransitive verb*
She read a book on the train. *prepositional phrase used as an adverb and placed after the direct object*
On January 1 we will mail you our new catalog. *prepositional phrase used as an adverb and placed at the beginning of the sentence*

avoid: Katy wore a dress to the party with multicolored sequins. *misplaced prepositional phrase*
use: Katy wore a dress with multicolored sequins to the party.
avoid: Peter repaired the dish before he ate breakfast with fast-setting cement. *misplaced prepositional phrase*

use: Before he ate breakfast, Peter repaired the dish
<u>with fast-setting cement</u>.

Use of Prepositions

Selecting the correct preposition to follow a verb is sometimes difficult. The reason is that the use of many prepositions is idiomatic—that is, there is no logical reason for choosing one over the other; usage alone determines such choices. It is easy enough to say *the paper is on the desk* or *by the desk* or *under the desk* and, by selecting one of these prepositions, give the correct meaning. But whether to say *he agreed with the proposal* or *he agreed to the proposal* is not such a simple choice.

This list contains some examples of idiomatic uses.

agree to...a proposal
agree with...a person
agree on...a plan

anger at...things, conditions,
  animals
anger with...a person
anger toward...a person
  (*exaggerates the offense*)

beside *by the side of*
besides *in addition to*

between *refers to two persons
  or things*
among *refers to three or more
  persons or things*

blame me for it
blame it on me

compare to *to discover
  similarities only*
compare with *to discover
  likenesses or differences*

comply <u>with</u> (*not* <u>to</u>)

convenient for...a purpose
convenient to...a person

correspond to...things
correspond with...persons

die <u>of</u> (*not* <u>with</u>)...disease

differ from (*or* with)...an
  opinion
differ about (*or* over)...a
  question

enter upon...duties
enter in...a record

free <u>from</u> (*not* of)

frightened <u>at</u> or <u>by</u> (*not* <u>of</u>)

graduate from...a school
graduate in...a year

impatient with...someone else
impatient of...restraint
impatient at...someone's
  conduct

inquire into...any matter
  demanding investigation
inquire about (*or* concerning)...
  the transaction
inquire of...one who can give
  information
inquire at...a place
inquire after...one's health

in search <u>of</u> (*not* <u>for</u>)

try to (*not* <u>and</u>)

unequal to (*not* for)

unmindful <u>of</u> (*not* <u>about</u>)

FROM/OFF   *From* is used with persons; *off,* with things.

Examples: I took dictation <u>from</u> Mr. Kerr.
The file was raised six inches <u>off</u> the floor.

AT, IN/INTO,   *In* is used to mean that something is surrounded or contained; *at*
TO   is used to mean at the site of something rather than inside it. *Into*
indicates motion from outside to inside. *To* suggests the journey to
and from a place; *at* suggests that someone or something is already
there.

Examples: We held our meetings <u>in</u> the Statler Hotel.
We met <u>at</u> the Statler Hotel.
Mary walked <u>into</u> Mr. Smith's office.
We are going <u>to</u> the office.
Mr. Lee left early; he is already <u>at</u> home.

INTO/IN TO,   The two-word forms of these one-word prepositions have a
ONTO/ON TO,   different meaning and function in the sentence. In the respective
UPON/UP ON   phrases *in to, on to,* and *up on, in, on,* and *up* are adverbs.

Examples: I drove <u>into</u> the parking lot.
George stopped <u>in to</u> see a customer.
She put the file <u>onto</u> Mr. Scott's desk. On *is preferable to*
onto *in most instances.*
Go <u>on to</u> the next letter if you cannot read your notes.
I made the decision <u>upon</u> the basis of his report.
The boy climbed <u>up on</u> the ladder.

Unnecessary Prepositions

Do not use prepositions that are not necessary. *Up* is frequently
added to verbs that already convey the idea of "up," such as *divide,
lift, drink, eat. Off* does not need *of* or *from* with it. In the examples
below, the underscored prepositions are unnecessary.

Examples: Where is my book <u>at</u>?
When are you going to start <u>in</u> working?
Where did my pen go <u>to</u>?
I attended the meeting <u>at about</u> eight o'clock. *Use one of
the prepositions, not both.*
The shingles blew off <u>of</u> (or <u>from</u>) the roof.
I hope Mr. Lee divides <u>up</u> the typing of the report.
I do not think they will eat <u>up</u> all the food.
Call me <u>up</u> when you are ready to leave.

Preposition Ending a Sentence

Although it was once considered poor usage to end a sentence with a preposition, it is now very often the natural word order. In fact, a sentence may become clumsy by avoiding a preposition at the end, as in: *This is the sort of nonsense up with which I will not put.* Short questions will often end with prepositions; for example, *What do you want this for?*

CONJUNCTIONS

Conjunctions introduce and connect clauses and join series of words and phrases.

Kinds of Conjunctions

Coordinating conjunctions connect grammatical elements of equal rank: words to words, phrases to phrases, independent clauses to independent clauses, and dependent clauses to dependent clauses. The principal coordinating conjunctions are *and, but, or, nor, for, yet.*

Coordinating conjunctions

Examples: Betty <u>or</u> Kate will drive me home. *connects word to word*
I walked to the store <u>and</u> to the bank. *connects phrase to phrase*
I walked to the store, <u>but</u> I drove to the bank. *connects independent clause to independent clause*
I said that the order was filled <u>and</u> that it was sent yesterday. *connects dependent clause to dependent clause*

Correlative conjunctions work in pairs to connect elements of equal grammatical rank. Some of these pairs are *either/or, neither/nor, not only/but (also) both/and, whether/or.*

Correlative conjunctions

Examples: <u>Both</u> Helen <u>and</u> Grace were ill.
<u>Neither</u> time <u>nor</u> effort helped the situation.

<u>WARNINGS:</u>

1. *Each member of a pair of correlative conjunctions must be followed by elements of equal grammatical rank.*

Example: *avoid:* I read both <u>in the office</u> and <u>while riding on the train</u>.
use: I read both <u>in the office</u> and <u>on the train</u>.

2. Correlatives must be placed immediately before the combinations they connect.

Example: *avoid:* You will either <u>attend the morning</u> or <u>afternoon session</u>.
use: You will attend either the <u>morning</u> or <u>afternoon session</u>.

Subordinate conjunctions

Subordinate conjunctions connect dependent (subordinate) clauses to independent clauses. Some common subordinate conjunctions are *after, although, as, as long as, because, before, unless, in order that, though.*

When relative pronouns introduce adjective clauses, they act as subordinate conjunctions. These relative pronouns are *who, whom, which,* and *that. That* may also act as a subordinate conjunction when introducing noun clauses.

Since dependent clauses are always noun, adjective, or adverb in use, the words introducing these clauses will always be subordinate conjunctions.

Examples:

Adverb Clauses:

Do not leave <u>until</u> I call you.
<u>Because</u> Mr. Smith is ill, he is not in the office.

Adjective Clause:

Mr. Smith, <u>who</u> is handling the matter, is not in the office.

Noun Clause:

Mr. Smith said <u>that he would be out of the office today.</u>

Conjunctive adverbs

Conjunctive adverbs (sometimes called *transitional* adverbs) connect independent clauses and show a relationship between the connected clauses. The fact that these are adverbs makes them different from simple conjunctions. Grammatically, the connected clauses are independent—but the clause introduced by the conjunctive adverb is dependent on the other clause for a complete meaning. Some of the conjunctive adverbs are *however, therefore, moreover, consequently, namely, likewise, nevertheless, so.*

Examples: I wanted to attend the meeting; <u>however</u>, I shall not be able to do so.

This plan will be difficult to put into operation; <u>nevertheless</u>, it still has some merit.

<u>WARNING:</u>

These connectives are more appropriate to formal writing than to general writing or business letters. They give a stilted tone to writing (with the exception of so) and should therefore be used sparingly.

Conjunction Warnings

While is a conjunction of time; it does not express contrast. For contrast use *although, though,* or *but.* Do not use *while* to express actions happening at the same time; use *and* instead.   WHILE

Examples: <u>While</u> I am working on the report, I shall not have time for any other work. *expresses time*

<u>Although</u> I wanted very much to go to the meeting, I stayed home and finished my work. *expresses contrast*

At nine o'clock the beginning class meets in Room 314 <u>and</u> the intermediate class meets in Room 214. *expresses actions happening at the same time*

And expresses something in addition; *but* expresses a contrast.   AND/BUT

Examples: I wanted him to do the work, <u>but</u> he was unable to do it.

I wanted him to do the work, <u>and</u> he did do it.

Use *whether* (often with *or*) in indirect questions and expressions of doubt. Do not use *if* because it introduces a condition.   WHETHER/IF

Examples: He does not know <u>whether</u> he can complete the work.

<u>If</u> he can complete the work, he will call us.

He asked <u>whether</u> I had read the fact in a magazine or a newspaper.

<u>If</u> I had read the fact in that magazine, I would remember it.

Use *that* to introduce noun clauses; do not use *where*. Remember, too, that *where* cannot introduce a definition.   THAT/WHERE

Examples: I read in the paper <u>that</u> there would be a big storm.

avoid: Proofreading is <u>where</u> you read material for errors.

use: Proofreading is a process of reading for errors.

AS, AS IF/LIKE   *Like* is a preposition, not a conjunction. This means that *like* cannot connect a dependent clause to an independent clause. Use *as, as if,* or *as though* to introduce dependent clauses. Use *like* to connect a noun or pronoun (object of the preposition) to a sentence.

Examples: It seems <u>as</u> if he has a good chance of getting the job.

My brother looks <u>like</u> me.

BEING THAT/   *Being that* and *being as* are not conjunctions; instead, use such
BEING AS   conjunctions as *since, because,* or *for* to introduce dependent clauses.

Examples: <u>Since</u> it was raining, I took a cab to work.

<u>Because</u> Mr. Scott is out of the office, I referred the matter to Mr. James.

AS   Do not use *as* in place of *because, for, since, that, which, who,* or *whether. As* is the weakest of the subordinate conjunctions used to indicate cause or reason; *because* is the most specific. *As* should not be used to introduce noun clauses.

Examples: <u>Because</u> I was asleep, I did not hear the phone ringing.

I do not know <u>whether</u> I can finish the work.

7. Punctuation

Punctuation is used for one purpose: to assist the reader in understanding what is written. Punctuation marks are signals in sentences; they indicate starts, stops, and pauses. There are instances when some punctuation does seem to be unnecessary; there are times, too, when the punctuation can be left to the discretion of the writer. But there are many cases where punctuation rules do apply—and apply without exception.

Many people excuse their inability to punctuate correctly by insisting that all punctuation is subject to the whims of the writer. On the contrary: Most punctuation follows definite rules and understanding these rules will help you to punctuate correctly.

7

END-OF-SENTENCE PUNCTUATION

Period

1. Use a period after declarative and imperative sentences.

Examples: I cannot complete the work by next Tuesday. *declarative*
Stay in the left lane. *imperative*

2. Use a period after simple requests.

Example: May I hear from you regarding the matter.

3. Use a period after an indirect question.

Example: I wonder whether or not he has read the report.

4. Use a period after initials and abbreviations, except for the two-letter state abbreviations.

171

Examples: C. R. Martin
           etc.
           KY

WARNING:

A contraction is not an abbreviation. An apostrophe shows where letters are omitted (doesn't, won't), and there is no period at the end of a contraction.

   5. Use a period as a decimal point.

Example: $4.50

   6. Use spaced periods to indicate an ellipsis (an omission of words within a sentence). Ellipses signify omissions in quotations, hesitation in dialogues or narratives, and separation of statements in advertising copy. Three periods indicate an omission of words at the beginning of or within a sentence; a fourth period, a question mark, or an exclamation point is used when the omission occurs at the end of the sentence.
   In typing ellipses, space once after the last word; then alternate periods and spaces. If the period ending the sentence precedes the ellipsis, no space is left before it.

Examples: Let's have the shutters up . . . before a man can say Jack
           Robinson.
                                                   —CHARLES DICKENS
           Progress, therefore, is not an accident, but a necessity. . . .
           It is a part of nature.
                                                   —HERBERT SPENCER
           This remarkable gasoline is superior in many ways—bet-
           ter performance . . . greater economy . . . longer life
           for your car.

WARNING:

Never end a sentence with two periods, even when the last word is an abbreviation.

Example: We buy our products from Jones & Lee, Inc.

Exclamation Point

Exclamation points are used after sentences or expressions to show strong emotion.

Examples: Oh!
Alas! It will soon be over!

WARNINGS:

1. *Don't overuse exclamation points; they lose their effect if placed lavishly throughout any writing.*
2. *Don't use double or triple exclamation points.*

Question Mark

1. Use a question mark after a direct question.

Examples: Is Mr. Smith in his office?
You can do the work, can't you?

2. Use a question mark to show doubt or approximation. Enclose such question marks in parentheses.

Example: Our college was founded in 1858 (?).

3. Use question marks in a series of short questions in the same sentence. Do not capitalize the first word of each question unless the questions are complete sentences.

Examples: Who will make the decision? the president? the vice president? the secretary?
Check these things in all letters: Are names spelled correctly? Are figures correct? Is the letter well centered? Are all parts of the letter included?

WARNING:

Avoid using a question mark to show humor, sarcasm, or irony.

Example: His short (?) speech lasted two hours.

Typing hint: Leave two spaces after any punctuation that ends a sentence.

INTERNAL PUNCTUATION

Comma

Commas are used for two purposes: to separate and to set off. To set off a part of the sentence, it is usually necessary to use a pair of commas; to separate, only one comma is needed.

1. TO SEPARATE CLAUSES OF A COMPOUND SENTENCE

If a comma is used to separate the clauses of a compound sentence:

a. these clauses must be joined by coordinate conjunctions— *and, but, for, or, nor, yet* (Always place the comma before the conjunction, never after it.)
b. none of the clauses should have internal punctuation (See section on semicolons, page 180.)
c. each clause should have its own subject

Examples: I wanted to read the latest issue of *Time,* but it was not available on the newsstand.
I wanted to read the latest issue of *Time* but was unable to do so. *no second subject*
I hurried to the meeting room, for I was already late.

2. TO SEPARATE ITEMS IN A SERIES

If a comma is used to separate items in a series:

a. the series should consist of three or more items
b. none of the items in the series should have internal punctuation (See section on semicolons, page 182.)

A series may consist of words, phrases, or clauses. A comma after the item that precedes the coordinate conjunction is optional. If the series contains *etc.* (*et cetera*), a comma should be placed *before* and *after* the *etc.* (unless, of course, the *etc.* comes at the end of the sentence).

Examples: I bought paper, erasers, and ink at the stationery store. *series of words* (The comma after erasers *is optional.*)
I walked to the market, to the post office, and to the bakery yesterday morning. *series of phrases*
I did my homework, I washed the car, and I cooked dinner. *series of clauses*
I read the book and the magazine on the train. *series of two; therefore, no comma*

Paper, pencils, pens, etc., are sold at the stationery store.
series containing etc.
Mr. Jones, as well as other members of our company, will be available to serve you.

WARNINGS:

1. If the conjunction in the series is repeated, do not separate the items by commas.

Example: Adults and children and dogs covered the beach.

2. Never place a comma after the item that follows the coordinate conjunction.

Example: *avoid:* I bought paper, pens, and pencils, at the stationery store.
use: I bought paper, pens, and pencils at the stationery store.

3. Since etc. *means "and others," do not use* and *before it.*

Example: *avoid:* Paper, pencils, and etc., are sold at the stationery store.
use: Paper, pencils, etc., are sold at the stationery store.

4. Etc. *in a series weakens the sentence; it takes away from the emphasis because it is vague and all-inclusive. Try to reword the sentence so that the list is preceded by a phrase like* such as *to indicate that the series is incomplete.*

Example: Such items as paper, pencils, and pens are sold at the stationery store.

Coordinate adjectives are adjectives of equal importance that usually precede the noun that is modified. A comma should *not* be placed between the last adjective in the series and the noun that is modified.

3. TO SEPARATE COORDINATE ADJECTIVES

Examples: The gray, weather-stained house is over fifty years old.
The building contained many new air-conditioned offices. *There are no commas in the series because these adjectives are not coordinate, or of equal importance;* new *modifies* air-conditioned offices; many *modifies* new air-conditioned offices.

4. TO
SEPARATE
REPEATED
WORDS, TWO
NUMBERS
COMING
TOGETHER,
TAG
QUESTIONS,
AND
INVERTED
NAMES

A comma is necessary to separate two numbers that come together, but the sentence can often be made more readable by changing the order so that the two numbers do *not* come together.

A tag question is a short direct question that follows a statement but is still part of the sentence.

Examples: Never, never turn the pointer on the dial backward.

In 1978, 4,500 people attended our exhibit.

In 1978 there were 4,500 people who attended our exhibit. *a clearer order*

David can finish the work, can't he?

Hale, William

5. TO SET OFF
CERTAIN
CLAUSES
AND
PHRASES
OUT OF
THEIR
NATURAL
ORDER

The natural position of an adverb clause is after the verb; if the clause comes at the beginning of a sentence, place a comma after it. Some subordinate conjunctions frequently used to introduce these clauses are *if, when, as, because, before,* and *since.* The comma after the introductory adverb clause may be omitted if the clause is short and closely related to the main clause—and especially in sentences in which both clauses have the same subject.

The natural position of infinitive and participial phrases is after the words they modify. Occasionally they will introduce a sentence and then should be followed by a comma.

Examples:

Adverb clauses out of their natural order:
When Mr. Graves returns, will you please call me.
If Mr. Graves returns before Friday, will you please let me know.
Mr. Scott, when he was in St. Louis, ordered two new typewriters.

Introductory adverb clause that does not require comma:
When I return I shall complete the report.

Participial phrase out of its natural order:
Standing apart from the crowd, Mr. Lee witnessed the entire incident.

Infinitive phrase out of its natural order:
To read the announcement, Betty had to stand on a chair.

A short introductory prepositional phrase is not followed by a comma; a long phrase may be followed by a comma.

Examples: On Friday Mr. Hale will be out of the office.

In the three years of using your services, we have had no complaints.

On January 2 our firm will begin the biggest sale in its history.

Nonrestrictive elements can be adjective clauses, infinitive or participial phrases, and occasionally adverb clauses. (Nonrestrictive means that the element can be taken out of the sentence without affecting the identity of the object that it describes.) In most instances, the nonrestrictive modifier is used as an adjective. Adjective clauses are introduced by one of the relative pronouns—*who, which,* or *that.* Adverb clauses in their natural order—after the verb—are occasionally nonrestrictive; when nonrestrictive, they are usually introduced by *as* and are set off by commas. They are, of course, set off by commas when they are out of their natural order.

6. TO SET OFF NON-RESTRICTIVE MODIFIERS

Examples: Mr. Williams, whom you met recently, is our new sales manager. *nonrestrictive adjective clause*
Our latest product, containing many secret ingredients, will be placed on the market in July. *nonrestrictive participial phrase*
Our sales for January fell below the yearly average, as you probably realize. *nonrestrictive adverb clause in its natural order*

Appositive elements come after a noun or pronoun and rename or supplement the noun or pronoun. One-word appositives are not set off by commas.

7. TO SET OFF APPOSITIVE ELEMENTS

Examples: Mr. Smith, the president of our company, is in Japan.
My brothers, John and Robert, left the meeting early.
My sister Kate is a secretary. *one-word appositive*

Parenthetical elements are words or groups of words that interrupt the sentence in which they occur. These elements may explain, qualify, or contrast some part of the sentence, but they are not grammatically necessary to the sentence. (Weak exclamations, such as *well, oh,* or *remember,* and *yes* and *no* are also considered to be parenthetical.) Some of the frequently used words, phrases, and short clauses that may be used parenthetically are:

8. TO SET OFF PAREN-THETICAL ELEMENTS

after all	fortunately	namely
again	however	nevertheless
as you know	I believe	of course
at any rate	I think	on the other hand
by the way	in fact	perhaps
finally	in short	to be sure

Examples: I was not, as you know, aware of the complaint.
I think, however, that Mr. Lee is the best qualified for the position.

The loss, <u>after all</u>, is not a large one.
It is my father, <u>not my uncle</u>, who lives in Washington.
<u>Yes</u>, you may use my name as reference.
<u>Remember</u>, we are here to help you.
Remember to return the form with your check. *Do not put a comma after* remember *in this instance;* remember *is not parenthetical—it is the main verb.*

9. TO SET OFF DIRECT ADDRESS

Direct address indicates the persons or objects addressed in speaking or writing.

Examples: <u>Ladies and gentlemen</u>, may I introduce our speaker.
I do not think, <u>Mrs. Carson</u>, that you would want your account to become delinquent.

10. TO SET OFF EXPLAN- ATORY ELEMENTS

The explanatory elements include geographic names, dates, degrees or titles, *Inc.* and *Ltd.*, and explanatory words accompanying direct quotations.

Examples: Portland, <u>Oregon</u>, is larger than Portland, <u>Maine</u>.
Robert Jones, <u>Ltd.</u>, is the manufacturer of our new line of appliances.
"I cannot," <u>Miss Ray said</u>, "finish the work by five o'clock."
Friday, <u>January 31</u>, is the deadline for turning in the report.
January 31, <u>1882</u>, was the birth date of Franklin D. Roosevelt.

WARNING:

Inc. and Ltd. are abbreviations, and they must have periods after them. They are rarely spelled out when used in firm names.

If the date consists of the month and year only, usage varies; commas may or may not be used.

Example: May 1983 is the date of his departure.
or: May, 1983, is the date of his departure.

Although titles and degrees after personal names (including *Jr.* and *Sr.*) are usually set off by commas, numbers such as *IV* or *2d* are not.

Examples: Raymond Taylor, <u>Ph.D.</u>, gave the commencement address.
William James, <u>Jr.</u>, is chairman of the committee.
but: Martin Fuller <u>IV</u> is our new president.

Sometimes words are omitted when the context of the sentence
makes the omitted words clearly understood; a comma is placed
where the omission occurs.

11. TO SHOW
OMISSION
OF
WORDS

Examples: Our sales increased 15 percent in January; in February,
10 percent; and in March, 15 percent.
To err is human; to forgive, divine.

There are specific instances when a comma is needed for clarity.
(But "clarity" should not be used as justification for a comma when
you do not otherwise know a rule for using one.) Take out the
commas in the examples below, and it will be obvious that the
commas are needed for clarity.

12. FOR
CLARITY

Examples: The week before, Christmas sales were exceeding all
records.
Outside, the building gave the impression of great size.

Commas are used in numbers of four or more digits, although
they are not used in years, page numbers, house numbers, telephone
numbers, serial numbers, decimal fractions, and ZIP codes.

13. IN
NUMBERS
OF FOUR
OR MORE
DIGITS

Examples: $1,500   2,785 pounds
page 1432   2421 Western Avenue
the year 1966   Order No. 314583

<u>WARNING:</u>

Do not use commas:
1. Between subjects and verbs

Example: *avoid:* Whoever left the safe unlocked, will be in
trouble.
use: Whoever left the safe unlocked will be in trouble.

2. Between verbs and direct objects or complements

Example: *avoid:* The reason that the company is moving, is to con-
solidate services.

use: The reason that the company is moving is to con-
solidate services.

3. Between two adjectives that are not coordinate

Example: *avoid:* The auction house sold many fine, old paintings.
use: The auction house sold many fine old paintings.

*4. Between two items in a series that are joined by a coordinate
conjunction*

Example: *avoid:* He wrote that he would be in Chicago next week,
and that he would call me.
use: He wrote that he would be in Chicago next week
and that he would call me.

*5. After dates, unless the date or the sentence would otherwise re-
quire a comma*

Example: *avoid:* On March 1, Mr. Harris will celebrate his eighti-
eth birthday.
use: On March 1 Mr. Harris will celebrate his eight-
ieth birthday.

Semicolon

Semicolons are the strongest of the internal punctuation marks;
in fact, they can frequently be used in place of periods. The function
of the semicolon in a sentence is to separate.

1. TO
SEPARATE
CLAUSES
OF A
COMPOUND
SENTENCE

If a semicolon is used to separate the clauses of a compound
sentence, one of these conditions must exist (See section on
commas, page 174):

a. there is no coordinate conjunction connecting the clauses
b. either or both clauses contain internal punctuation
c. a conjunctive adverb or a transitional phrase such as *for example* or *that is* is used to connect the clauses

Examples:

No coordinate conjunction:
I did not hear the telephone ringing; it had been ringing for some
time.
I wanted to see Mr. Smith; I needed his advice.

Internal punctuation in either or both clauses:

This is not, as a matter of fact, the best method; but it is the only
    workable one at the moment.

Mr. McNally, the president of our company, wrote the letter; but Mr.
    Hastings, the chairman of the board, signed it.

One of the company's top executives—Mr. Harper, in this instance—
    approved the new contract; and he believes it will greatly
    benefit the firm.

Clauses connected by a conjunctive adverb:

I did not want to make the complaint; however, I had no choice but to
    do so.

I do not want to drive in the commuter traffic; therefore, I shall leave
    before four o'clock.

Clauses connected by a transitional expression:

The report gives all of the necessary information except for one thing;
    that is, who will see that the plan is adopted?

The comma after the conjunctive adverb is a matter of choice; use it
only if the conjunctive adverb is considered to be parenthetical.
The comma after the transitional expression is considered necessary.

Semicolons are used before words or phrases that introduce
explanations and enumerations. Frequently used introductory expressions are *as, for example* (abbreviated *e.g.*), *for instance, namely,
that is* (abbreviated *i.e.*), and *that is to say.* Colons and commas can
also be used before the explanation or enumeration.

2. TO
SEPARATE
EXPLANATIONS
AND
ENUMERA-
TIONS

Examples: Mr. Lee would not sign letters containing errors; <u>for
example</u>, misspelled words.

Each month I read these magazines: that is, The <u>New
Yorker</u>, <u>Harper's</u>, and <u>The Atlantic Monthly</u>. *Use a
colon because the main clause introduces a listing.*

It is too late to get the letter in the last mail, that is, the mail
that is picked up at five. *Use a comma because the
explanation is appositive.*

If the enumeration occurs within the sentence, it may be set off
by commas, dashes, or parentheses.

Examples: A number of salesmen—for example, Mr. Scott, Mr.
Williams, and Mr. Stanley—received promotions last
year.

A number of salesmen, in this instance, Mr. Scott, Mr.
Williams, and Mr. Stanley, received promotions last
year.

Many of the errors (for example, typographical errors) were inexcusable.

---

3. TO SEPARATE ITEMS IN A SERIES

Semicolons separate items in a series if those items contain internal commas.

Examples: The salesperson's itinerary includes Portland, Oregon; Seattle, Washington; and Boise, Idaho.
The dates of July 1, 1984; August 1, 1984; September 7, 1984; and January 5, 1985, were on the invoices.

Quotation Marks

Quotation marks enclose *any* direct quotation, whether from a speaker or from written material. A direct quotation must be quoted exactly as spoken or written, even if it includes misspelled words, incorrect punctuation, or other errors.

1. PLACEMENT OF EXPLANATORY EXPRESSIONS

Since only the direct quotation is placed inside quotation marks, explanatory expressions will be outside the quotation marks. An explanatory expression can precede the quotation, fall within it, or be placed at the end. It is usually set off from the direct quotation by commas, but a colon is sometimes used when lengthy explanatory material precedes the direct quotation.

Examples: It was Churchill who said: "Never in the field of human conflict was so much owed by so many to so few."
"I do not think," Mr. Hill said, "that the company will show a profit for the year."
"I hope this plan meets with your approval," Mr. Hill dictated.

2. QUOTATIONS OF MORE THAN ONE PARAGRAPH

If the quotation consists of more than one paragraph, quotation marks are placed at the beginning of each paragraph but at the end of the last paragraph only.

3. QUOTATION WITHIN A QUOTATION

If a quotation is contained within a quotation, single quotation marks enclose the internal quotation. Should there be a quotation within the single-quoted matter, enclose this in double quotation marks.

Example: Mr. Evans said, "I quoted President Roosevelt's statement, 'The only thing we have to fear is fear itself.'"

If words are omitted in the quoted matter, three periods (an ellipsis) are used to indicate the omission. If the omission falls at the end of the sentence, a fourth period must be added to show the end of the sentence. (See also page 172.)

4. OMISSION OF QUOTED WORDS

Example: It was almost fifty years ago that Hitler wrote: ''. . . the great masses of people . . . will more easily fall victim to a great lie than a small one.''

When *etc.* follows a quotation, it is not a part of the quotation and should not be enclosed in the quotation marks.

5. ETC. WITH QUOTATIONS

Example: Mary began typing Lincoln's Gettysburg Address: ''Four score and seven years ago,'' etc.

The period and the comma always go *inside* closing quotation marks.

6. QUOTATION MARKS WITH OTHER MARKS OF PUNCTUATION

Example: ''It is not easy,'' Mr. Kay said, ''to find letters in that file.''

The colon and the semicolon always go *outside* closing quotation marks.

Example: I have just read ''Jabberwocky''; it is part of *Through the Looking Glass.*

The dash, the question mark, and the exclamation point may go either inside or outside closing quotation marks. Their positions are determined by whether or not the entire sentence or just the quotation is the question or exclamation or includes the dash.

Examples: The manager asked, ''Has Mr. Hughes left yet?''
Did the manager ask, ''Has Mr. Hughes left yet''?

Quotation marks are also used to enclose titles of short stories, poems, radio and television programs, lectures, articles, one-act plays, parts of chapters of books, and other literary works less than book length. Words used as words, unusual or technical terms, and words accompanied by their definitions may be enclosed in quotes; in print, these words often appear in italics.

7. OTHER USES

Examples: ''The Speckled Band'' is a Sherlock Holmes story.
''Dickens: The Two Scrooges'' is an essay by Edmund Wilson.

The words "affect" and "effect" are often confused.
A "spoonerism," an unintentional transposition of initial sounds, was named for an English clergyman.

WARNING:

Do not use quotation marks around an indirect quotation.

Example: He said that he was leaving early.

Colon

The colon is most frequently used to introduce something that follows. It is often used after or in place of *namely* or *as follows.*

1. BEFORE LISTED ITEMS   Colons are used before listed items that are introduced by such words as *the following* and *as follows* or by any other enumerating expressions. Do not use colons before series that function as predicate nominatives or direct objects.

Examples: Please send the following: 10 quires of stencils, 10 reams of paper, and 5 bottles of correction fluid.
The supplies needed for dictation are pencils, pen, and notebook. *predicate nominatives*

2. BEFORE LONG OR FORMAL QUOTA- TIONS   A colon is used before a long or formal quotation.

Example: I am quoting George Washington, who said in his Farewell Address: "It is our true policy to steer clear of permanent alliances with any portion of the foreign world."

3. TO SEPA- RATE TWO INDEPENDENT CLAUSES   A colon can be used to separate two independent clauses when the second clause explains or illustrates the first. The first word following the colon is usually capitalized when it begins a complete sentence.

Example: This is an excellent suggestion: Get Mr. Lee's approval before going ahead with the plan.

4. SPECIAL USES   Special uses of the colon include the following: (a) after the salutation in a business letter (mixed punctuation, see page 37); (b) to show hours, minutes, and seconds; (c) to separate chapter and

verse in biblical selections; (d) to separate volume and page in bibliographical references; (e) to express ratios.

Examples: Dear Mr. Morris:
The train leaves at 5:45.
The quotation is from Psalms 25:7.
Harper's 229:28
The vote was 4:1 in favor of the amendment.

Dash

The dash is used to indicate abruptness in thought or to set off
parenthetical elements. The usual way to type a dash is to use two
hyphens with no space before or after.

A dash is used to indicate an abrupt change in the thought or
structure of a sentence.

1. TO INDICATE AN ABRUPT CHANGE IN THOUGHT

Examples: She was—how shall I say it—a person one could not
easily forget.
She screamed—it was a bloodcurdling sound—at the
sight of the man.

Parenthetical or explanatory expressions are made more emphatic by using dashes rather than commas.

2. TO SET OFF PAREN-THETICAL EXPRESSIONS

Examples: Two of the auto industry's biggest manufacturers—Ford
and General Motors—signed the contract.
Our two top salesmen—that is, Mr. Jarvis and Mr.
Walker—are in New York.

A dash can precede the name of an author or source of a
quotation.

3. TO SHOW THE SOURCE OF A QUOTA-TION

Example: All animals are equal, but some animals are more equal
than others.
—GEORGE ORWELL

Parentheses

Parentheses set off matter that is not essential to the sentence;
they should *not* be used around matter that *is* essential to the
sentence. (The dash may also be used in such instances.)

1. TO SET OFF ABRUPT INTER- RUPTIONS

Parentheses set off parenthetical matter when the interruption is more abrupt than one usually set off by commas.

Example: He read a statement (I thought he would never finish!) on the company's new product.

2. TO SET OFF SUPPLE- MENTARY OR EXPLANATORY MATTER

Parentheses can set off supplementary or explanatory matter that is not a part of the sentence.

Examples: The plaintiff (Mr. Smith, in this instance) refused to give the information.

Read the chapter on pronouns (see page 14) before you do the exercises.

3. MECHAN- ICAL USES

Parentheses can be used mechanically, around such items as numbers in outlines and the source of a fact or statement.

Examples: The sections in the book are (a) nouns, (b) pronouns, and (c) verbs.

Cash is defined as bank deposits and certain readily negotiable paper (*Webster's Third New International Dictionary*).

4. OTHER PUNCTUA- TION WITH PARENTHESES

When other punctuation marks are needed with the matter in parentheses, place these marks after the ending parenthesis. If the parenthetical matter is a complete sentence, capitalize the first word and place the punctuation mark before the ending parenthesis. Do *not* place a comma before a beginning parenthesis.

Example: *avoid:* If you find an inactive file, (one that has not been used for a year) transfer it to storage.

use: If you find an inactive file (one that has not been used for a year), transfer it to storage.

Brackets

Brackets are used around corrections or inserted material that is added by someone other than the original author. Although they are not used often in business correspondence, they are sometimes used in reports.

The word *sic* (*thus, so*) is placed in brackets after an error in a direct quotation to show that the original source contained the error.

Example: The president's secretary wrote: ''The expence [*sic*] is too
great.''

Italics

To indicate words intended to be printed in italics, underline
once in writing or typing. Usage of italics varies, but listed below are
the more common uses.

Italics are used to show titles of books, periodicals, newspapers,   1. TITLES
musical works, plays, movies, paintings and works of art, legal
citations, and names of ships and aircraft.

Examples:

For Whom the Bell Tolls   *The Deputy*
The New York Times   *Mona Lisa*
The Saturday Review   *Brown v. Board of Education*
Beethoven's *Missa Solemnis*   *U.S.S. Arizona*

Italics are used to indicate foreign words—but not words that   2. FOREIGN
have a foreign origin and are now a part of the English language.   WORDS

Examples: *caveat emptor*   *ad hoc*
    but: camouflage   baton

Italics are used to make words or expressions stand out and for   3. EMPHASIS
emphasis.

Examples: *But* can be either a conjunction or a preposition.
    Do *not* leave the electric typewriter turned on.

8. Style or Mechanics

Style (or mechanics) deals with abbreviation, capitalization, and expressing numbers as words or in figures. Usage varies considerably, and business usage can vary from general usage; rules vary, too, from office to office. Follow the rules that are given here or consult with authorities such as the *United States Government Printing Office Style Manual, The Chicago Manual of Style,* and *Words into Type.* When style variations occur, select one form and follow it.

CAPITALIZATION

Capitalization practices vary. Proper names and adjectives are generally capitalized, as are the first words of such units as sentences, lines of poetry, and items in an outline. The term commonly used for small letters is *lower case.*

Capitalization Rules

Capitalize:

1. *Proper Names and Adjectives.* Personal names as the bearer of the name does, geographic names as they are officially presented, and proper adjectives that are derived from proper nouns (some proper nouns and adjectives when used to convey special meanings are commonly spelled with lower-case letters). An atlas or a dictionary can be helpful when questions arise.

Examples:

Proper nouns: McMillan *or* Macmillan   English Channel
                Vonderheit *or* von der Heit   Missouri River

Proper adjectives: French pastry
                  Elizabethan culture
                  American literature
          but: italic type, brussels sprouts

2. *Organizations.* Cap names of private and governmental organizations as well as *Government, Administration, Federal, Union, Nation,* and *Constitution* when used to refer to a specific country or to a part of an official name. Usage varies on whether *administration, government, federal, nation,* and *constitution* are capitalized when used alone. The tendency seems to be that they are not.

Examples: Quaker State Oil Refining Company
National Education Association
Federal Bureau of Investigation
United States Supreme Court, *but* a federal court

3. *Ethnic Terms.* Names of nationalities and specific names of races as well as all words referring to them. Do not capitalize names of skin colors.

Examples: Spanish   Israeli   Lebanese
Negro, American Indian, Oriental,
but: black, red, yellow

4. *Religious Terms.* References to the deity or deities and saints in all recognized religions, religious sects, books, holy days, and adjectives derived from these terms. General terms such as *biblical* and *godless* are not capitalized. Pronouns referring to the deity, other than *who, whose,* and *whom,* are sometimes capitalized.

Examples:

Koran	Easter	St. John	Protestant	Presbyterian
Bible	Christmas	Mohammed	Catholic	Rosh Hashanah

5. *Names of calendar divisions and holidays.* Names of calendar divisions and holidays but not names of seasons.

Examples: Friday   January   Labor Day
but: summer sales   winter skiing

6. *Geographic localities.* Names of geographic localities— nations, states, provinces, continents, bodies of water, mountains, cities, parks, and specific geographic regions—and points of the compass that refer to definite regions

Examples: Bulgaria   Australia   New Orleans
Idaho   Black Sea   Yellowstone Park
Alberta   Mount St. Helens the East Coast
but: We live north of San Francisco.

8

Do not capitalize geographic terms that are not a part of the name, are placed before the name, or are made plural.

Examples: the valley of the Willamette
Columbia and Snake rivers
the city of New York

7. *Trade names.* Trade names of products but not the names of the products

Examples: Sanka Coffee, *but* a can of coffee
Kodak film
a Buick car

8. *Personal titles.* Professional, business, civic, military, religious, and family titles immediately preceding personal names

Examples: Dr. William Davis   Grandmother Miller
General George Marshall   Rabbi Berkowitz
Senator Alan Cranston

9. *Course titles.* Specific names of educational courses and general names of such courses if the name is formed from a proper noun

Examples: Beginning Typewriting, *but* a course in typewriting
Elementary French, *but* a course in French

10. *Titles of literary works and art.* All beginning principal words in titles of books, magazines, newspapers, plays, poems, reports, pictures, and works of art

Examples: da Vinci's *The Last Supper*   *The New Yorker*
The New York Times   *Pioneer Women*
Death of a Salesman

11. *The pronoun "I" and exclamations.* The pronoun *I* and exclamations such as *oh, help,* and *ouch* when these words stand alone

12. *Nouns with numbers or letters.* Nouns followed by numbers or letters unless the noun refers to a minor item such as page, paragraph, line, or verse

Examples: Exhibit B   page 250, line 17
          Purchase Order No. 6741   Check 503

13. Abbreviations only if they would be capitalized when written in full. Some abbreviations such as *f.o.b., c.o.d., a.m.,* and *p.m.* are usually written in lower-case letters. The two-letter state abbreviations are written in all capitals and without periods.

Examples: etc.   U.S.A.   NY
          i.e.   U.S.S.R.

Typing Hint: Do not space after periods within an abbreviation; space once after the final period when the abbreviation is in the body of a sentence.

Examples: a.m.   P.T.A.
          e.g.   A.M.S.

14. *Initial Words.* The initial words of
    Any sentence
    A direct quotation
    Every line of poetry
    The salutation of a letter, as well as any nouns in the
        salutation
    The complimentary close of a letter
    Items in an outline
    Items following a colon in tabulated material

Examples: Thurber paraphrased the old proverb by writing:
              "Early to rise and early to bed
              Makes a male healthy and wealthy and dead."
          Dear Customer
          My dear Mrs. Wilson
          Very sincerely yours

Lower-case Rules

Do not capitalize:

1. Common names of persons, place, or things, such as foods, animals, plants, general geographic terms, and musical instruments

Examples: mother town maple mountain
     park   goat   daffodil clarinet
     coffee   creek   river   quarter horse

2. Names of job titles or occupations, with the exception of *Realtor,* which is always capitalized when the title refers to a member of the National Association of Real Estate Boards

Examples: personnel manager dentist   program director
     cost analyst   secretary psychologist

3. Names of diseases unless a proper name is part of the name of the disease

Examples: chicken pox Parkinson's disease
     tuberculosis arthritis

NUMERALS

Whether to write numbers as words or as figures is a matter of style. In business letters figures are used more often than words because they are easier to read; a quick glance will pick up *$5* more readily than *five dollars*. The important considerations are that you use a uniform style—do not write an amount of money, for example, in two different ways—and that the numbers can be read as easily as possible.

Unless you are instructed otherwise, follow these rules for writing numbers:

Numbers as Words

Write these numbers as words:

1. Numbers one through ten when such numbers are used individually

Examples: The president of the company wrote eight letters on the
     subject.
     Only five people attended the meeting on letter writing.

Large round numbers such as million and billion are usually spelled out: 5 billion; $20 million

2. Any number beginning a sentence. If the number is large, rewrite the sentence so that the number no longer comes at the beginning.

Example: *avoid:* Four hundred and fifty-five people came to the exhibit.
use: There were 455 people at the exhibit.

3. Round or indefinite numbers

Examples: Approximately a hundred people attended the meeting.
There were several thousand books in Mr. Lee's library.

4. Fractions standing alone

Examples: At least one third of the audience left early.
More than two thirds of the house was destroyed by fire.

5. A person's age when the number of years only is given

Example: Tom will be twenty-five next Friday.

6. Periods of time unless such figures are used in credit or interest rates

Examples: I will complete the work in fifteen minutes.
Mr. Jones has lived in that house for fifteen years.
but: The note was issued for 60 days.

7. Time of day when used with *o'clock*

Examples: twelve o'clock   one o'clock

8. Names of centuries and decades

Examples: The fifties (*but* the 1950's)
the twentieth century

9. Days of the month—first through tenth—when written *before* the month. Use the ordinal form.

Examples: sixth of June   first of July

Numbers as Figures

Write these numbers as figures:

1. Exact numbers over ten

Examples: I typed 14 letters before five o'clock.
There were 11 patients waiting to see the doctor.

2. Numbers that occur more than once in a sentence. If a number immediately follows another, usually the smaller number is spelled out and the larger one written in figures; however, if the numbers are unrelated, they can be separated by commas. All numbers in a series of three or more are written as figures, even though the numbers are less than ten.

Examples: 15 five-cent stamps
In 1984, 450 houses were built in that area.
Your orders for 3, 9, and 12 dozen typewriter ribbons have been received.

3. Days of the month when they come *after* the month. Do not use the ordinal endings, such as *13th, 23d.*

Examples: July 24   December 15   March 2

4. House numbers (except *One*) and street numbers over ten. Numbered streets up to ten use the ordinal endings—*First, Tenth*— but numbered streets over ten do not—*19, 45.*

Examples: 4031 Tenth Street   4031 - 19 Street
4031 East 19 Street

5. A person's age when given in years, months, and days. Commas are not used in this series.

Example: His age at the time the policy was written was 15 years 3 months and 16 days.

6. Exact time or when A.M. or P.M. is used

Examples: 5:15   4 P.M.

7. Amounts of money. Use the dollar sign when $1 or over; spell out the word *cents* when less than $1. Do not use the decimal

point and ciphers when the amount of money consists of dollars alone.

Examples: $25 $125.65 $5,000   25 cents   7 cents

In legal documents amounts of money are spelled out and the figures placed in parentheses.

Example: two thousand dollars ($2,000)

   8. Percentages; weights; measures; dimensions; distances; degrees; capacities; page numbers; person's age in months, days, and years; and bond and financial quotations. Note that the words with the figures are spelled out. Symbols (%, #) are not used unless space is limited.

Examples: 40 percent   5 miles   98.6 degrees
      6 percent   6 pounds   9 gallons
      page 85   IBM 5s at 525   25 kilometers
      25 years 6 months 4 days

WARNING:

Ordinal numbers written as figures are formed by adding -d, -st, or -th to a number.

Examples: 22d   31st   24th

ABBREVIATIONS

An abbreviation should not be used if there is the slightest possibility that it will be misunderstood. Consult a dictionary when questions arise, for dictionaries contain definitions and correct forms of abbreviations. A list of frequently used abbreviations is given in the Appendix, page 223.

Acceptable Abbreviations

   Accepted business abbreviations include:

   1. Abbreviations that come before and after personal names

Examples: Dr.   Mr./Messrs.   Sr.

          Esq.   Mrs./Mmes.   St.   (before   a   saint's
                                                  name)

          Jr.   Ms./Mses. *or* Mss.

2. Earned or honorary degrees or special awards, such as B.A., M.A., Ph.D., D.D.S., C.P.A., C.P.S., D.S.C. (Distinguished Service Cross)

Do not repeat titles; that is, a person with the degree of *M.D.* would not be addressed as *Dr.* and also have *M.D.* after his or her name. *Esquire* is the equivalent of a courtesy title; therefore, use one or the other—not both. *Esquire* is more commonly used in Great Britain than in the United States. American usage seems to be confined to certain professions—law, architecture, and consulate.

Titles such as *Honorable, Professor,* and *Reverend* may or may not be abbreviated. *The* usually precedes both *Honorable* and *Reverend.* If only the surname is used with the title, the name usually includes a courtesy title as well.

Miss is not an abbreviation and should not have a period after it.

Examples: St. Anthony

          Dr. William Harvey *or* William Harvey, M.D.

          Miss Margaret Tully

          Jeremy R. Hawkins, Jr., Esq.

          Professor (or Prof.) Mary Ellen Spears

          The Honorable (or Hon.) James K. Stone

          The Honorable Mr. Stone

3. Abbreviations in firm names if the firms show such abbreviations and *Ltd.* and *Inc.* following firm names. Use the ampersand (&) in place of *and* only if the firm uses it.

Examples: Valspar Corp.   Roberts & Co.

          William Kirk, Ltd.   Mason & McConnell, Inc.

4. These abbreviations are used to designate time:

A.D. (anno Domini—in the year of
     our Lord)   A.D. 1950

B.C. (before Christ)   33 B.C.

                                (Note that A.D. precedes and B.C. follows the year.)

a.m. (ante meridiem) *or* AM   10 a.m. *or* 10 AM

p.m. (post meridiem) *or* PM   11 p.m. *or* 11 PM

M.   (meridies)—this is the abbreviation for noon; however, it is less
confusing to write 12 noon or 12
midnight

EST (Eastern Standard Time), CST (Central Standard Time), MST
(Mountain Standard Time), and PST (Pacific Standard Time)
DST (Daylight Saving Time), EDST (Eastern Daylight Saving Time),
and so on

    5. Letters used in place of complete names of various well-
known organizations, either government or private. They are often
written without periods. Radio and television station letters are not
abbreviations; they are call letters and are written in all capitals
without periods.

Examples: CIO   Y.M.C.A.   KNBR (radio station)
              NATO   FBI

    6. Compound compass points (northeast, southwest) as part
of street addresses. The periods after the abbreviations are optional.

Examples: 345 S.E. 35 Street
              345 Seventh Avenue SE

    7. States and Canadian provinces as part of addresses. Use
the two-letter ZIP Code abbreviations for both states and provinces.
See the list in the Appendix (page 224) for the correct abbreviations.

Example: Ms. Virginia Davis
             1890 Steiner
             San Francisco, CA 94100

    8. Latin words and phrases used in general and business
writing. Use English equivalents if possible.

Examples: etc.   i.e.   et al.

    9. Number (No.) when followed by a number

Examples: Order No. 734478   Social Security No. 123-18-4567

    10. Metric system terms

    Below are some of the abbreviations for these terms. These ab-
breviations do not require periods or additions to form plurals, nor

should they be capitalized unless shown with capital letters. (See pages 225–226 for further information on the metric system.)

centimeter cm	meter m	metric ton t	Celsius C
decimeter dm	milligram mg	milliliter ml	
millimeter mm	kilogram kg	kiloliter kl	
kilometer km	gram g	liter l	

To square a unit, put a superior 2 above the unit.
To cube a unit, put a superior 3 above the unit.

Examples: m^2 m^3

Abbreviations to Avoid

Avoid these abbreviations:

1. Titles (other than those listed in Item 1, page 195) when used with surnames only. When a title precedes a complete name, usage varies.

Examples: Governor Smith   Professor Hatch
General Taylor   The Honorable Mr. Pine

2. Compass points—north, south, east, west. See Item 6, page 197, for abbreviation of compound compass points.

Examples: 234 East 54 Street   1000 Seventh Avenue North

3. Personal first names

Examples: *avoid:* Wm.   Robt.
use: William   Robert

4. Days, months, and seasons

Examples: *avoid:* The 18th of Jan. will be a Mon.
use: The 18th of January will be a Monday.

5. Streets, avenues, boulevards, courts, and other such designations unless there are space limitations or they are used in computer addresses

Examples: computer addresses:
367 Ocean Boulevard   367 OCEAN BLVD
4700 California Street   4700 CALIFORNIA ST

5. Foreign addresses, with the exception of U.S.S.R.

Examples: Dublin, Ireland   Liverpool, England
    but: Moscow, U.S.S.R.

7. Weights and measurements

Examples: *avoid:* hrs., ft., lbs.
          use: hours, feet, pounds

Special Points

Here are some special points to observe about abbreviations:

1. Plurals of abbreviations are formed in a number of ways:

a. In most instances *s* is added to the singular form.

Examples: No./Nos.   hr./hrs.   lb./lbs.

b. Some abbreviations are the same form for both singular and plural.

Examples: ft.—foot/feet   min.—minute/minutes

c. If the abbreviation consists of letters with internal punctuation, the plural is formed by adding either *s* or an apostrophe and *s*.

Examples: M.D.'s *or* M.D.s   f.o.b.'s *or* f.o.b.s

d. Some single-letter abbreviations double the letters for the plural forms.

Example: p.—page   pp.—pages

2. Many abbreviations that would not ordinarily be accepted in general business writing are used in tabulated material or in limited space. These include latitude and longitude; names of countries, including the United States; weights and measurements; and measurements of time. In fact, any standard dictionary abbreviation could be used under such circumstances.

9. Spelling

Learning to spell correctly is more a matter of alertness than anything else. There are rules—given below—but because of the many origins of English words, there are also many exceptions. These rules can guide you; however, if there is ever any doubt, you should consult the dictionary.

SPELLING RULES

1. Nouns and Verbs Ending in Y

A noun ending in *y* preceded by a consonant forms its plural by dropping the *y* and adding *ies;* a verb ending in *y* preceded by a consonant forms its present tense, third person singular by dropping the *y* and adding *ies.*

Examples: baby/babies   marry/marries
sky/skies   copy/copies

A noun ending in *y* preceded by a vowel forms its plural by adding *s;* a verb ending in *y* preceded by a vowel forms its present tense, third person singular by adding *s.*

Examples: attorney/attorneys   journey/journeys
turkey/turkeys   delay/delays

Exceptions: colloquy/colloquies   obloquy/obloquies
soliloquy/soliloquies

2. IE or EI

In words with *ie* or *ei*, when the sound is long *e*, use *i* before *e* except after *c*.

200

Examples: achieve, relieve, ceiling

Exceptions: either, weird, leisure, neither, seize

3. Final Silent E

A word ending in *silent e* generally drops the e before a suffix beginning with a vowel, but it keeps the e before a suffix beginning with a consonant.

Examples: hope/hoping/hopeful   guide/guidance/guided

Exceptions:
After c or g, if the suffix begins with a or o, the e is kept.

Examples: change/changeable   notice/noticeable

The e is kept when dropping it would cause confusion with another word.

Examples: dye/dyeing   singe/singeing

If the word ends in *oe*, the e is retained.

Examples: shoe/shoeing   hoe/hoeing

4. Doubling the Final Consonant

In words of one syllable and words accented on the last syllable—in each case ending in a single consonant preceded by a single vowel—*double the final consonant* before a suffix beginning with a vowel.

Examples: drop/dropped   control/controlled
          confer/conferred

Exception:
Do not double the final consonant if the word ends in x.

Example: taxing

5. Final L

One-syllable words ending in *l* are usually spelled with two *l's*; words of more than one syllable ending in *l* are usually spelled with one *l*.

Examples: pill/kill/still
until/propel/control

6. Sede, Ceed, and Cede

Only one word ends in *sede: supersede.* Three words end in *ceed: exceed, proceed, succeed.* All other words end in *cede: accede, antecede, concede, cede, intercede, precede, recede, se- cede.*

WARNING:

The derivatives of these words may not be spelled the same as the root words.

Examples: success, procession, procedure, excess

WORDS FREQUENTLY MISSPELLED

The marks within these words show where the words may be di- vided in typed material. Because word division does not always fol- low syllabication (see pages 214–215), these words are not marked at all syllables. For example, *absence* has two syllables (ab-sence), but it should not be divided.

absence	advan.ta.geous	ath.lete
accep.tance	already	autumn
accom.mo.date	ama.teur	
accom.pa.ni.ment	among	
accom.pany	analy.sis	begin.ning
accu.mu.late	apol.ogy	believe
achieve.ment	appar.ent	bene.fi.cial
acknowl.edg.ment	appear.ance	budget
acquaint	argu.ment	bul.le.tin
acquain.tance	arrange.ment	busi.ness

com.ing
com.para.tive
com.pe.ti.tion
con.fi.dent
con.trol
con.trolled
con.trolling
con.ven.ience
con.ven.ient
cour.te.ous
criti.cism
criti.cize

def.inite
describe
descrip.tion
develop
diction.ary
dif.fer.ence
dis.ap.point
dis.as.trous

eighth
eli.gi.ble
elimi.nate
embar.rass
endeavor
equip
equip.ment
equipped
espe.cially
excel.lent
exer.cise
exis.tence
expense
experi.ence
explain
expla.na.tion
extrava.gance

fami.liar
February
fed.eral
finally
for.eign

forty
friend

gov.ern.ment
gov.er.nor
gram.mar
grate.ful
guar.an.tee
guard
guid.ance

hand.ker.chief
har.ass
height
hop.ing

igno.rance
imme.di.ate
inde.pend.ence
indis.pen.sa.ble
influ.ence
intel.li.gence
inter.est
inter.fere
inter.rupt
irre.sis.ti.ble

judg.ment

knowl.edge

lab.o.ra.tory
lei.sure
library
license
lik.able

main.te.nance
man.age.ment
mathe.mat.ics
medi.cine
mis.cel.la.ne.ous
mis.chie.vous
moral
morale

nec.es.sary
nickel
ninety
ninth
notice.able

occa.sion
occa.sion.ally
occur
occurred
occur.rence
omis.sion
omit
omit.ted
oper.ate
oppor.tu.nity
origin

paid
pam.phlet
par.al.lel
per.ma.nence
per.ma.nent
per.mis.si.ble
per.suade
pleas.ant
prac.ti.cal
pre.fer
pre.ferred
privi.lege
proba.bly
psy.chol.ogy
pur.sue

qual.ity
quan.tity
ques.tion.naire

real.ize
receipt
receive
rec.og.nize
rec.om.mend
refer
ref.er.ence

refer.ring

repe.ti.tion

res.tau.rant

safety

sched.ule

sec.re.tary

seize

sepa.rate

simi.lar

strictly

sub.tle

sur.prise

tem.po.rary

thor.ough

truly

undoubt.edly

unnec.es.sary

until

unu.sual

use.ful

using

usu.ally

vari.ous

vol.ume

vol.un.tary

weather

Wednes.day

wel.fare

whether

wholly

write

writ.ing

writ.ten

yield

10. Word Usage

ONE-WORD, TWO-WORD, AND HYPHENATED FORMS

Although today's trend is toward use of the one-word form, whether to write any given word as one or two words or to hyphenate presents so many inconsistencies that there is only one reliable solution: Consult a dictionary. Be sure that your dictionary is up-to-date because usage is constantly changing. A word that cannot be found in the dictionary is probably written as two words. (Also review pages 111–112 on compound nouns and page 156 on compound adjectives.) *Webster's Third New International Dictionary* is the authority for the information given here.

1. Prefixes

As a general rule, write prefixes in combination with other syllables as one word. Such prefixes include:

afternoon
antipolitical[1]
anything (*but:* any more)
bipartisan
cooperate (*but:* co-worker,
                    co-venture)
everyone (*but:* every time)
extraordinary
interstate
into
nonessential

nowhere (*but:* no one)
outside
overcoat
postmaster (*but:* post office)
prehistoric
rename
semicolon[1]
someone
subconscious
today
undertake
withdraw

---

[1] If these prefixes are followed by a root beginning with *i*, hyphenate.
   Examples: anti-intellectual   semi-independent

205

1. Prefixes before proper nouns or adjectives are hyphenated.

Examples: un-American   semi-Gothic   pre-Incan

2. Words with the prefix *re* are sometimes hyphenated to avoid confusion with another word that has the same spelling but a different meaning.

Examples: re-act (to act again) *but* react (to respond)
re-ally (to ally again) *but* really (in actual fact)
re-collect (to collect again) *but* recollect (to remember)

3. *Self* as a prefix is usually hyphenated; *self* as a suffix is joined to the root without hyphens.

Examples: self-control   self-esteem   herself

Exceptions: selfsame   selfish (*and its derivatives*)

2. One- and Two-Word Forms

The following are written as one word:

already	cannot	meantime	percent	weekday
airmail	furthermore	meanwhile	policyholder	weekend
businesslike	goodwill	paycheck	proofread	worthwhile
businessman	letterhead	payday	trademark	yearbook

The following are written as two words:

all right   daylight saving   down payment   inasmuch as   a lot

3. Hyphenated Numbers

Compound numbers (for example, *forty-six*) and fractions (for example, *one third*) cause confusion in hyphenation. Follow this rule: Hyphenate compound numbers from twenty-one to ninety-nine. Hyphenate a fraction when it is used as an adjective before its modifier, but not when it is used as a noun.

Examples: One half of the secretaries left before five o'clock. *noun*
A one-half inch margin is not wide enough. *adjective*

EXPRESSIONS TO AVOID

Listed below are expressions that are either misused or overused in business writing and should therefore be avoided. Some expressions were borrowed from the legal profession and do not belong in business writing; others use several words when one would be sufficient. Some are used incorrectly in place of other words, and others are merely trite or overused. This list is not complete, but it does include some of the more obvious expressions to be avoided. (Check the dictionary for any others about which you may have doubts.)

Examples

above
above listed
above mentioned
the above

avoid: The above-mentioned items are being sent by registered mail.
Please send the above items.
use: These items are being sent by registered mail.
Please send these items.

aforementioned
aforesaid

avoid: The aforementioned report cannot be found in our files.
use: The report mentioned earlier cannot be found in our files.

along these lines
line

avoid: He worked in this line for many years.
use: He has done personnel work for many years.

and/or

avoid: The client and/or his attorney may reply to the charge.
use: Either the client or his attorney may reply to the charge.

appreciate

avoid: We should appreciate your taking care of this matter immediately.
use: We should like to have you take care of this matter immediately.

as per

avoid: We are shipping your order by airmail as per your instructions.
use: We are shipping your order by airmail as you instructed.

as to whether   *avoid:* I am doubtful as to whether he can handle the assignment.

use: I doubt that he can handle the assignment.

attached herewith   *avoid:* Attached herewith is my check for $50.

use: Attached is my check for $50.

be good enough   *avoid:* Would you be good enough to take care of this matter immediately.

use: Would you please take care of this matter immediately.

close proximity   *avoid:* The towns are in close proximity to each other.

use: The towns are close to each other.

earliest convenience   *avoid:* Please return the application at your earliest convenience.

use: Please return the application promptly (soon, immediately).

enclosed herewith   *avoid:* Enclosed herewith is our check for $50.

use: Enclosed is our check for $50.

feel free to   *avoid:* If you would like our catalog, please feel free to ask for one.

use: If you would like our catalog, we will send it to you on request.

he is a man who   *avoid:* He is a man who has held many important positions.

use: He has held many important positions.

if and when   *avoid:* Please return the application if and when you have completed it.

use: Please return the application when you have completed it.

in the course of   *avoid:* We discussed the subject in the course of our meeting.

use: We discussed the subject <u>during</u> our meeting.

in the event that   *avoid:* We will have to take further action <u>in the event that</u> we do not hear from you.

use: We will have to take further action <u>if</u> we do not hear from you.

in the last analysis   *This is a meaningless expression and should not be used.*

meet with your approval   *avoid:* We hope that this <u>meets with your approval</u>.

use: We hope that you <u>approve</u> of our action.

oftentimes   *avoid:* <u>Oftentimes</u> we are not able to find addresses for old customers.

use: <u>Often</u> we are not able to find addresses for old customers.

party   *avoid:* The <u>party</u> who purchased the car is unknown.

use: The <u>person</u> who purchased the car is unknown.

reason is because   *avoid:* The <u>reason</u> for his dismissal <u>is because</u> he was often late.

use: The <u>reason</u> for his dismissal <u>is that</u> he was often late.

subsequent to   *avoid:* <u>Subsequent to</u> his dismissal, he moved to Los Angeles.

use: <u>After</u> his dismissal, he moved to Los Angeles.

take the liberty of   *This is a trite expression and should not be used.*

thanking you in advance, I remain   *This expression is out-of-date and should not be used.*

this is to inform you that   *This is a meaningless expression since obviously the information is for the reader.*

WORDS OFTEN CONFUSED

Homonyms

Homonyms (also called *homophones*) are words that are pronounced alike but are spelled differently and that have different meanings. These homonyms are frequently confused in business writing.

ad (noun) *commonly used form of* advertisement
add (verb) to join

allowed (verb) permitted
aloud (adv.) said or spoken audibly

ascent (noun) the act of going upward
assent (noun or verb) consent

bare (adj.) uncovered
bear (verb) to carry

billed (verb) charged
build (verb) to construct

capital (adj.) major, main; (noun) funds; a city or town that is the seat of government in a state or nation
capitol (noun) the building in which legislators meet

carat (noun) unit of weight
caret (noun) mark in writing or printing indicating a place where something is inserted
carrot (noun) vegetable

cite (verb) to summon before a court, quote as authority
sight (noun) something that is seen; (verb) to inspect
site (noun) a place or position

complement (noun) something that fills up; (verb) to fill up or complete
compliment (noun) a formal expression of admiration; (verb) to express respect or admiration

forth (adv.) onward
fourth (adj.) number four in countable series

guarantee (verb) to be responsible for; (noun) a pledge to be responsible
guaranty (noun) a pledge to be responsible

passed (verb) moved on
past (adj.) at a former time, gone by; (noun) former time

peace (noun) harmony
piece (noun) a part of a whole

principal (adj.) most important; (noun) chief, head
principle (noun) general or fundamental truth

role (noun) part played by performer; function performed by someone or something
roll (noun) list of names; (verb) to move by turning over and over

stationary   (adj.) fixed
stationery   (noun) material for writing or typing

their   (pron.) *3d person plural possessive*
there   (adv.) in or at that place
they're   (pron. and verb) *contraction of* they are

threw   (verb) hurled, tossed
through   (prep.) along or across an object, substance, or space

to   (prep.) indicating direction toward
too   (adv.) in addition
two   (noun) two units

vary   (verb) to make different; to differ
very   (adv.) extremely; (adj.) actual, precise

wait   (verb) to remain inactive
weight   (noun) quantity of heaviness

ware   (noun) manufactured articles or farm produce, goods, commodities
wear   (noun) use; (verb) to bear or have upon the person

your   (pron.) *2d person possessive*
you're   (pron. and verb) *contraction of* you are

Words that Sound Alike

Because the words listed below have similar sounds, they too are often confused.

accede   (verb) to give consent
exceed   (verb) to surpass

accept   (verb) to take or receive
except   (prep.) with the exclusion of

access   (noun) entrance
excess   (noun) surplus

adapt   (verb) to make suitable
adept   (adj.) highly skilled
adopt   (verb) to take as one's own

addition   (noun) an increase
edition   (noun) form in which a written work is published

advice   (noun) an opinion or judgment
advise   (verb) to give counsel or opinion

affect   (verb) to produce an influence upon
effect   (noun) a result or outcome; (verb) to produce as a result, to accomplish

biannual   (adj.) twice a year
biennial   (adj.) every two years

choose   (verb) *present tense of* choose, *to select*
chose   (verb) *past tense of* choose, *to select*

coma (noun) unconsciousness

comma (noun) *mark of punctuation*

conscience (noun) the sense of right or wrong

conscious (adj.) aware

consul (noun) an official appointed to a foreign country

council (noun) an administrative body

counsel (verb) to recommend a course or policy; (noun) consultation; a lawyer engaged to give legal advice

continual (adj.) repeated at intervals (*used of events*)

continuous (adj.) uninterrupted (*used of time and space*)

eminent (adj.) outstanding

imminent (adj.) near at hand

eraser (noun) object used for removing ink or pencil marks

erasure (noun) a place where an ink or pencil mark has been removed

formally (adv.) in prescribed or customary form

former (adj.) first in a series of two

formerly (adv.) beforehand, previously

last (adj.) at the end, final

latest (adj.) most recent

latter (adj.) second in a series of two

later (adv.) after a time

loose (adj.) not fastened

lose (verb) to fail to keep

loss (noun) the act of losing or failing to keep, the state of being lost

reality (noun) the actual state of things

realty (noun) real estate

respectfully (adv.) in a courteous manner

respectively (adv.) singly, in the order named

than (conj.) *introduces statements of comparison or preference*

then (adv.) at that time, in the future or past

weather (noun) state of the atmosphere; (verb) to expose to the open air

whether (conj.) *introduces an indirect question involving alternatives*

One- and Two-Word Pairs

These pairs of words have different meanings when written as one word or as two words.

Examples

all most   all very much

We are *all most* satisfied with the typewriter.

almost   (adv.) nearly

We are *almost* finished with the typing.

all ready   all prepared

The letters are *all ready* to be mailed.

already   (adv.) previously

The letters had *already* been mailed when the error was discovered.

all together   all in one place

The letters were *all together* in the file.

altogether   (adv.) entirely

I am not *altogether* satisfied with my new typewriter.

all ways   by all means

He has tried *all ways* to solve the difficulty.

always   (adv.) at all times

The letters are *always* ready for mailing by five o'clock.

any one   any person of a group

Any one of the secretaries could have taken the folder.

anyone[1]   (pron.) any person

Anyone could have taken the folder.

a while   (noun plus article) a period of time; *a while* is usually part of a prepositional phrase (*in a while, for a while*)

Think about it for *a while* before you make a decision.

awhile   (adv.) for some time

Rest *awhile* before you do the typing.

may be   a *verb phrase*

Mr. Ross *may be* out of town on Friday.

maybe   (adv.) perhaps

Maybe we should call Mr. Ross about the order.

some time   (adj. plus noun) part of a specified period

At *some time* in the future we shall need that information.

sometime   (adv.) at some unspecified or indefinite time

Sometime yesterday the office was burglarized.

some times   specified periods

Some times in history are harder than others.

sometimes   (adv.) now and then

Sometimes letters are not answered promptly.

---

[1] Most of the indefinite pronouns can be written as one or two words. When written as one word, they are indefinite pronouns; when written as two, they represent part of a group—for example, *nobody / no body; someone / some one; everyone / every one.* The two-word form is usually followed by *of.*

WORD DIVISION

Basic Rule

When possible, avoid dividing words. When word division is necessary, divide at the syllable. Therefore, one-syllable words cannot be divided. It is better to have a short line on a page than a long one.

Additional Rules

1. Carry over at least three letters to the second line.

Example: Occasionally *could not be divided* occasional-ly.

2. Do not divide the last word on a page or the last word of the last full line of a paragraph. Do not divide words on more than two consecutive lines.

3. Do not divide after a one-letter or two-letter syllable that begins a word.

Examples: ahead *not* a-head   begin *not* be-gin

4. It is better not to divide between two proper nouns; however, there are times when this cannot be avoided.

Example: William Cunningham; San Francisco, California (*not* William/Cunningham; San Francisco,/California)

5. Divide hyphenated words only at the hyphen.

Example: self-/control   (*not* self-con-trol)

6. Do not divide before a single-vowel syllable.

Example: Accompani-ment   (*not* accompan-iment)

Exceptions:
a. If there are two consecutive single vowels, divide between the vowels.

Example: abbrevi-ation

b. Divide before the single-vowel syllable when it is the first syllable of a root word.

Example: dis-unite

c. If the single-vowel syllable is part of the suffixes *able, ible, icle,* or *ity,* divide before the vowel.

Example: secur-ity

7. Generally, divide between double letters. However, if the root word would be destroyed by dividing between the double letters, divide after the double letters.

Examples: fol-low, control-ling
     but: bill-ing

8. Abbreviations, figures, and words containing apostrophes cannot be divided.

Examples: doesn't $25,000   N.Y.C.

Appendix

CORRECT FORMS OF ADDRESS

GOVERNMENT OFFICIALS

OFFICIAL OR DIGNITARY	ENVELOPE AND INSIDE ADDRESS	SALUTATION[1]	COMPLIMENTARY CLOSE[1]
President of the United States	The President The White House Washington, DC 20500	Mr. President Dear Mr. President My dear Mr. President	Very respectfully yours Respectfully yours Respectfully
Vice President of the United States	The Vice President or The Honorable (full name) Vice President of the United States The United States Senate Washington, DC 20510	Mr. Vice President Dear Mr. Vice President My dear Mr. Vice President	Respectfully Very truly yours Sincerely yours
Chief Justice	The Chief Justice of the United States or The Chief Justice The Supreme Court Washington, DC 20543	Sir Dear Mr. Chief Justice My dear Mr. Chief Justice	Respectfully Very truly yours Sincerely yours
Associate Justice	Mr. or Madam Justice (full name) The Supreme Court Washington, DC 20543	Sir or Mr. or Madam Justice Dear Mr. or Madam Justice My dear Mr. or Madam Justice Dear Mr. or Madam Justice (surname)	Very truly yours Sincerely yours
Cabinet member	The Honorable the Secretary of (name of department) Washington, DC ZIP Code	Sir or Madam My dear Sir or Madam	Very truly yours

[1] Listed in order of decreasing formality.

OFFICIAL OR DIGNITARY	ENVELOPE AND INSIDE ADDRESS	SALUTATION[1]	COMPLIMENTARY CLOSE[1]
	or The Honorable (*full name*) Secretary of (*name of department*) Washington, DC ZIP Code	Dear Sir or Madam My dear Mr. or Madam Secretary Dear Mr. or Madam Secretary	Sincerely yours
Senator, United States	The Honorable (*full name*) The United States Senate Washington, DC 20510	Sir or Madam Dear Sir or Madam Dear Senator (*surname*)	Very truly yours Sincerely yours
Representative, United States	The Honorable (*full name*) House of Representatives Washington, DC 20515	Dear Sir or Madam My dear Mr., Ms., Mrs., or Miss (*surname*) Dear Mr., Ms., Mrs., or Miss (*surname*)	Very truly yours Sincerely yours
Governor of a state	*In Massachusetts and New Hampshire, and by courtesy in some other states:* His or Her Excellency, The Governor of (*name of state*) City, State ZIP Code *In other states:* The Honorable the Governor of (*name of state*) or The Honorable (*full name*), Governor of (*name of state*) City, State ZIP Code	Sir or Madam My dear Sir or Madam Dear Sir or Madam My dear Governor (*surname*) Dear Governor (*surname*) Dear Mr., Ms., Mrs., Miss (*surname*)	Respectfully yours Very truly yours Sincerely yours
State Senator	The Honorable (*full name*) The State Senate City, State ZIP Code	Sir or Madam My dear Sir or Madam Dear Sir or Madam My dear Mr. or Madam Senator My dear Senator (*surname*) Dear Senator (*surname*)	Very truly yours Sincerely yours

Member of the State Assembly	The Honorable (full name), Member of the Assembly House of Representatives or The State Assembly The State Capitol City, State ZIP Code	Sir or Madam Dear Sir or Madam My dear Mr., Ms., Mrs., Miss (surname)	Very truly yours Sincerely yours
Mayor	The Honorable (full name), Mayor of (name of city) or The Mayor of the City of (name) City Hall City, State ZIP Code	Sir or Madam Dear Sir or Madam Dear Mr. or Madam Mayor My dear Mr. or Madam Mayor Dear Mayor (surname)	Respectfully yours Very truly yours Sincerely yours

RELIGIOUS DIGNITARIES

Pope	His Holiness Pope (full name) Vatican City Rome, Italy	Most Holy Father Your Holiness	Respectfully yours
Cardinal	His Eminence (given name) Cardinal (surname) Archbishop of (name of archdiocese) City, State ZIP Code or His Eminence Cardinal (surname) Archbishop of (name of archdiocese) City, State ZIP Code	Your Eminence My dear Cardinal (surname) Dear Cardinal (surname)	Respectfully yours Sincerely yours
Bishop, Archbishop (Catholic)	The Most Reverend (full name) Bishop (or Archbishop) of (name of diocese) City, State ZIP Code	Your Excellency	Respectfully yours

1 Listed in order of decreasing formality.

OFFICIAL OR DIGNITARY	ENVELOPE AND INSIDE ADDRESS	SALUTATION[1]	COMPLIMENTARY CLOSE[1]
Bishop (Protestant Episcopal)	The Right Reverend (full name) Bishop of (name of diocese) City, State ZIP Code	Right Reverend Sir My dear Bishop (surname) Dear Bishop (surname)	Respectfully yours Sincerely yours
Bishop (Methodist)	The Reverend (full name) City, State ZIP Code	Reverend Sir Dear Sir My dear Bishop (surname) Dear Bishop (surname)	Respectfully yours Sincerely yours
Minister (Protestant)	The Reverend (full name) or The Rev. Dr. (full name) or The Reverend (full name), D. D.[2] Address	Dear Sir or Madam Reverend Sir or Madam My dear Mr., Dr., Ms., Mrs., or Miss (surname) Dear Mr., Dr., Ms., Mrs., or Miss (surname)	Sincerely yours
Rabbi	Rabbi[3] (full name) Address	My dear Rabbi (surname) Dear Rabbi (surname)	Respectfully yours Sincerely yours
Monsignor	The Right Reverend Monsignor (full name) Address	Right Reverend Monsignor (surname) Dear Monsignor (surname)	Respectfully yours
Priest (Catholic)	The Reverend (full name, followed by initials of religious order if appropriate) Address	Reverend Father Dear Father (religious name or surname)	Respectfully yours Sincerely yours

Priest (Episcopal)	The Reverend (full name) Address	Dear Mr., Dr., Mrs., Ms., or Miss (surname) Dear Father (surname) (if masculine)	Respectfully yours Sincerely yours
Sister	Sister (religious name or full name, followed by initials of religious order) Address	Dear Sister Dear Sister (religious name or given name)	Respectfully yours Sincerely yours

MILITARY OFFICERS

Naval officer	Admiral[4] (full name), U.S.N. Address	Dear Admiral[4] (surname)	Very truly yours Sincerely yours
Naval officer below rank of Commander	Full title or rank (full name), U.S.N. Address	Dear Mr. (surname) or (if woman): Dear Ensign (or other title) (surname)	Very truly yours Sincerely yours
Army officer	Colonel[4] (full name), U.S.A. (or U.S.A.F.)	Dear Colonel[4] (surname)	Very truly yours Sincerely yours

[1] Listed in order of decreasing formality.
[2] If he or she holds doctor's degree.
[3] If he or she holds doctor's degree, Dr. may be substituted for Rabbi.
[4] Use appropriate name of rank.

PROOFREADERS' MARKS

INSTRUCTION	MARK IN MARGIN	MARK IN TYPE	CORRECTED TO READ
Align	‖	‖ Correct all errors. ‖ Correct all errors.	Correct all errors. Correct all errors.
Capitalize	cap	correct all errors.	Correct all errors.
Close up space	⌒	Cor rect all errors.	Correct all errors.
Delete	ℓ	Correct all errors.	Correct errors.
Delete and close up space	ℓ	Correct all errors.	Correct all errors.
Insert apostrophe	⌄	Correct Lees errors.	Correct Lee's errors.
Insert colon	⊙	Correct these errors	Correct these errors:
Insert comma	⌃	He made errors errors errors.	He made errors, errors, errors.
Insert em dash	ⅰ/M ⅰ/M	Find and correct all errors.	Find—and correct—all errors.
Insert hyphen	=	error free copy	error-free copy
Insert parentheses	(/)	Correct errors page 1	Correct errors (page 1).
Insert period	⊙	Correct all errors	Correct all errors.
Insert quotation marks	⟨⟨/⟩⟩	Correct the error hte.	Correct the error "hte."
Insert semicolon	⌃;	Find all errors correct all errors.	Find all errors; correct all errors.
Insert space	#	Correct all errors.	Correct all errors.
Insert indicated material	all	Correct errors.	Correct all errors.
Let it stand	stet	Correct all errors.	Correct all errors.
Make lower case	lc	Correct All errors.	Correct all errors.
Move left	[	[Correct all errors.	Correct all errors.
Move right	]	Correct all errors.	Correct all errors.
Run in (no new paragraph)	run in	Find all errors. Correct all errors.	Find all errors. Correct all errors.
Spell out	sp	3 errors	three errors
Start paragraph	¶	Find errors; correct errors.	Find errors; correct errors.
Transpose	tr	Correct errors all	Correct all errors.

FREQUENTLY USED ABBREVIATIONS

This is a list of some commonly used abbreviations. Many of them are found in bibliographies and footnotes.

abbr.	abbreviation	ibid.	ibidem (in the same place)
A.D.	anno Domini	i.e.	id est (that is)
a.k.a.	also known as	id.	idem (the same)
a.m.	ante meridiem (before noon)	Inc.	Incorporated
bcc	blind carbon copy	l.c.	lower case (no capitals)
B.C.	before Christ	loc. cit.	loco citato (in the place cited)
cc	carbon copy	Ltd.	Limited
ch.	chapter	m.	meridies (noon)
c.o.d.	cash on delivery	ms., mss.	manuscript, manuscripts
col.	column	MDT	Mountain Daylight Time
CDT	Central Daylight Time	MST	Mountain Standard Time
CST	Central Standard Time	OCR	Optical Character Reader
EDT	Eastern Daylight Time	op. cit.	opere citato (in the work cited)
EST	Eastern Standard Time	p., pp.	page, pages
e.g.	exemplia gratia (for example)	par.	paragraph
et al.	et alii (and others)	p.m.	post meridiem (afternoon)
et seq.	et sequens (and the following)	PDT	Pacific Daylight Time
etc.	et cetera (and so forth)	PST	Pacific Standard Time
f., ff.	and following page (pages)	viz.	videlicet (namely)
fig.	figure	vol.	volume
f.o.b.	free on board	ZIP Code	Zone Improvement Plan Code

UNITED STATES POSTAL ABBREVIATIONS

Alabama	AL	Kentucky	KY	Ohio	OH
Alaska	AK	Louisiana	LA	Oklahoma	OK
Arizona	AZ	Maine	ME	Oregon	OR
Arkansas	AR	Maryland	MD	Pennsylvania	PA
California	CA	Massachusetts	MA	Puerto Rico	PR
Colorado	CO	Michigan	MI	Rhode Island	RI
Connecticut	CT	Minnesota	MN	South Carolina	SC
Delaware	DE	Mississippi	MS	South Dakota	SD
District of		Missouri	MO	Tennessee	TN
Columbia	DC	Montana	MT	Texas	TX
Florida	FL	Nebraska	NE	Utah	UT
Georgia	GA	Nevada	NV	Vermont	VT
Hawaii	HI	New Hampshire	NH	Virginia	VA
Idaho	ID	New Jersey	NJ	Washington	WA
Illinois	IL	New Mexico	NM	West Virginia	WV
Indiana	IN	New York	NY	Wisconsin	WI
Iowa	IA	North Carolina	NC	Wyoming	WY
Kansas	KS	North Dakota	ND		

CANADIAN POSTAL ABBREVIATIONS

Alberta	AB	Nova Scotia	NS
British Columbia	BC	Ontario	ON
Labrador	LB	Prince Edward Island	PE
Manitoba	MB	Quebec	PQ
New Brunswick	NB	Saskatchewan	SK
Newfoundland	NF	Yukon Territory	YT
Northwest Territories	NT		

METRIC SYSTEM

In order to standardize its weights and measures with the rest of the world, the United States is gradually moving to the metric system. The chart on the next page is intended to give general metric information; for additional information, consult a reference source such as *The American Heritage Dictionary* or one of the encyclopedias.

Eventually all typewriters will have metric scales rather than scales marked in inches. The following information will be helpful in using a typewriter with a metric scale:

1 inch = 2.5 centimeters

   10 pica spaces = 2.5 centimeters   XXXXXXXXXX (10 pica) = 2.5 cm

   12 elite spaces = 2.5 centimeters   XXXXXXXXXXXX (12 elite) = 2.5 cm

6 vertical line spaces = 2.5 centimeters

8½ × 11-inch paper = 21.5 × 28 centimeters

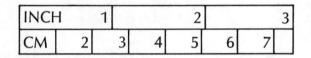

INCH		1			2		3
CM	2	3	4	5	6	7	

Equivalents of present system:

1 inch = 2.54 centimeters

1 foot = 0.3048 meter, 30.480 centimeters

1 yard = 0.9144 meter

1 mile (5280 feet) = 1.609 kilometers

1 ounce avoirdupois = 28.35 grams

1 pound = 453.6 grams, 0.453 kilogram

1 ton (U.S. 2000 pounds) = 907.2 kilograms, 0.907 metric ton

1 fluid ounce = 30 milliliters

1 liquid quart (U.S.) = 0.946 liter

1 liquid gallon (U.S.) = 3.785 liters

1 square inch = 6.452 square centimeters

1 square foot = 929 square centimeters

1 square yard = 2.5899 square kilometers

1 acre (43,560 square feet) = 0.405 hectare, 4047 square meters

METRIC MEASURES AND EQUIVALENTS

PRINCIPAL UNITS:	EQUIVALENT IN PRESENT SYSTEM:

LENGTH—Meter (m)[1]

10 millimeters (mm)	= 1 centimeter (cm)	1 millimeter = 0.03937 inch
100 millimeters		
10 centimeters	= 1 decimeter (dm)	1 centimeter = 0.3937 inch
10 decimeters		1 decimeter = 3.937 inches
100 centimeters	= 1 meter (m)	1 meter = 39.37 inches (1.0936 yards)
10 meters	= 1 decameter (Dm)	1 decameter = 393.7 inches (10.936 yards)
10 decameters	= 1 hectometer (Hm)	
10 hectometers		
1000 meters	= 1 kilometer (km)	1 kilometer = 0.6214 mile

AREA (Surface)—Square Meter (m²)

100 square millimeters (mm²) = 1 square
   centimeter (cm²)
10,000 square centimeters = 1 square meter (m²)
100 square meters = 1 are (a)
10,000 square meters = 1 hectare (ha)

1 square millimeter = 0.00155 square inch
1 square centimeter = 0.155 square inch
1 square meter = 10.764 square feet
1 are = 1076 square feet
1 hectare = 107.650 square feet

WEIGHT (Mass)—Metric Ton (t)

1000 milligrams (mg) = 1 gram (g)
1000 grams = 1 kilogram (kg)
1000 kilograms = 1 metric ton (t)

1 gram = 0.3527 ounce avoirdupois[2]
1 kilogram = 2.2048 pounds avoirdupois
1 metric ton = 2204.6 pounds

CAPACITY (Small volume)—Liter

1000 milliliters (ml) = 1 liter
1000 liters = 1 kiloliter (kl)

1 liter = 1.0567 U.S. quarts (0.2642 U.S. gallon)

VOLUME (Large volume)—Cubic Meter (m³)

1000 cubic millimeters (mm³) = 1 cubic
   centimeter (cm³)
1000 cubic centimeters = 1 cubic decimeter (dm³)
1,000,000 cubic centimeters = 1 cubic meter (m³)

TEMPERATURE
Fahrenheit = $\frac{9}{5}$ Celsius temperature +32
Celsius (Centigrade) = (Fahrenheit − 32) $\frac{5}{9}$

[1] Official symbols for metric measures given in parentheses.
  These symbols do not require periods or the addition of an -s for plural forms.
[2] Avoirdupois—16 ounces per pound

  Meanings of terms: deci, deca (deka)—tens   centi, hecto—hundreds   kilo, milli—thousands

REFERENCE SOURCES

No office worker is expected to be able to answer all questions likely to arise in an office, but he or she should be able to *find* the answers to such questions—either in the reference books in the office or in the library.

The list below, although not comprehensive, does suggest some useful sources of information.

Dictionaries and Word Sources

1. *The American Heritage Dictionary of the English Language.* New College Ed. Boston: Houghton Mifflin, 1980.
2. Leslie, Louis A. *20,000 Words.* 7th Ed. New York: McGraw-Hill, 1977. (Pocket-sized book for spelling and word division.)
3. *Roget's International Thesaurus.* 4th Ed. New York: Thomas Y. Crowell, 1977.
4. *Webster's New Collegiate Dictionary.* 8th Ed. Springfield, MA: G. and C. Merriam, 1980. (Desk-sized.)
5. *Webster's Collegiate Thesaurus.* Springfield, MA: G. And C. Merriam, 1976.
6. *Webster's Third New International Dictionary of the English Language* (Unabridged). Springfield, MA: G. and C. Merriam, 1976.
7. *The Word Book.* Boston: Houghton Mifflin, 1976.

Grammar and Style Manuals

1. Ebbitt, Wilma R., and David R. Ebbitt. *Writer's Guide and Index to English.* 7th Ed. Chicago: Scott, Foresman, 1981.
2. Fowler, H. W. *A Dictionary of Modern English Usage.* 2d Ed. Revised by Sir Ernest Gowers. London: Oxford University Press, 1965.
3. Himstreet, William C., and Wayne M. Baty. *Business Communications.* 6th Ed. Boston: Kent Publishing, 1981.
4. Hodges, John C., and Mary E. Whitten. Harbrace College Handbook. 9th Ed. New York: Harcourt Brace Jovanovich, 1982.
5. *The Chicago Manual of Style.* 13th Ed. Chicago: University of Chicago Press, 1982.
6. Skillin, Marjorie E., and Robert M. Gay. *Words into Type.* 3d Ed. Englewood Cliffs, NJ: Prentice-Hall, 1974.
7. *United States Government Printing Office Style Manual.*[1] Rev. Ed. Washington, D.C.: Superintendent of Documents, 1979.
8. Whalen, Doris H. *Handbook for Business Writers.* New York: Harcourt Brace Jovanovich, 1978.

---

[1] In addition to this book, the Superintendent of Documents of the United States Government Printing Office has available a variety of materials—from leaflets to hard-bound books—in a truly amazing range of subjects and in prices from a few cents to several dollars. It is possible to have your name added to the mailing list to receive listings of the publications by sending a postal card with your name and address to: Superintendent of Documents, United States Government Printing Office, Washington, D.C. 20402. Libraries have indexes of the publications available. Research in these indexes will often disclose valuable sources of information.

General Sources

1. Bartlett, John. *Familiar Quotations*. 15th Ed. Boston: Little, Brown, 1980.
2. *Encyclopaedia Britannica*, 14th Ed. Chicago: Encyclopaedia Britannica, 1980.
3. *The New Columbia Encyclopedia*. 4th Ed. New York: Columbia University Press, 1975. (One Volume.)
4. McWhirter, Norris and Ross. *Guinness Book of World Records*. New York: Sterling Publishing Co. (Published annually.)
5. *The New York Times Index*. New York: The New York Times. (Published semimonthly.)
6. Post, Elizabeth. *Emily Post's Etiquette*. 12th Ed. New York: Funk & Wagnalls, 1975.
7. *Reader's Guide to Periodical Literature*. New York: H. W. Wilson. (Published semimonthly September to June; monthly July and August.)
8. *Statistical Abstract of the United States*. Washington, D.C.: United States Bureau of the Census. (Published annually.)
9. Wallechinsky, David, and Irving Wallace. *The People's Almanac #3*. Garden City, NY: Doubleday, 1980.
10. *Who's Who*. London: A. & C. Black. (Published annually.)
11. *Who's Who in America*. Chicago: Marquis. (Published biennially.)
12. *World Almanac and Book of Facts* (Luman H. Long, ed.). New York: Newspaper Enterprise Association. (Published annually.)

Directories

1. Business and professional directories
2. City directories (primarily a listing of names and addresses of residents of a city or area. Usually published annually by commercial firms but no longer published in certain large cities [New York and Los Angeles, for example].)
3. *Official Congressional Directory*. Washington, D.C.: United States Government Printing Office. (Published annually.)
4. Telephone directories (both local and out of town)

Postal, Shipping, Travel, and Geographical Sources

1. *Bullinger's Postal and Shippers Guide for the United States and Canada*. New York: Bullinger's Monitor Guide. (Published annually, with a supplement six months after publication.)
2. *National Zip Code Directory*. Washington, D.C.: United States Government Printing Office, 1979.
3. *The New International Atlas*. Chicago: Rand McNally, 1980.
4. *Official Hotel Red Book*. New York: American Hotel Association Directory Corp. (Published annually.)
5. *Official Airline Guide*. Oak Brook, IL: Donnelley Corp. (Published monthly.)

6. *The Postal Manual.* Washington, D.C.: Superintendent of Documents, United States Government Printing Office. (Kept up-to-date by supplements.)

Financial Information Sources

1. *Manual of Investments, American and Foreign.* New York: Moody's Investors Service. (Published annually with semiweekly supplements.)
2. *Reference Book.* New York: Dun & Bradstreet. (By subscription.)
3. *Standard Corporation Records.* New York: Standard & Poor's Corporation Services. (Published currently in loose-leaf form.)

Records Management Sources

1. Johnson, Mina M., and Norman F. Kallaus. *Records Management.* 2d Ed. Cincinnati: South-Western, 1981.
2. Maedke, Wilmer O., and others. *Information and Records Management.* 2d Ed. Encino, CA: Glencoe, 1981.
3. *Rules for Alphabetical Filing.* Prairie Village, KS: Association of Records Managers and Administrators, Inc., 1972.

Secretarial Handbooks

1. Anderson, Ruth I., and others. *The Administrative Secretary.* 3d Ed. New York: Gregg Division/McGraw-Hill, 1976.
2. Clark, James L., and Lyn Clark. *How 3: A Handbook for Office Workers.* 3d Ed. Boston: Kent, 1982.
3. Dallas, Richard J., and James M. Thompson. *Clerical and Secretarial Systems for the Office.* Englewood Cliffs, NJ: Prentice-Hall, 1975.
4. Doris, Lillian, and Besse Miller. *Complete Secretary's Handbook.* 4th Ed. Englewood Cliffs, NJ: Prentice-Hall, 1977.
5. Hanna, J. Marshall, and others. *Secretarial Procedures and Administration.* 7th Ed. Cincinnati: South-Western, 1978.
6. House, Clifford R., and Kathie Sigler. *Reference Manual for Office Personnel.* 6th Ed. Cincinnati: South-Western, 1981.
7. Janis, J. Harold, and Margaret Thompson. *New Standard Reference for Secretaries and Administrative Assistants.* New York: Macmillan, 1972.
8. Nanassy, Louis C., and others. *Reference Manual for Office Workers.* Encino, CA: Glencoe, 1977.
9. Sabin, William A. *The Gregg Reference Manual.* 5th Ed. New York: Gregg Division/McGraw-Hill, 1977.
10. *Webster's Secretarial Handbook.* Springfield, MA: G. and C. Merriam, 1976.

abbreviation A shortened form of a word or phrase used in writing to represent the complete form.

absolute adjective An adjective that cannot be compared as it represents the highest degree of a quality.

absolute phrase A phrase modifying a sentence or clause as a whole but not joined by a connective to the sentence.

active voice A verb form that has a direct object and is used to show that the subject is acting.

adjective A part of speech that describes, restricts, or limits a noun or pronoun.

administrative secretary A secretary who handles administrative responsibilities; in word processing, a secretary who has administrative responsibilities and composes and edits rough-draft copy.

adverb A part of speech that describes, restricts or limits a verb, an adjective, or another adverb.

agreement Correspondence in form (number, gender, person) of certain parts of speech with other parts (for example, a subject with its verb or a pronoun with its antecedent).

antecedent A word or a group of words to which a pronoun refers.

anticipatory subject (expletive) The word *it* or *there* used as a sentence beginning that anticipates the true subject that follows.

antonym A word with a meaning approximately the opposite of another word.

apostrophe (') A mark of punctuation used to show possessive case in nouns and indefinite pronouns, to indicate omission of letters in contractions, and to form plurals of nouns in some instances (figures, letters of the alphabet, and words used as words).

appositive The placing of a noun or pronoun next to another noun or pronoun so that the second completes or supplements the first.

article A word used before a noun to signal that a certain noun is to follow. There are three articles: *a, an* (indefinite) and *the* (definite). Articles are classified as adjectives.

attention line A part of the inside address of a letter that directs the letter to the attention of a specific person or department within an organization.

automatic typewriter (text-editing) An electric typewriter equipped with a medium such as a magnetic card or tape that stores material as it is being typed. The typewriter will automatically type the material stored on the medium.

auxiliary verb A verb helper in a verb phrase. It is always placed before the main verb and indicates such things as voice or tense.

bibliography A list of reference sources (for instance, books, periodicals, newspapers, films, television programs) consulted or quoted in writing.

body The part of the letter containing the message.

brackets ([ ]) A pair of symbols used to enclose a correction or an insert of something other than the writer's own words.

carbon-copy notation The initials *cc* or the words *copy(ies) to* placed below the identification initials of a business letter to show that a carbon copy of that letter is being sent to a person or persons listed after the *cc.*

case The change in form of a noun or pronoun to indicate relationship to other words in the sentence. There are three cases: *nominative, objective,* and *possessive.*

chain feeding A process for quickly inserting and typing cards or envelopes.

clause A group of words that are made up of a subject and a predicate. There are two types of clauses: *independent* and *dependent.*

coding A filing term meaning the marking of a piece of correspondence to show the name under which it will be filed.

collective noun A noun made up of a group or collection of persons or things.

colon (:) A mark of punctuation used to introduce something that follows, such as listed items or a direct quotation.

comma (,) A mark of punctuation used (1) to separate a single word or group of words from the rest of the sentence or (2) to set off parts of the sentence.

comparison of adjectives and adverbs Changes in the simple form of adjectives or adverbs to show a greater or lesser degree of the characteristic than the adjective or adverb expresses.

comparative degree An adjective and adverb form change used to compare two items. It is formed by adding *-er* to the positive form, by changing the positive form to another word, or by adding *more* or *less* to the positive form.

complement A noun or adjective completing the meaning of a linking verb and either modifying or renaming the subject. It is also the noun or pronoun that completes the infinitive *to be.*

complex sentence A sentence with one independent clause and one or more dependent clauses.

complimentary close A short courteous phrase used to end a letter.

compound adjective An adjective made up of two or more descriptive words serving as a single adjective and that is usually connected by hyphens.

compound-complex sentence A sentence with two or more independent clauses plus one or more dependent clauses.

compound noun A noun consisting of two or more words, usually a noun plus qualifying words. It can be written as one or two words, or it can be hyphenated.

compound sentence A sentence made up of two or more independent clauses.

compound subject A subject with two or more nouns or pronouns joined by coordinating conjunctions.

compound verb A verb consisting of two or more verbs joined by conjunctions.

conjugation All the forms of any verb.

conjunction A connecting word that introduces or connects clauses or joins series of words, phrases, or clauses.

conjunctive adverb A conjunction that connects independent clauses and shows a relationship between them.

contraction A word or words shortened by omitting or combining some of the letters or sounds.

coordinate conjunction A conjunction that connects elements of equal grammatical rank, such as dependent clause to dependent clause or infinitive phrase to infinitive phrase. The five principal coordinate conjunctions are *and, but, or, nor, for.*

correlative conjunction A pair of words that connect elements of equal grammatical rank, for example, *either/or* and *neither/nor.*

correspondence secretary The person who does the transcribing and typing (keyboarding) in a word processing center.

cross-reference A filing term meaning a notation or direction at one file name referring to another name where information is filed.

dangling modifier A modifier that is placed in the sentence so that it cannot reasonably apply to the word it is intended to modify, or there is nothing in the sentence that it can modify.

dash (—) A mark of punctuation used to indicate abruptness either in thought or in setting off parenthetical elements.

demonstrative adjective One of two pairs of adjectives—*this/these* and *that/those*—used before nouns to point out or limit.

demonstrative pronoun One of four pronouns that point out: *this/these* and *that/those.* These words may also function as demonstrative adjectives, but a demonstrative pronoun is not followed by a noun.

dependent clause A clause that cannot stand by itself and is dependent for its meaning on some other part of the sentence. There are three types: *adjective, adverb,* and *noun.*

direct address (nominative of address) A noun or pronoun used to address a person (or object) in speaking or writing.

direct object (object of a transitive verb) A noun or pronoun that receives the action of a verb; it answers the question *whom* or *what* about the verb.

direct quotation A passage taken from a written work or from direct speech and that must appear exactly as it was written or spoken.

double negative Two negative statements in the same sentence or clause but used to express a single negative.

electronic typewriter A computerized typewriter with memory and limited word processing functions.

ellipsis (. . .) A clearly understood omission of words from a sentence. Spaced periods are used to show an elliptical omission in direct quotations.

enclosure notation A notation placed at the end of a letter to indicate that something is enclosed in the envelope with the letter.

exclamation point (!) A mark of punctuation used after sentences or expressions to show strong emotion.

expletive See *anticipatory subject.*

footnote A note placed at the bottom of a page of manuscript to add a comment or to give a reference to a source.

full-block letter A business-letter style in which every line of writing is begun at the left margin.

future tense A verb form used to express action that will take place in the future. The future tense uses *shall* or *will* as an auxiliary.

gender A form of a noun or pronoun that indicates sex or the absence of sex.

gerund A verb form ending in *-ing* that functions as a noun, never as a verb.

homonym One of two or more words with the same sound and spelling but different meanings.

homophone One of two or more words with the same sound but different spellings and meanings.

hyphen (-) A mark of punctuation between parts of a hyphenated compound word or between syllables of a word divided at the end of a line.

identification initials A notation placed at the end of a business letter to indicate who dictated the letter and who typed it.

idiom An expression that is grammatically acceptable even though it cannot be translated literally or may violate established rules of grammar.

imperative (mood) The form of a verb that gives a command or makes a request.

indefinite pronoun (adjective pronoun) A pronoun that does not name any particular individual or thing.

independent (main) clause A group of related words containing both a subject and a predicate and able to stand by itself as a simple sentence.

indexing A filing term meaning the determining of the name under which a piece of correspondence will be filed.

indicative (mood) The form of a verb that states a fact or asks a question.

indirect object A noun or pronoun used with verbs that ask or give and that names the receiver.

infinitive A verb form consisting of *to* plus the present tense and that functions as an adjective, an adverb, or a noun—never as a verb.

inside address A part of a business letter that indicates the name and address of the addressee.

intensive (reflexive) pronoun A pronoun formed by adding the suffix *-self* (singular) or -*selves* (plural) to a personal pronoun in order to express emphasis.

interjection A part of speech that expresses strong emotion in the form of an exclamation.

interoffice memorandum A business form used for messages within a company.

interrogative pronoun One of the pronouns *who, which,* or *what;* used in asking questions.

intransitive verb A verb that does not require an object to complete its meaning. It describes the subject or expresses a condition or state of being.

irregular verb A verb that does not follow standard rules for forming its past tense and past participle—that is, by adding -*d* or -*ed* to the present tense.

italics A style of printing type used to set off a word or passage distinctively within a text. In typing italics are indicated by underscoring.

itinerary A chronological listing of planned hotel and travel arrangements, places to be visited, persons to be seen, and things to do.

leaders (. . .) Spaced periods in tabulations that guide the reader to the various columns.

letterhead Stationery printed with a person's or firm's name and address, and—sometimes—the telephone number and cable address.

linking (copulative) verb An intransitive verb that needs a predicate nominative or predicate adjective to complete it; it relates the subject to the subject complement.

mailing notation A notation on a letter and its envelope indicating that the letter is being sent by special postal service.

manuscript A typewritten version of a report, book, article, etc., usually typed according to specifications and often intended for publication.

metric system A decimal system of weights and measures based on the meter and gram.

mixed punctuation A business-letter style of punctuation that places a colon after the salutation and a comma after the complimentary close.

modified-block letter A business-letter style in which the date and the closing lines are placed at the right margin or are centered; paragraphs may be blocked or indented.

modifier Any word or word group functioning as an adjective or an adverb.

mood The form of a verb that indicates the manner of action expressed by that verb. There are three moods: *indicative, imperative,* and *subjunctive.*

nominative (subjective) case The case form of a noun or pronoun showing it as the subject of a sentence or a clause or as a word identified with the subject (such as a predicate nominative).

nonrestrictive modifier A modifying phrase or clause not essential to the meaning of a sentence. The modifier is usually set off by commas.

noun A part of speech that names a thing, person, animal, place, quality, idea, or action.

noun clause A dependent or subordinate clause used as a noun.

number The form of a noun, pronoun, demonstrative adjective, or verb that indicates whether the word is singular or plural.

object of a preposition A noun or pronoun joined to the sentence by a preposition.

objective (accusative) case The case form of a noun or pronoun indicating that it is the direct object of a verb, the subject of any infinitive, or the object of a preposition.

open punctuation A business-letter style of punctuation in which no punctuation is placed after the salutation or complimentary close.

outline A listing of main points, organized as a plan for writing.

parentheses (( )) A pair of punctuation marks used to mark off explanatory or qualifying remarks within a sentence.

part of speech Classification of any word by its function in the sentence.

participle A verb form that ends either in -*ing* (present participle) or in -*ed* (past participle) and that functions as an adjective—never as a verb.

passive voice A verb characteristic used to show that the subject is receiving the action of the verb. It consists of a form of the verb *be* plus the past participle.

past tense A verb form indicating that action has already taken place.

perfect tense A verb form that combines a form of *have* with the past participle to indicate action or state of being that is completed at the time of speaking or at a time spoken of.

period (.) A mark of punctuation indicating a full stop. It is placed at the end of declarative sentences, indirect questions, abbreviations, and other statements considered to be complete.

person The form of a verb or a pronoun that indicates whether a person is speaking (first person), spoken to (second person), or spoken about (third person).

personal pronoun A pronoun that refers to persons (or animals) and that indicates by form whether the person is speaking, spoken to, or spoken about.

phrasal preposition Two or more words used as a preposition.

phrase A sequence of two or more related words not having a subject and a predicate but functioning as a single part of speech.

plural A form of a noun, pronoun, or verb indicating more than one.

positive degree The simple form of an adjective or an adverb.

possessive (genitive) case The form of nouns and pronouns that shows ownership.

postage meter A machine with prepaid postage that both seals the envelope and prints the correct amount of postage on it.

postscript A message added at the end of a letter below the signature.

predicate The part of a sentence or clause that expresses something about the subject; it consists of the verb plus any complements, objects, or modifiers.

predicate adjective An adjective that comes after a linking verb and describes the subject.

predicate nominative (predicate noun, subject complement) A noun or pronoun that comes after a form of the verb *be* and renames the subject.

preposition A single word or a group of words used to connect a noun or pronoun to some other word in the sentence.

prepositional phrase A phrase consisting of a preposition, its object, and any modifiers.

present tense A verb form indicating action that is taking place now. It also indicates general or permanent truths, or habitual action.

principal parts of a verb The forms of any verb from which the various tenses are derived. The principal parts are *present, past,* and *past participle.*

progressive verb A verb phrase made up of the auxiliary—a form of *be*—and the present participle. It expresses continuous action or state of being.

pronoun A word used for or in place of a noun.

proofreaders' marks Marks made on manuscripts or printed proof indicating changes, deletions, or additions made in the text.

proper adjective An adjective derived from a proper noun and usually capitalized.

proper noun A noun that designates a particular person, place, or thing. A proper noun is always capitalized.

question mark (?) A punctuation mark that asks a direct question when placed at the end of a sentence or that shows doubt or approximation when placed in parentheses.

quotation marks (" ") Punctuation marks used to enclose written or spoken quotations.

reciprocal pronoun There are two reciprocal pronouns: *each other* and *one another*. *Each other* refers to two, and *one another* refers to three or more. They are used only as objects of verbs and as objects of prepositions.

reflexive (intensive) pronoun Those pronouns formed by adding the suffixes *-self* (singular) or *-selves* (plural) to personal pronouns and used to reflect verb action toward a noun or pronoun already used.

relative clause A dependent adjective clause introduced by a relative pronoun—*that, which, what,* or a form of *who*—that refers to the antecedent of the relative pronoun.

relative pronoun A pronoun used to join a dependent adjective (relative) clause to the antecedent of that relative pronoun. The relative pronouns are *who* (*whom* or *whose*), *which, that, what, whoever, whomever, whatever.*

restrictive modifier A modifying phrase or clause that is essential to the meaning of the sentence.

salutation A part of the letter that serves as the greeting, as ''Dear Mr. Lee.''

semicolon (;) A mark of punctuation used to separate clauses of a compound sentence, items in a series containing internal punctuation, explanations, and enumerations from the rest of the sentence.

sentence A group of related words that constitute a complete thought, which may be a statement, a question, a command, or an exclamation.

signature A part of a letter that includes the penwritten signature of the person writing the letter and, in a business letter, the typed name and title of the signer.

Simplified letter A business-letter style in which every line is blocked at the left margin, and the salutation and complimentary close are omitted.

sorting A filing term meaning arranging documents in the order in which they will be filed.

split infinitive An infinitive with an adverb between the *to* and the rest of the infinitive.

subject The person or object about which something in the sentence is said or asked.

subject line A part of the body of a business letter that tells what the letter is about.

subject of an infinitive The noun or pronoun that does the action of the infinitive. The subject of an infinitive is always in the objective case.

subjunctive (mood) The verb form indicating wish, possibility, or doubt. It changes for certain forms of the verb *be* and in the first and third person singular.

subordinate (dependent) clause A clause that cannot stand by itself and is dependent for its meaning upon some other part of the sentence. There are three kinds: *adjective, adverb,* and *noun.*

subordinate conjunction A conjunction that connects a dependent clause to an independent clause.

superlative degree An adjective or adverb form that compares three or more items. It is formed by adding *-est* to the positive, by changing the positive to another word, or by placing *most* or *least* before the positive.

synonym A word with a meaning similar to that of another word.

tense A verb form that express distinctions of time.

transitive verb A verb requiring an object to complete its meaning.

typewriter carriage The part of a typewriter that moves as the keys of the machine are struck. (The IBM Selectric has no carriage.)

typewriter platen The roller of the typewriter, against which the keys are struck.

typewriter scale The scale of the typewriter, marked and numbered to show number of spaces and length of writing line. The typewriter scale is used in straightening the paper.

verb A part of speech that makes a statement, asks a question, or gives a command.

verb phrase A phrase consisting of a main verb and one or more auxiliaries. The auxiliary verb or verbs are always first, followed by the main verb.

verbal A verb form used as one of three parts of speech—adjective, noun, or adverb.

voice The verb characteristic used to show whether the subject is acting or receiving an action. The two voices are *active* and *passive*.

window envelope An envelope with a transparent section through which the inside address typed on the letter can be seen, thus eliminating the need to type an address on the envelope.

word originator A term in word processing to indicate the person who dictated or wrote the material being typed on the automatic typewriter.

word processing A system of transcription that involves the use of automatic typewriters and of material stored on electronic media.

ZIP (Zone Improvement Plan) Code A code system used by the United States Postal Service to identify geographic localities of all United States post offices.

Exercises

EXERCISE **1**   **KINDS OF SENTENCES**

Identify the following sentences as simple, complex, compound, or compound-complex. Write the identification in the blank at the right. Underline the dependent clauses and identify them as adjective, adverb, or noun clauses by writing *adj., adv.,* or *noun* below the underlined clause.

Example: Work <u>that is not completed by four o'clock</u>
adj.
will be placed in this file basket.   _____complex_____

1. According to my figures, the balance in my checking account at the end of the month should be $275.   _____

2. The house on the other side of the river belongs to Mr. Shaw.   _____

3. The man to whom you wrote is no longer with our company, but I shall be happy to help you if I can.   _____

4. When Mr. Curtis returns, give him my message.   _____

5. I bought a new car, but I cannot get delivery until September 1.   _____

6. The old mansion, which has 87 rooms, is more than a hundred years old.   _____

7. Mr. Warren is a person whom I can trust.   _____

8. I wanted to read my book without being interrupted by the telephone's ringing.   _____

9. Judy thought that Mr. Gray was out of the office.   _____

10. However late you are, call me when you return.   _____

11. The movie that I saw last night was shown at two local theaters.   _____

12. He said that he would call me and that I should wait for the call.   _____

EXERCISE **2**   **SENTENCE FAULTS**

Identify the sentence faults in these sentences and write the kind of fault in the blank to the right. Correct the fault by writing a correct sentence on the blank lines below it. If the sentence is correct, mark it C.

Example: By endorsing the check.   _____fragment_____

> I was able to receive payment by endorsing the check.

1. Waiting in the outer office.   _____

_____

_____

2. I cannot find the Maxwell file, however, I think it
   has been misplaced in the file.   _____

_____

_____

3. Mary said that she looked for the file yesterday,
   she also said that she could not find the Martin
   file.   _____

_____

_____

4. Our filing system, it seems, is very inefficient.   _____

_____

_____

5. Although we recently purchased new filing
   equipment, we seem to have trouble locating
   files, our filing supervisor will try to correct the
   problems.   _____

_____

_____

6. Perhaps we should revise our methods of checking out files.   _____

_____

_____

7. To improve the filing system.   _____

_____

_____

8. Because the supervisor has had many years of experience.   _____

_____

_____

9. The filing system for our company must be able
   to store a large number of records many employees use the files every day.   _____

   _____

   _____

10. The files contain our records for the past ten
    years, we need to be able to find records quickly
    and easily.   _____

    _____

    _____

EXERCISE 3   **CHOICE OF PRONOUNS**

Underline the correct pronoun in each set of parentheses.

Example: People (<u>who</u>, which) live in glass houses shouldn't throw stones.
1. (This, These) kind of test is very difficult.
2. John bought tickets to the play for Mark and (me, myself).
3. (That, Those) persons who are tardy will be marked absent.
4. All of the nurses helped (each other, one another) with sterilizing the equipment.
5. I do not like (this, these) kind of pen for shorthand.
6. Mr. Miller and (I, myself) are going to do the filing.
7. All persons (that, which) are able to complete the test before the end of the hour may leave early.
8. Will everyone turn to page 17 of (his or her, their) text.
9. James and Barbara helped (each other, one another) with their home-work.
10. One of the men took my coat and left (his, theirs) in its place.
11. (That, Those) sort of story is unbelievable.
12. Mr. Ball ordered the taxi to come for (him, himself) at five o'clock.
13. Fresh vegetables, (that, which) are more abundant in the summer, should be a part of everyone's diet.
14. (Those, These) students who do not register by September 1 may not be admitted to the college.
15. All of the people who are attending the lecture may check (his or her, their) coat(s) in Room 45.

EXERCISE 4   **PLURALS OF NOUNS I**

Indicate in the first blank whether the following nouns are singular or plural; then give the singular form if the noun is plural or the plural form if the noun is singular. If there is no singular or plural form for the noun, indicate this by writing the word *none* in the second blank.

	Singular/Plural	Other Form
Example: media	plural	medium
1. data		
2. alumnus		
3. sister-in-law		
4. Ms.		
5. selves		
6. salmon		
7. F.O.B.		
8. cupful		
9. Mary		
10. company		
11. mice		
12. turkey		
13. half		
14. safes		
15. foxes		
16. lunch		
17. veto		
18. salesperson		
19. economics		
20. branch manager		

PLURALS OF NOUNS II   EXERCISE **5**

	Singular/Plural	Other Form
1. bosses		
2. university		
3. chimney		
4. analysis		
5. portfolio		
6. moose		
7. attorney general		
8. #'s		
9. teaspoonful		
10. bunches		
11. mumps		
12. trousers		
13. appendixes		
14. staffs		
15. district manager		
16. bookcases		
17. life		
18. Jones		
19. airline		
20. potatoes		

EXERCISE **6**   **GENDER, PERSON**

Indicate in the first blank the gender of the following nouns and pronouns. Then, if the word is masculine or feminine, give the corresponding feminine or masculine form. If the word is neuter, there is, of course, no corresponding form, and the word *none* should be written in the second blank.

	Gender	Other Form
Example: boy	masculine	girl
1. he	_____	_____
2. businessman	_____	_____
3. alumna	_____	_____
4. her	_____	_____
5. brother	_____	_____
6. Messrs.	_____	_____
7. host	_____	_____
8. table	_____	_____
9. bride	_____	_____
10. landlord	_____	_____

Indicate the person of the following nouns and pronouns by writing *1*, *2*, or *3* in the blanks that follow.

Example: him ___3___

1. I	_____	6. she	_____
2. us	_____	7. David	_____
3. you	_____	8. it	_____
4. we	_____	9. dog	_____
5. him	_____	10. them	_____

EXERCISE **7**   **CASE OF PERSONAL PRONOUNS   I**

Underline the correct pronoun in each set of parentheses.

Example: I told (<u>him</u>, he) to wait for me.

1. Their employers, the customers, and (they, them) will benefit by the decision.
2. Neither (she, her) nor (I, me) used the ink.
3. He asked Miss Brown and (she, her) to write the letters now.
4. You, Marianne, and (I, me) are to share the same office.
5. Both (they, them) and (we, us) are to attend the meeting next week.
6. The letters were mailed to Mr. Little and (he, him) yesterday.
7. They hired Jones and (I, me) for the job.
8. They assumed it was (she, her) whom we expected today.
9. I should never have expected the callers to be (they, them).
10. I am supposed to be (he, him) who is in charge.
11. I thought the new director to be (he, him), but I was wrong.

12. If you were (he, him), would you accept the offer?
13. Is it (he, him) whom you wish to see?
14. It could not have been (they, them) who gave us the information.
15. Why do you think it was (she, her)?
16. If anyone wins in this case, it will be (I, me).
17. Was it (they, them) who called yesterday?
18. The evidence indicates it to be (they, them) who should be held responsible for the error.
19. You will receive full instructions from your employer and (I, me).
20. May I ask Anne and (she, her) to help type the reports?
21. Are you willing for Mr. Case and (I, me) to decide the matter?
22. The money will eventually be divided between Miss Lynn and (I, me, myself).
23. The delegates to the convention were Tom and (he, him).
24. Davis sent notices for Andrews and (I, me, myself) to report for interviews.
25. I do not wish to dismiss either (she, her) or (he, him).
26. (We, Us) salespeople do everything possible to satisfy our customers.
27. I'm sure it was (he, him) who spoke on Monday.
28. Mr. Perkins was uncertain whether to appoint you or (he, him) to be chairman.
29. The manager asked all of (we, us) clerks to sign the form.
30. I thought Judy to be (she, her).
31. I was thought to be (she, her).
32. Mrs. Wilson thought Jerry to be (I, me).
33. I told (he, him) to meet me at six o'clock.
34. She left earlier than (I, me).
35. Mary is as pleased as (we, us).
36. When he called, I thought Mr. Black to be (he, him).
37. I wished (he, him) to attend the meeting.
38. I asked him if the girl was (she, her) who answered the phone.
39. It was not (she, her) whom you interviewed yesterday.
40. Between Hazel and (she, her) they have $5.
41. This work is to be completed by you and (he, him).
42. I believed the woman to be (she, her) who took the message.
43. It is (he, him) who is standing by the window who is my uncle.
44. The general public, as well as (he, him), believed the investment to be a sound one.
45. Did you say it was (they, them) who deposited the money?
46. I told Grace and (she, her) to finish the typing by five o'clock.
47. Will you ask Ruth and (he, him) if they can do the work?
48. Mr. Baxter wanted (she, her) to be his secretary.
49. The president called upon (we, us) typists for extra help.
50. I told Jack and (he, him) to leave early.

CASE OF PERSONAL PRONOUNS II   EXERCISE **8**

1. I gave the message to either Jan or (her, she).
2. (We, Us) students wish to submit a petition.

3. I doubt very much that it was (she, her) who signed the letters.
4. If you were (I, me), would you do the extra typing?
5. You will get checks from both Mr. Farrell and (I, me, myself).
6. Does Mr. Hull want Margaret and (I, me) to help with the filing?
7. Marian thought the president of the club to be (he, him).
8. I do not believe it could be (he, him).
9. Miss Lambert assumed that it was (I, me) who wrote the memo.
10. Jane believed Mr. Allen to be (he, him) who left the safe unlocked.
11. This is a good mystery; I should not have suspected the murderer to be (he, him).
12. Anne waited for Jerry and (he, him) to do the duplicating.
13. Barbara is later for our appointment than (I, me).
14. I am (she, her) who called for an appointment.
15. The company hired both Ralph and (I, me) as salesmen.
16. The coffee break was welcomed by all of (we, us) stenographers.
17. Do you think it was (she, her) who called?
18. It could not have been (she, her) who called.
19. If anyone goes to the ball game, it will be (he, him).
20. Susan mailed copies of the report to Mr. James, Mr. Harrison, and (he, him).
21. Mr. Ray had to choose between you and (he, him).
22. We thought you to be (she, her).
23. Please divide the work among John, Frank, and (he, him).
24. The stockholders and the officers, as well as you and (I, me), will profit from the increased dividend.
25. Mr. Newman does not wish to see either (she, her) or (he, him).
26. If you had been (he, him), how would you have handled the matter?
27. The filing must be completed by you and (she, her) before five o'clock.
28. I do not think it will be (we, us) who are chosen to go to New York.
29. Katherine believed (he, him) to be (I, me).
30. I would not wish to be (he, him) when Mr. Ward discovers the error.

EXERCISE **9** **CASE OF PERSONAL PRONOUNS III**

1. Did you think it was (I, me)?
2. The Christmas bonus was given to (we, us).
3. Can you and (she, her) help me find the error in the trial balance?
4. If you were (he, him), you would have finished the work before you left.
5. Mr. Jameson does not want either Janet or (she, her) to handle the matter.
6. Jane arrives at the office earlier than (I, me).
7. It was (he, him) who was thought to be (I, me).
8. It was hoped that (we, us) employees would not go on strike.
9. Patricia left the paychecks for Mr. Marsh, Mr. Wall, and (he, him) in the file basket.
10. There are so many errors in the work that I cannot believe it was (she, her) who typed it.
11. We think Mr. Kay gave the report to either Marie or (she, her).
12. Linda did not recognize us; she thought (I, me) to be Kate and Kate to be (I, me).

13. The duplicating must be finished by either (she, her) or (he, him) before lunch.
14. I cannot find my friend; is that (he, him) across the street?
15. I hurt (I, me, myself) on the open desk drawer.
16. We, my employer and (I, me), finished checking the figures before three o'clock.
17. I saw Mr. Williams and (he, him) standing by the elevator.
18. Mrs. Hale considered (he, him) to be the best qualified for the job.
19. Joan denied that it was (she, her) who started the rumor.
20. Mr. Jones and (I, me, myself) are going to be on a panel to discuss numeric filing.
21. The matter to be discussed is between Mrs. Scott and (I, me, myself).
22. My sister is taller than (I, me).
23. The new secretary helped Phyllis and (I, me) with the sorting of the mail.
24. I do not think Mr. Kane wanted his new secretary to be (she, her).
25. Miss Lane told Nell and (she, her) to begin the typing immediately.

POSSESSIVES OF NOUNS I

Fill in the blanks with the singular possessive and the plural possessive of the following nouns.

	Singular Possessive	Plural Possessive
Example: woman	woman's	women's
1. company		
2. editor in chief		
3. season		
4. man		
5. attorney		
6. sister		
7. sheriff		
8. boss		
9. businesswoman		
10. nation		
11. vice president		
12. doctor		
13. employee		
14. accountant		
15. wife		
16. year		
17. hostess		
18. Henry		
19. stenographer		
20. committee		
21. army		
22. month		
23. architect		

24. child
25. fox

EXERCISE **11** **POSSESSIVES OF NOUNS II**

	Singular Possessive	Plural Possessive
1. actress		
2. lady		
3. navy		
4. brother		
5. week		
6. calf		
7. airline		
8. secretary		
9. lawyer		
10. wolf		
11. girl		
12. dog		
13. ballplayer		
14. baby		
15. policeman		
16. merchant		
17. alumnus		
18. father		
19. professor		
20. racketeer		
21. family		
22. astronaut		
23. student		
24. gentleman		
25. stepson		

EXERCISE **12** **POSSESSIVE PRONOUNS**

Fill in the blanks with the correct possessive form of the personal pronoun.

Example: Which book is ___his___ (3d person masc. sing.)?

1. Give me _____ (1st person sing.) coat.
2. That desk is _____ (3d person fem. sing.).
3. I received _____ (2d person sing.) letter Friday.
4. I think _____ (3d person masc. sing.) answer is wrong.
5. I do not believe _____ (3d person pl.) story.
6. The job is _____ (3d person masc. sing.) if he wants it.
7. _____ (1st person pl.) company is a small one.
8. Many of _____ (1st person pl.) customers shopped early.

9. I believe this design is _____ (2d person sing.).
10. _____ (3d person pl.) answers were correct.

Underline the correct form of *who* to complete the following sentences.

1. (Whose, Who's) book are you using?
2. (Whose, Who's) calling, please?
3. (Whose, Who's) car are you driving?
4. (Whose, Who's) driving that car?
5. (Whose, Who's) the taller of the two boys?

AGREEMENT I

Underline the correct word in each set of parentheses.

Example: The jury reached (its, their) verdict in two hours.

1. The company held (its, their) picnic at the state park.
2. The band played (its, their) last number at ten o'clock.
3. Anyone who finishes the test early may turn in (his or her, their) paper(s) and leave.
4. Will everyone pass (his or her, their) paper(s) forward.
5. All items of the data (is, are) incorrect; (it, they) must be corrected before we leave.
6. Will all students sign (his or her, their) name(s) to the roll sheet.
7. One of the girls left (her, their) pen(s) on my desk.
8. This is one of those pens that (is, are) guaranteed for a year.
9. Over a third of the girls (was, were) late because of the storm.
10. Half of the magazine (is, are) torn away.
11. Each man and boy (is, are) expected to do (his, their) work.
12. There (is, are) many days when all of the work is not finished.
13. The crises in the newly formed government (is, are) frequent and disturbing.
14. One of the men left (his, their) typewriter(s) uncovered.
15. I bought one of those dresses that (is, are) on sale at the Emporium.
16. Neither the girls nor Mrs. Ames (is, are) going to the city.
17. Neither Mrs. Ames nor the girls (is, are) going to the city.
18. Half of the papers (was, were) missing from the files.
19. Each secretary and typist (is, are) doing (his or her, their) share of the work.
20. Every book and magazine (was, were) returned to (its, their) proper place.
21. Either Tom or John will lend you (his, their) tennis racket.
22. Either Bill or James (is, are) completing the report.
23. My sister Jean, as well as my mother and father, (is, are) out of town at this time.
24. Anne gave the message to the sales manager who (is, are) handling the matter.
25. Anne gave the message to one of the salesmen who (is, are) handling such matters.

EXERCISE **14**   **AGREEMENT   II**

1. One of the students turned in (his or her, their) paper without putting (his or her, their) name on it.
2. Every house and building (was, were) destroyed in the hurricane.
3. Half of the letters from the files (was, were) lost.
4. I bought one of the new erasers that (is, are) guaranteed to erase without smudging.
5. Eleanor, as well as two other girls in the office, (has, have) received a promotion.
6. The criteria for evaluating the work (is, are) too demanding.
7. The number of students attending the rally (was, were) very small.
8. The company (has, have) (its, their) headquarters in Chicago.
9. Spaghetti and meatballs (is, are) Tom's favorite food.
10. Neither Elizabeth nor the stenographers (has, have) completed all of the dictation.
11. Neither the stenographers nor Elizabeth (has, have) completed all of the dictation.
12. The order was given to one of the salesmen who (is, are) promoting our new product.
13. One of the salesmen (was, were) given an order for our new product.
14. There (is, are) many things to discuss at the meeting.
15. The committee members may park (his or her, their) car(s) in this lot.
16. A number of errors (was, were) found in the report.
17. In my desk (was, were) the missing file folder.
18. The accountant and office manager (is, are) out of the office.
19. The accountant and the office manager (is, are) out of the office.
20. Either Ted or Bob (is, are) handling the campaign.
21. No one can enter the building unless (he or she, they) (sign, signs) the register.
22. We recently purchased one of those electric typewriters that (has, have) a choice of typefaces.
23. One of our new electric typewriters (has, have) a choice of typefaces.
24. We recently purchased an electric typewriter that (has, have) a choice of typefaces.
25. The company has expanded (its, their) advertising campaign.

EXERCISE **15**   **AGREEMENT   III**

1. The council (decides, decide) how the matter will be handled.
2. Our company (is, are) unable to ship your entire order.
3. Parentheses (is, are) used throughout the report.
4. The subject of federal taxes (is, are) discussed in detail in the textbook.
5. The alumni (is, are) opposing the appointment of a new dean.
6. No one (knows, know) better than he that failure to study (has, have) disastrous results.
7. The Messrs. March and Lambert (is, are) attorneys at law.
8. The class (was, were) so small that the instructor canceled future meetings.

9. He is one of those people who never (knows, know) the right answers.
10. The number of errors in the letter (is, are) truly unbelievable.
11. The person who (is, are) able to invent a typewriter that can spell will become famous.
12. I am going to buy one of those records that (teaches, teach) me while I sleep.
13. A large crowd of students and faculty members (has, have) gathered in the auditorium.
14. Neither Nancy nor the twins (is, are) going to the party.
15. Either Peg or one of her friends (has, have) the measles.

WHO/WHOM I

EXERCISE **16**

Underline the correct form of *who* or *whom* in each set of parentheses.

Example: I saw Mr. Burns, (<u>who</u>, whom) I thought was out of town.

1. I shall be happy to learn (who, whom) will be chosen to take my place.
2. One of the applicants is a person (who, whom) I am very sure is reliable.
3. She is one person (who, whom) I think could become a good typist.
4. (Who, Whom) did you write to?
5. List the names of those (who, whom) you think will be present at the meeting.
6. She is a secretary (who, whom) we know can take dictation at 120 words per minute.
7. (Who, Whom) do you think will be elected as our new supervisor?
8. It is difficult to tell (who, whom) will be chosen to accompany Mrs. Smith to the convention.
9. (Who, Whom) shall I call in case of an emergency?
10. They wanted to know (who, whom) the visitor was.
11. It is a wise salesperson (who, whom) studies daily market fluctuations.
12. Have you decided (who, whom) should supervise the work?
13. (Who, Whom) will give me the keys to the building?
14. Mr. Carter, (who, whom) I have met many times, is an interesting person.
15. The man (who, whom) I wished to speak to is not here.
16. We bought our supplies from the merchants (who, whom) we thought gave us the best values.
17. Will you give me the address of the person (who, whom) you think can give me this information?
18. Mr. Jones, (who, whom) we met yesterday, is manager of Smith and Company.
19. I should like to ask (who, whom) you consider the best secretary in your office.
20. I am not quite certain (who, whom) is to be appointed president.
21. Mr. Green is a man (who, whom) can be trusted.
22. Mr. Green is a man (who, whom) I know to be trustworthy.
23. Mr. Green is a man (who, whom) I know is trustworthy.
24. I don't know (who, whom) he is supposed to be.
25. I saw the man (who, whom) is said to be the leader of the group.

26. Mr. Davis is the man (who, whom) I hope will be elected.
27. Mr. Davis is the man (who, whom) I hope to see elected.
28. Mr. Davis, (who, whom) was confident of election to the presidency, did not win.
29. It was he (who, whom) I wished to see.
30. We are glad to promote those (who, whom) we find to be capable.
31. We shall be glad to give you the names of several men (who, whom) you will be likely to interest in handling your product.
32. Mr. Williams, (who, whom) you saw on the elevator, is a well-known attorney.
33. Be careful (who, whom) you nominate for president.
34. It is hard to tell (who, whom) they will elect as vice president.
35. Labels on the folders indicate to (who, whom) they belong.
36. (Who, Whom) will take care of the incoming calls?
37. I do not know (who, whom) took the message.
38. We shall be glad to give the appointment to the person (who, whom) you think would be best suited to the job.
39. He is a person (who, whom) I assume can do the job efficiently.
40. Give the letters to one of the executives (who, whom) are dictating.
41. I do not know the man to (who, whom) you refer.
42. The person (who, whom) is mentioned in the report is Mr. Kay.
43. The secretary is a person (who, whom) is thought to be very efficient.
44. My secretary, (who, whom) is very efficient, typed the report in less than an hour.
45. The name of the envelope showed for (who, whom) the letter was intended.
46. All (who, whom) are admitted to the room must have permits to enter.
47. Those (who, whom) pay their bills before the tenth of the month may take a 5 percent discount.
48. The girl, (who, whom) I saw from across the street, disappeared in the crowd.
49. (Who, Whom) did you call about the appointment?
50. He is a man (who, whom) I think would make a fine president.

EXERCISE 17   WHO/WHOM II

1. (Who, Whom) will take Mr. Baker's dictation?
2. I do not know (who, whom) you are.
3. Mr. Williams recommended several men (who, whom) he thought could do the work.
4. We do not know (who, whom) is going to do the filing.
5. (Who, Whom) did you call about the error?
6. He is not the person (who, whom) I believe to be the best qualified for the job.
7. The secretaries (who, whom) were hired before September 1 will be eligible for Christmas bonuses.
8. Was it Kate to (who, whom) Mr. Kenyon gave the report?
9. (Who, Whom) did you say was going to write the letter?
10. I do not know (who, whom) will do it.

11. I know it will not be I (who, whom) will write the letter.
12. Mr. Hale hoped to find a person (who, whom) would be able to set up the training program.
13. (Who, Whom) is calling?
14. We have no proof that he is the one (who, whom) started the rumor.
15. (Whoever, Whomever) started it has caused a lot of trouble.
16. Miss Horton, (who, whom) I think is unknown to you, has been promoted to assistant buyer.
17. Miss Horton, (who, whom) I do not think you know, has been promoted to assistant buyer.
18. Ask (whoever, whomever) you see for the file.
19. The credit manager, (who, whom) makes the decision in such matters, would not approve the purchase.
20. (Whoever, Whomever) typed the report should have a carbon copy of it.
21. Give the book to (whoever, whomever) answers the door.
22. Please let me know (who, whom) is going to handle the claim.
23. (Who, Whom) do you consider to be best qualified for the job?
24. (Whoever, Whomever) is hired will have a difficult job.
25. It would not be so difficult for someone (who, whom) has had some experience in merchandising.
26. The person (who, whom) called Mr. Baker was Susan.
27. The person (who, whom) Mr. Baker called was Susan.
28. We would not have thought him to be the one (who, whom) could finish the work.
29. (Who, Whom) shall I say offered to do the work?
30. (Whoever, Whomever) is late will be asked to give an explanation.

REVIEW OF PRONOUNS

EXERCISE **18**

Underline the correct pronoun in each set of parentheses.

Example: Give the book to (whoever, whomever) wants it.

1. You will report to either Mr. Jones or (I, me).
2. Every voter should understand the issues before marking (his or her, their) ballot(s).
3. (We, Us) accountants do not want shorter lunch periods.
4. I thought it was (she, her) (who, whom) answered Mr. Riley's telephone.
5. Everyone (who, whom) has seen the movie has been enthusiastic in (his or her, their) praise of it.
6. I believed Jerry to be (he, him) (who, whom) said the office would be closed Monday.
7. I was thought to be (he, him) (who, whom) said the office would be closed Monday.
8. Both Peter and (she, her) checked the file for the letter.
9. If you were (I, me), would you sign the contract?
10. He asked Mr. West and (I, me) to be responsible for locking the safe.
11. My brother Ted is taller than (I, me).
12. Mr. Foster did not know whether you or (she, her) would be chosen for the position.

13. Lee denied that it was (he, him) (who, whom) left the office door unlocked.
14. I asked (they, them) to give the final report to Mr. Reed and (I, me).
15. Is it (she, her) to (who, whom) you gave the books?
16. Anyone (who, whom) witnessed the accident should give (his or her, their) name(s) to the police.
17. I do not know for (who, whom) the message was intended.
18. We hope to employ only those (who, whom) wish to remain with the company.
19. It is difficult to know for (who, whom) to vote.
20. It will be difficult to find a person (who, whom) is qualified for the position.
21. Mr. Kelly selected the person (who, whom) he thought should be awarded the prize.
22. Was it (they, them) to (who, whom) you referred?
23. The family left (its, their) car in the parking lot.
24. The work was distributed among Jane, Betty, and (she, her).
25. Are you (he, him) (who, whom) called earlier?
26. Anyone (who, whom) wishes to be placed on the mailing list should sign (his or her, their) name(s) to the sheet.
27. Neither Tom nor John completed (his, their) assignment.
28. No one but (she, her) could solve the difficult problem.
29. It could not have been (he, him) (who, whom) found the error in the accounts.
30. Give the material to (whoever, whomever) wants it.

EXERCISE **19** **VERBS AND VERB PHRASES**

In the following sentences, draw one line under the main verbs and two lines under the auxiliary verbs.

Example: Joan should have read the assignment.

1. The man was seen in the library.
2. Have you read the assignment?
3. I walked home through the park.
4. The children played and laughed in the amusement park.
5. After Mr. Smith dictated the letters, his secretary typed them.
6. Mr. Smith has been dictating all afternoon.
7. I do not want to be disturbed.
8. I shall have finished my work by four o'clock.
9. Jean did not believe that I had finished the typing.
10. Peg taught herself to type.

EXERCISE **20** **TRANSITIVE/INTRANSITIVE I**

Underline the verbs in the following sentences. Write *T* in the blank if the verb is transitive and *I* if the verb is intransitive. If the sentence contains a direct object, draw two lines under it.

Example: I read the assignment last Friday.   T

1. Her secretary takes dictation at 120 words per minute. —
2. The sun sets in the west. —
3. I received a bill for my car repairs. —
4. The notebook contained many important addresses. —
5. Many important addresses were in the notebook. —
6. I do not have any carbon paper. —
7. I am happy with the results of the examination. —
8. There is no excuse for his conduct. —
9. Mr. Evans laid the papers on his desk. —
10. Sally always arrives on time at the office. —
11. We did not believe the story about the accident. —
12. School begins at eight o'clock each morning. —
13. Close the door quietly. —
14. The bag was full of walnuts. —
15. The president made a speech. —
16. The girl is Susie. —
17. The missing papers were on the desk in full sight of everyone. —
18. Mr. Lee does not need the papers until Monday. —
19. The telephone rang late at night. —
20. The flood waters rose rapidly. —

TRANSITIVE/INTRANSITIVE II   EXERCISE **21**

1. The stone rolled down the hill. —
2. Bill rolled the stone to the boy. —
3. The concert began at eight o'clock. —
4. The pianist began the concert at eight o'clock. —
5. Check your figures carefully. —
6. These figures are not accurate. —
7. Whom did you see about the error? —
8. The customer waited for an hour. —
9. My sister left her books in my car. —
10. My sister left at four o'clock. —
11. I am happy about my promotion. —
12. There was no reason for his tardiness. —
13. The typewriter needs a new ribbon. —
14. Many addresses became out-of-date with the postal changes. —
15. Jane laid the letters on Mr. Scott's desk. —
16. The letters lay on the desk overnight. —
17. Who is responsible for taking the dictation? —
18. My brother looks like me. —
19. I saw myself in the mirror. —
20. The number of accidents is small. —

VERB TENSE   EXERCISE **22**

Determine the correct past or perfect tense form of the verb that is given in the parentheses and write that form in the blank to the right.

Example: I (write) the assignment before I went to class.   _____wrote_____

1. He (dive) from the board into the pool. _____
2. I have (begin) the assignment many times. _____
3. The water (freeze) in the radiator of the car. _____
4. The tree (grow) much higher than we expected. _____
5. He (leave) his coat in the office. _____
6. I (speak) to Mr. Wells as he was leaving. _____
7. Mr. Thomas has (choose) Miss Webster to be his secretary. _____
8. He (hang) his coat on the hook in the closet. _____
9. Betty (rise) from her chair to answer the door. _____
10. I (lend) my pen to a customer who did not return it. _____

EXERCISE **23**   **ACTIVE AND PASSIVE VOICE I**

Underline the verbs in the following sentences. Write *A* in the blank following the sentence if the voice of the verb is active and *P* if the voice is passive.

Example: The boy <u>pushed</u> the bicycle up the hill.   _A_

1. Read the directions carefully. ___
2. Karen read the directions carefully. ___
3. The directions on the carton should be read carefully. ___
4. The freeway is posted for 55 miles per hour. ___
5. I drove 70 miles per hour on the freeway. ___
6. I drove my car on the freeway. ___
7. Jane is bringing three guests to the party. ___
8. Jane brought three guests to the party. ___
9. Three guests were brought to the party. ___
10. Donations were made for the victims of the hurricane. ___
11. The hurricane victims received donations of money and food. ___
12. Donations for the hurricane victims have been made by many people. ___
13. Many people have made donations for hurricane victims. ___
14. I am just finishing the assignment. ___
15. The assignment was finished on time. ___
16. Mary finished the assignment yesterday afternoon. ___
17. The pine tree grew three feet in one year. ___
18. The roots of the pine tree are growing under the street. ___
19. The gardener planted the pine tree ten years ago. ___
20. The pine tree was planted to shade the house. ___

EXERCISE **24**   **ACTIVE AND PASSIVE VOICE II**

Example: The boy pushed the bicycle up the hill.   _A_

1. I was offered an opportunity to invest in a foolproof plan to double my money. ___

2. School begins at eight o'clock.   —
3. Much has been said about proper dress for office workers.   —
4. We waited an hour for the storm to subside.   —
5. The escaped prisoner was found a mile from the prison.   —
6. They found the escaped prisoner a mile from the prison.   —
7. The notebook, as well as the pen, was on the desk.   —
8. I set my watch by the clock at City Hall.   —
9. The book was laid on the desk.   —
10. The book was lying on the desk.   —

TROUBLESOME VERBS I

Fill in the blanks in the following sentences with the correct forms of *lay* or *lie*.

Example: The architect ____laid____ the plans for the house.

1. _____ down, Fido.
2. The king's yacht is _____ in the harbor.
3. _____ those parcels on the floor.
4. The check has_____ in Mr. Eliot's file for so long that I think he has forgotten about it.
5. The confidential report _____ in plain sight yesterday morning.
6. Mr. Martin _____ it there and then forgot about it.
7. _____ the book on the table.
8. The book _____ on the table.
9. I _____ down yesterday.
10. I have _____ in bed for two weeks.
11. I have _____ the book on Mr. Fisher's desk.
12. The book was _____ under the table.
13. I _____ the carbon copies right there.
14. He has _____ down the rules for me.
15. He is _____ the foundation for a more practical system.
16. To the left of the typewriter _____ the typing book.
17. It was _____ there yesterday, too.
18. His coat and hat have been _____ on the couch all day.
19. In the attorney's office _____ the file folder for the Jones case.
20. Last week the office manager _____ down the procedure for accepting cash payments.
21. Margaret _____ down during her lunch hour.
22. Carbon paper should be _____ carefully in the folder.
23. I _____ awake last night for two hours.
24. I hope our case will be _____ before the office manager.
25. He told her to _____ the child down.
26. My check had fallen from the desk and was _____ on the floor.
27. The property that is for sale _____ west of the town.
28. The children's lunch bags were _____ on the playground.
29. My sweater was _____ on the back seat of Ruth's car.
30. I _____ the newspaper on the desk for Mr. Locke to read.

Fill in the blanks in the following sentences with the correct forms of *rise* or *raise*.

Example: I do not think that issue should be _____raised_____.

1. Please _____ your hand if you have the correct answer.
2. The river has _____ a full ten inches.
3. I have _____ the window.
4. The temperature in the room was _____ rapidly.
5. There was complete silence as Mr. Grant _____ to speak.
6. How did he ever _____ to his present high position?
7. It might be that he is successful at _____ money.
8. Did the bread _____?
9. The bread has _____.
10. Do not _____ your hand at the auction unless you wish to bid.
11. Mr. Julian _____ an objection to the plan.
12. We are gradually _____ our standards.
13. Each one in favor of this motion should _____ his right hand.
14. Do you think the river will _____?
15. Do not let him _____ that objection to the ruling.

Fill in the blanks in the following sentences with the correct forms of *sit* or *set*.

Example: Little Miss Muffet _____sat_____ on a tuffet.

1. The house _____ on a hilltop.
2. Before we were seated in the restaurant, the waiter _____ the table.
3. I _____ at the typewriter until I finished the work.
4. I have _____ a time limit for the job.
5. I want you to know that Mr. Hastings is still _____ in the reception room.
6. Jim seems to do nothing but _____ idly in his office.
7. He is incapable of _____ the pace for us.
8. He does not know how to _____ up the letter.
9. The boy _____ through the movie for two showings.
10. Sally is _____ the type now.
11. Mr. Bryant _____ the requirements for all stenographers.
12. _____ your machine for double spacing.
13. I _____ the clock for six o'clock.
14. Yesterday he _____ the milk bottle outside the door.
15. I like to _____ in that chair; it is very comfortable.

EXERCISE **26**   **TROUBLESOME VERBS II**

Fill in the blanks in the following sentences with the correct forms of *lay* or *lie*.

Example: Do not _____lay_____ the letters on the counter.

1. He _____ aside his plans and assumed the new job.
2. After the storm, the ship was _____ on its side.
3. As David stood on the hill, he saw the harbor _____ before him.
4. The cat _____ contentedly by the open fire.
5. The sleeping child seemed to be _____ in an awkward position.
6. I carefully _____ the wet paint brush on the paper.
7. The workmen _____ the carpet in three hours.
8. My pen was on the desk; it had been _____ there all morning.
9. It was necessary to get the rug to _____ straight before we could place the furniture.
10. _____ the letters on the desk as soon as they are completed.
11. The mason was _____ bricks for the patio.
12. After the earthquake, the city was _____ in ruins.
13. I am not tired; I do not wish to _____ down.
14. He was accused of "_____ down" on the job.
15. I don't think I can _____ such a proposal before Mr. Jones.

Fill in the blanks in the following sentences with the correct forms of *rise* or *raise*.

Example: The fish _____rose_____ to the bait.

1. Before such questions are _____, plans should be made for handling them.
2. The river _____ so rapidly that floods were inevitable.
3. The temperature _____ 20 degrees in an hour.
4. It was a difficult task for the committee to _____ $25,000.
5. The elevator _____ quickly to the ninth floor.

Fill in the blanks in the following sentences with the correct forms of *sit* and *set*.

Example: She did not want to _____sit_____ by the open window.

1. He _____ forth detailed instructions on the procedures that should be followed.
2. The dessert _____ quickly in the refrigerator.
3. He could not _____ in that chair; it was too uncomfortable.
4. Lee _____ impossible goals for himself.
5. I _____ near the 50-yard line at the football game.

SHALL/WILL; SHOULD/WOULD; MAY/MIGHT; CAN/COULD EXERCISE **27**

Underline the correct word in each set of parentheses.

Example: I (<u>shall</u>, will) read the chapter tonight.

1. Mr. Hughes (shall, will) not be in the office today.
2. I have not completed the report, but it (shall, will) be finished by five o'clock.
3. The assignment (shall, will) be due on Friday.

4. (May, Can) I telephone you about the matter?
5. I (should, would) have returned the book more quickly than I did.
6. My father promised that he (should would) take care of the matter.
7. All letters (should, would) be typed on letterhead stationery.
8. The handwriting is so illegible that I (cannot, may not) read the message.
9. You (shall, will) not have time to finish the income-tax form.
10. I (shall, will) do it tomorrow. (*a promise*)
11. This desk is a strong one; it (can, may) support the typewriter.
12. Mr. Shaw is determined that you (shall, will) be hired for the position.
13. I (could, might) give you an appointment at either four or five o'clock.
14. We (shall, will) take care of the matter promptly.
15. Either Mr. Scott or Mr. Lambert (shall, will) rewrite the report of the meeting.

EXERCISE **28**   **VERBALS I**

Underline the verbals in the following sentences; in the blanks to the right, identify the verbals as *gerunds, participles,* or *infinitives,* and give their part of speech.

	Verbal	*Part of Speech*
Example: I want to read this book.	infinitive	noun
1. I am unable to complete the letters by five o'clock.	_____	_____
2. Numbering the invoices required several hours of work.	_____	_____
3. The neatly typed report was lost in the mail.	_____	_____
4. I am able to take the dictation now.	_____	_____
5. I want to take the dictation now.	_____	_____
6. I do not believe he wants to quit his job.	_____	_____
7. Hurrying across the street, Mary slipped on the wet pavement.	_____	_____
8. We sent a check to pay the bill.	_____	_____
9. I heard him call.	_____	_____
10. By correcting the error, Mary was able to mail the letter.	_____	_____
	_____	_____
11. Jack and Jill Went up the hill To fetch a pail of water; Jack fell down And broke his crown And Jill came tumbling after.	_____	_____
	_____	_____

12. The sizzling steak was a gourmet's delight.   _____ _____

13. The private detective, aided by the obvious clues, quickly located the embezzler.   _____ _____

14. I gained a half hour by taking the shortcut.   _____ _____

15. Daydreaming, she decided, was a fine way to spend the afternoon.   _____ _____

VERBALS II

Verbal	Part of Speech

1. I wanted to see the new movie.   _____ _____

2. His plan, to pass the course by cheating, was somewhat like shooting elephants with a BB gun.

     _____ _____
     _____ _____
     _____ _____

3. The selling price of the diamond ring is twice the cost of it.   _____ _____

4. The old man passed the time by watching television.   _____ _____

5. I thought the story was an interesting, if unlikely, one.   _____ _____

6. Jan studies to raise her grades.   _____ _____

7. My sister is planning to leave on Friday for New York.   _____ _____

8. I watched the secretary operating the computer.   _____ _____

9. I am going to take the Civil Service examination.   _____ _____

10. The child, injured by a careless driver, is still in the hospital.   _____ _____

DANGLING PARTICIPLES

In the following sentences, underline the dangling participles and the words they modify. If there is more than one dangling participle in a sentence, underline the second and its modifier twice. Insert a caret between the two words where the participial phrase should be placed. If the sentence needs rewriting, use the blank line.

Example: ∧Joe∧ hit the child <u>swinging the bat with all his strength</u>. *The participial phrase can be placed either before or after Joe.*

1. Careening wildly down the highway, the motorist was unable to control his car.

_____

2. Crowded to capacity, the girl was unable to get on the bus.

_____

3. Mr. Rand worked frantically on the report, faced with a two-hour deadline.

_____

4. Jane could not see the movie, having lost her contact lenses.

_____

5. Striking midnight, Cinderella ran from the ballroom at the sound of the clock, losing her slipper.

_____

6. Breaking his leg in two places, the freshly waxed floor caused Mr. Davis to fall.

_____

7. Mary raced down the hill, riding on the skateboard.

_____

8. The library is not open in the evenings, causing problems for many students.

_____

9. Many famous paintings were donated to the museum, requiring more space than was available.

_____

10. Blinded by the headlights, the car plunged over the embankment.

_____

EXERCISE **31**   **POSSESSIVE CASE BEFORE GERUNDS**

Underline the correct word in each set of parentheses.

Example: Do you object to (him, <u>his</u>) going to Hawaii?

1. The clerk objected to (Jane, Jane's) asking for a sample.
2. The thief overheard (you, your) calling the police.
3. My employer disliked (me, my) leaving early.
4. The problem was solved by (Mr. Smith, Mr. Smith's) buying a new typewriter.

5. He was surprised at the (speaker, speaker's) understanding of the question.
6. There is no reason for (me, my) getting upset about the matter.
7. While I waited, I watched (him, his) arranging the material for the display.
8. The (Senator, Senator's) investigating the matter caused consternation.
9. (Bill, Bill's) whistling disturbed everyone in the office.
10. I heard (Betty, Betty's) telephoning for an appointment.
11. I bought the television set without (him, his) knowing about it.
12. I watched (him, his) typing the contract.
13. I saw (him, his) typing of the contract.
14. Mr. Hale was surprised at (us, our) leaving the decision to him.
15. (You, Your) winning the contest is almost impossible.

REVIEW OF NOUNS, PRONOUNS, AND VERBS

Underline the correct word in each set of parentheses.

Example: It (don't, <u>doesn't</u>) require much work to file the letters.

1. One of my friends (believe, believes) that the old mansion on the hill is haunted.
2. The stockings were (hung, hanged) by the chimney with care.
3. Neither Susan nor her friends (has, have) seen the movie.
4. The secretary (laid, lay) the letters on Mr. Smith's desk.
5. The dough (raised, rose) over the top of the pan.
6. My pen is the kind that (is, are) used by many stenographers.
7. His (mother-in-law's, mother's-in-law) house (sits, sets) on a hill overlooking the city.
8. This pen is one of those that (is, are) used by many stenographers.
9. His coat was folded and (laid, lain) on the back seat of the car.
10. (Is, Are) one of your instructors going to supervise the club?
11. The alumni (is, are) planning to (raise, rise) $50,000.
12. The store sells electric (knifes, knives) that (make, makes) carving quite easy.
13. The man (who, whom) (write, writes) the sports column in the paper is a former football player.
14. It was (he, him) (who, whom) you met in the park.
15. (Messrs., Mrs., Misters) Jones and Scott (is, are) planning to form a partnership.
16. I would not want to be (she, her) when Mr. Kirby discovers her mistake.
17. Put two (cupfuls, cupsful) of sugar in the bowl.
18. (Paul's, the tailor; Paul, the tailor's) shop is in the Jordan Building.
19. I thought Mr. Hull to be (he, him) (who, whom) called earlier.
20. I called Mr. Stewart (who, whom) I thought would be able to take care of the matter.
21. Either Mr. Mays or one of his assistants (check, checks) each order before it goes out.
22. The committee (is, are) meeting at (its, their) usual time.

23. Toast and jam (is, are) not enough for breakfast.
24. Over one half of the job applications (is, are) not legibly written.
25. The new air conditioner is one of the models that (is, are) thermostatic-ally controlled.
26. I want Pat and (she, her) to finish the mimeographing.
27. It was not (I, me) (who, whom) forgot to lock the door.
28. After the storm, the apples were (lying, laying) on the ground.
29. I (done, did) my report last night.
30. One half of the book (was, were) missing.
31. I could not find my car in (its, it's, its') usual place.
32. (Who's, Whose) pen are you using?
33. I object to (him, his) reading my letters.
34. (Senator Smith, Senator Smith's) voting for the measure is highly un-likely.
35. I saw (him, his) typing very quickly with only two fingers.
36. (You, Your, You're) being late made Mr. Miller quite angry.
37. I (should, would) be very glad if he (was, were) handling the matter.
38. Mr. Williams, as well as several other salesmen, (is, are) attending the convention in Los Angeles.
39. The letter from the employment agency, in addition to several carbon copies of Mr. Martin's letters, (was, were) missing from the files.
40. If I (was, were) (he, him), I should be more careful of typographical errors.
41. I thought you to be (he, him) (who, whom) took care of new accounts.
42. I cannot believe it was (she, her) (who, whom) I saw.
43. The missing papers were (laying, lying) in plain sight on (Mr. Ross', Mr. Ross's) desk.
44. My employer, (who, whom) I believe you met recently, is in Paris.
45. There (is, are) one of my sisters.
46. The switchboard operator and typist (is, are) Jane.
47. David, as well as his two brothers, (is, are) spending the summer in Europe.
48. He said that water (boils, boiled) at 212° Fahrenheit.
49. Jack (run, ran) around the track.
50. Someone left (his or her, their) book in the classroom.

EXERCISE **33**   **ADJECTIVES**

Write in the blank the correct degree of comparison of the adjective in parentheses.

Example: Her letters look (good) than mine do.   _____better_____

1. Of the two typewriters, I prefer the one with (small) type.   _____
2. Which city is the (large)—Los Angeles or Chicago?   _____
3. Betty is the (young) student in her class.   _____
4. The (tall) building in the United States is located in Chicago.   _____

5. I have (little) money than you have.   _____

6. This pen is the (bad) I have ever used.   _____

7. This assignment is (difficult) than the one I did yesterday.   _____

8. This new car is advertised as being (big), (fast), and (good) than any other car on the market.   _____
_____
_____

9. There must be a (good) way of solving the problem than the way you suggest.   _____

10. I thought the view of the mountains was the (beautiful) I had ever seen.   _____

11. The clown at the circus gave the (funny) performance I have ever seen.   _____

12. This book is (up-to-date) than the (early) edition.   _____
_____

13. The method you propose to use is (easy) than my method.   _____

14. Which of the Big Ten football teams has the (good) chance of playing in the Rose Bowl?   _____

15. The robbery must have been planned by the (clever) of thieves.   _____

Place hyphens in any adjectives that require them.

Example: I bought a <u>25-page</u> notebook.

1. The house was a three story, old fashioned, Victorian mansion.
2. Joan did a first rate job of typing the ten page manuscript.
3. The new one way streets caused confusion to motorists.
4. The two groups agreed to a sixty day cooling off period.
5. He constructed the radio from a do it yourself kit and a self teaching manual.
6. Do you plan to rent a three or four room apartment?
7. The credit manager called to remind us of our past due account.
8. Because I had not received a statement, I was not aware that the account was past due.
9. Mr. Dawson angrily paced back and forth in the small office.
10. Since it is a 45 inch box, it can be sent by fourth class mail.

In the following sentences, insert any words that are needed and cross out words that are not needed. If the sentence is correct, mark C in the blank at the right.

other
Example: My cat is older than any ∧ cat in the neighborhood.   ____

1. Of all my acquaintances, Susan is the most likely to become famous.   ____

2. Margaret plays tennis better than any girl in the class. ___

3. *The New York Times* is more widely read than any newspaper in the United States. ___

4. Of all my other friends, I like Tony the best. ___

5. Without a doubt, Miss Tracy is the best secretary I have ever had. ___

6. This machine is better than any machine we have tried. ___

7. When all of the other facts are considered, the need for reorganization is most urgent. ___

8. Of all the candidates, Mr. Shaw is the most likely choice for president. ___

9. Mr. Shaw has better qualifications than any candidate. ___

10. I learned more in that class than I learned in any class! ___

Correct any improperly used articles in the following sentences by (1) crossing out those that are not needed, (2) changing those that should be changed, or (3) supplying any missing articles. If the sentence is correct, mark C in the blank to the right.

Example: I shopped for a silk and a̸ cotton dress. (one dress) ___

1. Mr. Lane, the president and the manager, left at five o'clock. ___

2. I shopped for a silk and a cotton dress. (two dresses) ___

3. What kind of a plant is that? ___

4. The dog is characterized as "man's best friend." ___

5. The house and garage is on the north side of the street. ___

6. What style of a house are you building? ___

7. The president and the manager, Mr. Lane and Mr. Fredericks, left at five o'clock. ___

8. They wanted to form an union of the two companies. ___

9. The tiger is a handsome animal. ___

10. I bought a green and a white swimsuit. (one suit) ___

Underline the correct word in each set of parentheses.

Example: I like (this, these) pen for writing shorthand.

1. (That, Those) kind of injury does not heal quickly.

2. (This, These) varieties of trees are extremely hardy in cold climates.

3. I shall finish (them, those) letters as soon as I can.

4. (That, Those) sort of person is very dependable.

5. I cannot finish reading (them, those) books by Friday.

Underline the adjective clauses in these sentences. If any are misplaced, write the correct sentence on the blank line.

Example: I bought a coat for my mother <u>that is too small</u>.

<u>   I bought my mother a coat that is too small.   </u>

1. The fugitives needed a place where they could hide.

   _____

2. Do not use any abbreviations in your writing that cannot be easily understood.

   _____

3. He said that my overtime pay would be included in my weekly check, which is actually half of my salary.

   _____

4. Many of our company executives fly in private jet planes, who must travel a lot.

   _____

5. Writing is good writing that cannot be misunderstood.

   _____

ADVERBS

Underline the correct word in each set of parentheses.

Example: Jane does not type very (good, <u>well</u>).

1. I am (real, very) pleased about my new job.
2. This milk tastes (sour, sourly).
3. This car is (some, somewhat) bigger than your old car.
4. I felt (bad, badly) when I discovered that I had lost my watch.
5. The transistor radios were (bad, badly) made.
6. The music from the next apartment is (sure, surely) loud.
7. It was a (real, really) pleasure to see the ballet.
8. Production of our new equipment is going very (good, well).
9. It was (awful, very) late when Sue arrived at the office.
10. The chair is too new to be a (real, really) antique.
11. Mr. Kay worked (some, somewhat) faster than Mr. Steel.
12. The doctor quickly decided that Mr. Hale was not a (good, well) man.
13. It was (real, very) cold on Christmas morning.
14. It is (sure, surely) embarrassing to be in such a position.
15. Is there any (real, really) excuse for his conduct?
16. The slipper (easy, easily) fit Cinderella's foot.
17. The letters that she types always look (neat, neatly).

18. She (had, hadn't) scarcely time to finish the work.
19. The schedule for vacations (could, couldn't) hardly please everyone.
20. Mr. Jones did not want (anyone, no one) but Sally to take his dictation.

Insert carets in the following sentences to indicate the position of each adverb in parentheses. (The words in italics indicate what meaning the adverb has in the sentence.)

Example: ∧ He failed the course. (only) *No one else failed the course.*

1. Mr. Stevens teaches evening classes. (also) *In addition to other classes*
2. Mr. Stevens teaches evening classes. (only) *No other instructor teaches evening classes.*
3. Mr. Stevens teaches evening classes. (only) *Evening classes are all he teaches.*
4. The salesman said that he had one car for sale. (only) *No more than one*
5. I wrote to Mr. Wilson. (also) *In addition to other persons to whom I wrote*
6. He paid half the bill. (only) *That is all he paid.*
7. I wrote to Mr. Wilson. (also) *I was not the only person who wrote him.*
8. Mr. Curtis is late for work. (frequently)
9. I use that typewriter. (rarely)
10. My car will not start in the morning. (occasionally)
11. He spoke about the topic. (frankly)
12. He drove on the crowded freeway. (safely)

EXERCISE **35**   **REVIEW OF ADJECTIVES AND ADVERBS**

Correct any errors in the following sentences by rewriting the sentence on the blank line. If correct, mark C.

Example: This is the kind of a pen that is used for accounting.
_____This is the kind of pen that is used for accounting._____

1. I feel badly about Jane's resigning.

_____

2. This detergent is more economical than any detergent on the market.

_____

3. Of all the detergents on the market, this brand is the most economical.

_____

4. I am real glad that Jane is feeling some better today.

_____

5. She prepared a ham and cheese sandwich for lunch. (one sandwich)

_____

6. If I answer those letters, all of the correspondence will be up-to-date.

_____

7. Mr. Hayes only read the last paragraph of the letter. (*Meaning: He did not read all of the letter—just the last paragraph.*)

_____

8. I type badly when someone watches me.

_____

9. The company furnishes cars for Mr. Scott and Mr. Brown, but Mr. Scott's car is newest.

_____

10. Does the car have a four or a six cylinder engine?

_____

11. These kind of eraser works best.

_____

12. The newly formed chapter of the organization held a meeting at the Mountain Inn.

_____

PREPOSITIONS

EXERCISE **36**

Underline the correct word in each set of parentheses. Cross out any unnecessary prepositions within the sentences.

Example: (In, At) what city were you employed at?

1. Call me up when you know whether or not Jones is (at, to) work.
2. These totals do not correspond (to, with) my figures.
3. Mr. Lee always inquires (after, into) my father's health.
4. Where were you going to when you stopped to talk (with, to) Mr. Johnson?
5. He is able to converse intelligently (with, about) many subjects.
6. The work was divided (between, among) the three stenographers.
7. Miss Stevens wrote me (about, in regard to) the insurance.
8. I do not agree (to, with) Mr. Hale that the file should be inside of the office.
9. No one but Susan and (her, she) has access to the safe.
10. The book fell off of the shelf and (onto, in) the top of my desk.
11. He parted (from, with) the $10 reluctantly.
12. We can put the suitcase on the seat between you and (I, me).
13. He greatly disliked complying (to, with) the company's rules.
14. Go (in, into) the file room and get the Brown folder.

15. I thought he was angry (at, with) me for making the error.
16. I was graduated (at, from) the University of California in 1977.
17. We inquired (at, of) the service station for directions to Mary's house.
18. He is very skillful (in, with) adding long columns of figures.
19. This carbon paper is not adequate (for, to) typing many copies.
20. Whatever you wish to do, I shall abide (by, with) your decision.

Insert a caret in each of the following sentences to indicate the position of the prepositional phrase in parentheses.

Example: The rain fell∧all night. (without interruption)

1. I live in the white house at the end of the street. (with the red roof)
2. The pages were on my desk. (with all of the figures for the contract)
3. After his car ran out of gasoline, he walked to the gas station. (for two hours)
4. He climbed to rescue the cat. (over the fence)
5. Mary worked for four hours. (without stopping)

EXERCISE **37**   **CONJUNCTIONS**

Underline the correct word in each set of parentheses.

Example: I wanted to leave early, (and, <u>but</u>) it was not possible to do so.

1. My brother did not attend college (as, like) I hoped he would.
2. Neither Beth (nor, or) Janet has time to type the report.
3. There is no question (but what, that) he is working hard.
4. Please try (and, to) finish the work by four o'clock.
5. My sister looks (as, like) me.
6. (Because, Being that) this is her first job, she works slowly.
7. Do not use the phone (unless, without) Miss Scott gives you permission.
8. Not only Jane (and, but) Sarah looked for the letter.
9. He had hardly completed the work (but, when) his employer gave him another assignment.
10. You look (as if, like) you are ill.
11. He said that he would try (and, to) attend the meeting.
12. You may prefer that typewriter, (and, but) I prefer this one.

Correct any errors in the following sentences by rewriting the sentence on the blank line. If correct, write C.

Example: I think working with figures is easier than to write letters.
            <u>I think working with figures is easier than writing letters.</u>

1. I both wish him a Merry Christmas and a Happy New Year.

_____

2. To find the letter in the file and answering it took all afternoon.

_____

3. I have neither the time or the money to pursue the matter.

_____

4. He is one of those people who either know the answer or know where to find it.

_____

5. All the secretaries had not only extra work, but also many of the file clerks had additional tasks.

_____

6. When hiring new employees, we hope you will give our agency both the consideration that its reputation and record have earned.

_____

7. Joan is a pretty girl with red hair, and she has blue eyes.

_____

8. Being that there was a storm, I expected him to be late and that he would call me.

_____

9. That company has a good reputation for both honesty and fair dealing.

_____

10. I either want him to take care of the matter or to transfer it to someone else.

_____

REVIEW OF PREPOSITIONS AND CONJUNCTIONS   EXERCISE **38**

Underline the correct word in each set of parentheses.

Example: Either Betty (nor, <u>or</u>) Sue has the report.

1. I read in the paper (that, where) there will be a tax increase.
2. The child was frightened (by, of) the loud noise.
3. (Although, While) I planned to be on time for the appointment, I was ten minutes late.
4. He doubts (if, whether) he can finish the report by five o'clock.
5. We stepped (in to, into) the elevator as quickly as possible.
6. Mr. Lee works (at, in) Los Angeles, but he lives (at, in) Glendale.
7. It seems (as if, like) this plan is a good one.
8. He drove his car (on, on to, onto) the ferry.
9. The company wrote that it was unable to comply (to, with) my request.
10. If you buy our new dishwasher, you will be free (from, of) the drudgery of washing dishes by hand.
11. I made the decision (up on, upon) his recommendation.

12. (Since, Being that) you are in the office, perhaps Mr. Jones can see you.
13. I was angrier (at, with) John than I cared to admit.
14. (Before, Prior to) his appointment to this office, he worked in the mail room.

EXERCISE **39**   **REVIEW OF THE PARTS OF SPEECH I**

Underline the correct word in each set of parentheses.

Example: It was (he, him) who answered the phone.

1. His (fathers-in-law's, father-in-law's) car was damaged in the accident.
2. The recipe calls for two (cupsful, cupfuls) of sugar.
3. (Who's, Whose) typewriter was left uncovered?
4. Many (companys, companies) pay for life insurance for their employees.
5. The analyses of the product (was, were) quickly completed.
6. Neither Jane nor her sisters (know, knows) how to solve the problem.
7. Everyone should know (his or her, their) Social Security number.
8. Mary thought us to be (they, them).
9. I shall vote for (whoever, whomever) is nominated.
10. I shall vote for (whoever, whomever) I consider to be a good candidate.
11. (Betty's and Alice's, Betty and Alice's) mother is out of town.
12. Each club should write (its, their) own constitution.
13. It was not (I, me) who took the message.
14. It might have been (she, her) who took the message.
15. Do not (lay, lie) anything on the freshly painted desk.
16. Do you think you should (lay, lie) down before dinner?
17. This is one of the best books that (has, have) been published all year.
18. (We, Us) programmers would rather not work on Saturday.
19. He received one (weeks, week's, week) vacation this year.
20. There is no doubt about (his, him) getting the promotion.
21. You can depend on (my, me) being there.
22. The store attempted to collect its (past due, past-due) accounts.
23. Many a famous person (has, have) come from this area.
24. Jane is the person (who, whom) sorts the incoming mail.
25. (Who, Whom) do you think should attend the conference?
26. The key was (laying, lying) in the desk drawer.
27. He found Denver to be higher than (any, any other) city in Colorado.
28. You look (like, as if) you are tired.
29. Mr. Stanley gave (he, him) and (I, me) the supplies for the office.
30. The alumni (is, are) making plans for the reunion.
31. Either Nell or one of the students (is, are) studying late.
32. The bread is (raising, rising) quickly in the warm room.
33. I like to (sit, set) on the patio while I read the morning paper.
34. I (did, done) my assignment in a half hour.
35. (Karl's, the weaver; Karl, the weaver's) shop is four blocks away.
36. (This, Those) kinds of shoes are not comfortable.
37. Mr. Brown's daughter, as well as two of her friends, (is, are) getting a scholarship to the university.
38. The (children's, childrens') toys were (laying, lying) on the playground.

39. (Who's, Whose) car was stolen?
40. It cannot be (she, her) to whom Mr. Smith referred.
41. A number of changes (is, are) being made in the contract.
42. (Messrs., Mrs., Misters) Hill and Martin signed the agreement.
43. I did not know it was (he, him) who sent the telegram.
44. When the suit had been pressed, it was (laid, lain) carefully on the chair.
45. (Mary, Mary's) singing was pleasant to hear.
46. The secretary and treasurer (is, are) leaving early today.
47. I cannot finish (them, those) accounts by five o'clock.
48. What (kind of, kind of a) person would make such careless errors?
49. The chair felt (comfortable, comfortably) after sitting on the hard bench.
50. It was (real, very) late by the time I finished the work.
51. I felt (bad, badly) about breaking the vase.
52. (Being that, Since) I had an appointment, I could not stay for the meeting.
53. I was impatient (with, at) my employer.
54. I could not agree (with, to) his proposal for handling the matter.
55. Neither Jane (or, nor) Kate (is, are) in the office.
56. Of the many plans available, this is the (better, best).
57. The victim of the accident is (some, somewhat) better today.
58. He made arrangements with Bob and (he, him) to finish the extra work.
59. Every man and woman (is, are) willing to help.
60. I would not want to be (he, him).
61. (Who, Whom) do you think should become president?
62. Mr. Mason wanted Peg and (I, me) to make coffee.
63. The abandoned ship is (laying, lying) in the cove.
64. There were two (Harries, Harrys) in the class.
65. The (Lynch's, Lynches') house is at the end of the street.
66. My (boss', boss's) desk was covered with papers.
67. One of the salesmen (is, are) being promoted.
68. (Who, Whom) posted the notice on the bulletin board?
69. In Western movies the villain is often (hanged, hung).
70. I (haven't, havn't) read the morning paper.
71. He wrote me (in regard to, about) the invoice.
72. The (raising, rising) flood waters caused much anxiety.
73. It was not (they, them) whom you met.
74. The clerks, (he, him) among them, voted for a salary increase.
75. John is the (older, oldest) of the two boys.

REVIEW OF THE PARTS OF SPEECH II

EXERCISE 40

Underline the correct word in each set of parentheses.

Example: The jury reached (its, their) verdict in two hours.

1. Was it Mary and (he, him) (who, whom) you saw at the concert?
2. (Their, They) awarding us the contract is unlikely.
3. Anyone (who, whom) cannot finish the examination should give (his or her, their) name(s) to the instructor.

4. No one but (he, him) is permitted to visit the accident victim.
5. This book is one of those that (has, have) programmed exercises.
6. He (lay, laid) his swim trunks in the sun to dry.
7. Parentheses (is, are) often used around numbers in an outline.
8. (Who's, Whose) taking Mr. Lee's dictation?
9. Mr. Jones thought it would be (he, him) (who, whom) would receive the promotion.
10. Either Betty or one of the other secretaries (is, are) working Saturday.
11. At least one half of the students (is, are) absent today.
12. The curtain (raised, rose) promptly at eight o'clock.
13. Marian wrote both Mr. Lee and (he, him) (about, in regard to) the (past due, past-due) account.
14. Do not go (in, into) Mr. Tyler's office (unless, without) his permission.
15. He looked (as if, like) he was feeling (bad, badly).
16. Mr. Hill, Mr. Carter, and (I, me, myself) attended the conference.
17. Try (and, to) get a message to Mr. Hale.
18. Last year all employees received three (weeks, week's, weeks') vacation.
19. (Them, This, Those) kinds of trees are deciduous.
20. Every book and magazine (has, have) been returned to (its, their) place.
21. (Bill and Tom's, Bill's and Tom's) father is president of the bank.
22. This is one of the best references that (are, is) available.
23. Neither Sue nor her friends (is, are) going to the party.
24. My (brother-in-law's, brother's-in-law) car was stolen last night.
25. Joe was (laying, lying) on the floor in front of the television set.
26. Mrs. Martin can sit between you and (I, me).
27. I like this typewriter better than (any, any other) typewriter in the office.
28. The (newly-formed, newly formed) company is already making a profit.
29. The traffic noise is (sure, surely) loud.
30. I do not believe that ring has a (real, really) diamond in it.
31. I saw (him, his) running down the street.
32. It was not (she, her) (who, whom) was asked to make the speech.
33. Is that (he, him) by the door?
34. The clouds appeared to be (laying, lying) over the hills.
35. The stapler is not in (it's, its', its) usual place.
36. Miss Taylor said that she is feeling (some, somewhat) better today.
37. One of my friends (is, are) going to use my typewriter.
38. (Who, Whom) do you think should do the work?
39. A number of employees (is, are) on vacation.
40. I do not think you can depend on (him, his) taking care of the matter.
41. The company made (its, their) usual financial report.
42. The (Smith's, Smiths') house (sits, sets) on a hill above the city.
43. The cost of living is (raising, rising) steadily.
44. The unpopular leader was (hanged, hung) in effigy.
45. Are you angry (at, with) me?
46. The two girls helped (each other, one another) with the work.
47. This author is a (well known, well-known) authority on the subject.
48. (Fewer, Less) typing errors were made by Amy than by Nan.
49. No one but (her, she) knows the combination of the safe.
50. It could not have been (he, him) (who, whom) I saw in the elevator.

END-OF-SENTENCE PUNCTUATION

Supply any periods, exclamation points, and question marks needed in the following sentences. Circle any punctuation marks not needed. (Some of the sentences may be correct.)

Example: I asked if Mr. Lee would call me(?).

1. May we hear from you promptly.
2. Mr. J. M. Lane is the new president, isn't he
3. What time will the meeting start   six o'clock   seven o'clock   eight o'clock
4. Please return the enclosed form.
5. The secretary called at 4 P.M..
6. Will you please send us the order blanks by November 1?
7. Congratulations   You have won a television set
8. Do you think Mr. Lynn will return by five o'clock
9. I wonder whether Mr. Lynn will return by five o'clock
10. That story is a true one, is it not
11. I doubt that Mr. Gray is in his office
12. I think I owe Jones and Company $50(?).
13. Park College for Women began classes in 1900. (*This year may not be correct.*)
14. Act immediately   Tomorrow may be too late
15. Ask Mr. James for the key to the files!
16. Please ask Mr. Ramsey if he will see me?
17. What color is your new car   red   blue   white
18. No   I shall never go there again
19. I am not sure when I can finish the work
20. I wonder if you would please return the form to me

COMMAS THAT SEPARATE

In the following sentences, insert the missing commas. (Some of the sentences may be correct.)

Example: The new ten-story building was finished last fall, and it was completely occupied before Christmas.

1. Mr. Kay is out of the office but he said that he expected to return by five o'clock.
2. I saw many beautiful tables lamps and chairs at the furniture store.
3. In 1983 our company sold five hundred air-conditioning units.
4. We wish to fill your order promptly but it is impossible to do so.
5. I read two books four magazines and several newspapers while on vacation.
6. Our customer wrote that he had not received his order and that he needed it immediately.
7. I cannot give you Mr. Thompson's telephone number but will call you as soon as I find it.
8. This key unlocks the doors to Mr. Scott's office the reception room and the supply room.

9. Doctor Hall did not say when he would return nor did he leave a number where he could be reached.
10. Birthdays anniversaries holidays etc. can be remembered by using our calendar pad.
11. This special plastic typing shield helps make erasing easier quicker and neater.
12. His life-long ambition was to own the biggest shiniest and brightest automobile in town.
13. No one uses the manual typewriter for everyone prefers the new electric.
14. I walked across the campus and bought a new notebook at the bookstore.
15. I walked across the campus through the library and up the steps of the Chemistry Building.
16. Mr. James paid for the invoice by Check No. 500 but he later stopped payment on it.
17. Janet typed the letters Mr. Scott signed them and Beth mailed them at five o'clock.
18. The receptionist told me that Mr. Carr was out of town and that he would not return until Monday.
19. The children shouted laughed and sang on the playground.
20. In 1930 the company was near bankruptcy but it now has assets of over a million dollars.

EXERCISE **43** **COMMAS THAT SET OFF**

In the following sentences, insert any missing commas.

Example: When in Rome, do as the Romans do.

1. If you do not accept this offer immediately you will lose the opportunity of a lifetime!
2. My uncle who is retiring in June has worked thirty years for one company.
3. You will I think find the booklet that we sent you most interesting.
4. Mr. Adams who will be out of the office until Friday left detailed instructions for signing the contract.
5. Because Mr. Adams will be out of the office until Friday he left detailed instructions for signing the contract.
6. This is not after all a matter that I think is of great importance.
7. As the amount involved is so small Mr. Harper we are sure you have forgotten to send us your check.
8. All returns must be filed by Friday April 15 in order to avoid penalties.
9. John Russell Jr. lives in Pittsburgh Pennsylvania; his father John Russell Sr. lives in Pittsburg California.
10. Sitting high on a hill the house commands a spectacular view of the city.
11. When I heard the phone ring I knew that Janet would answer it.

12. I received an A on the first test; on the second test a B; and on the third a D.
13. Inside the house was alive with people who seemed to be rushing in all directions.
14. Before Mr. Ash returns and after Mr. Shaw gives you the information type a rough draft of the report.
15. This report as you probably know must be finished by Monday July 31.

ALL COMMAS

EXERCISE **44**

In the following sentences, insert the missing commas. (Some of the sentences may be correct.)

Example: This is not, I believe, the best way to handle the matter.

1. Jones and Wellington Ltd. and Scott Manufacturing Company Inc. are the companies handling our product.
2. If we do not hear from you by Friday Mr. Hastings it will be necessary to turn your account over to our attorneys.
3. Fortunately we are in a position to settle this matter immediately.
4. You have placed our company its stockholders and its employees in an awkward position.
5. I do not believe that assuming these figures are correct the costs could have been so high.
6. We have not heard from Mr. Jason and doubt that we will.
7. My sister Janet who is employed in New York was here recently.
8. However unless Mr. Mason signs the letters immediately it will be too late to get them into the outgoing mail.
9. The sales contract containing many complicated clauses was not signed by the customer.
10. Paintings lithographs etchings etc. were on display in the gallery.
11. June 30 1984 and July 31 1984 were mentioned as possible meeting dates.
12. Mr. Brady made 25 percent of the total sales; Mr. Harris 18 percent; and Mr. Wills 13 percent.
13. This is not as you know the best way of handling the situation.
14. To leave the office early Jerry had to work through the lunch hour.
15. The old dilapidated building will soon be torn down and replaced by a new up-to-date one.
16. I wanted to get to the meeting early but the traffic was so heavy that this was impossible.
17. Before the secretary left she covered the typewriter and locked her desk.
18. At any rate Mr. Watson you will be pleased to know that our product lives up to our advertising claims.
19. Mr. Hill who recently left our company is now working in Chicago.
20. The girl crossed the street while the light was red and nearly caused an accident.

EXERCISE **45** **COMMAS AND SEMICOLONS**

In the following sentences, insert any commas and semicolons that are necessary.

Example: Reno, Nevada; Boise, Idaho; Spokane, Washington; and Portland, Oregon, are west of the Rockies.

1. This is the best pen for writing shorthand however it is no longer being manufactured.
2. I do not believe Mr. Perry wrote that letter in fact I am sure he did not.
3. The letters dated January 21 1983 March 21 1983 May 29 1983 and August 17 1983 are missing from the file.
4. Careless errors for example typographical errors omission of words and uneven margins are inexcusable.
5. It is inexcusable to have careless errors for example typing errors omission of words and uneven margins.
6. When Mr. Dawson returns ask him to call me for it is necessary that he sign the contract before five o'clock.
7. I must find Mr. Dawson immediately he did not sign the contract.
8. The check is for $50,000 however unless it is presented for payment by July 1 it will be worthless.
9. After Mr. Sherman read the mail he said that he would dictate the letters and that he would sign them before he left.
10. Marian did not read the directions therefore she had difficulty using the machine.
11. Since Connie is ill today it will be necessary for someone else to take Mr. Lee's dictation for it is important that his mail be answered promptly.
12. The shipment was not in the afternoon delivery we do not know where it is.
13. His typing errors are transposition errors that is *hte* for *the ofr* for *for* and *fo* for *of.*
14. Friday October 29 Saturday October 30 and Monday November 1 are the dates of our annual sale.
15. Molly did not file the Morrison letters nevertheless she found them quickly for Mr. Hanna.

EXERCISE **46** **QUOTATION MARKS, COLON, DASH, PARENTHESES**

Supply any missing punctuation marks in the following sentences.

Example: "You are old," said the youth, "and your jaws are too weak
For anything tougher than suet
Yet you finished the goose with the bones and the beak—
Pray, how did you manage to do it?"

—LEWIS CARROLL

1. Collection letters Mr. Parker wrote should be carefully planned before they are dictated. They should also he continued be read very carefully before they are signed and mailed.

2. He did not say that he had not done the work he said that he would not do it.
3. I stopped abruptly I could not believe what I saw when I entered the room that was devastated by the fire.
4. Did he say George is late for work again (*direct quotation*)
5. Mrs. Evans told the editors the following story When Winston Churchill was criticized on a printer's proof for having ended a sentence with a preposition he is supposed to have commented This is the sort of impertinence up with which I will not put.
6. While you were at the Louvre did you see the Mona Lisa
7. I follow this plan always proofread a letter before it is removed from the typewriter.
8. The question that was used in the examination was taken from the text see page 94
9. Please omit the following items from the report paragraph 6 page 8 paragraph 2 page 12 paragraph 1 page 20.
10. Abraham Lincoln paraphrased the Bible Mark 3 25 when he said A house divided against itself cannot stand.
11. Mrs. Palmer asked Did you proofread the letter to Mr. Rhodes before you signed it
12. Mr. Day told his secretary Do not ever mail a letter without first checking all names and addresses Then he added In fact it would be a good idea to check names and addresses on anything that is written.

REVIEW OF ALL PUNCTUATION I

EXERCISE **47**

Supply any missing punctuation marks in the following sentences.

Example: I do not want to write the letter now; but if I do not do it, the mail will not go out on time.

1. Mr Richards is not in his office is he
2. I cannot find the letter that gives the amount of the invoice but I am sure that it was filed recently
3. I shall continue to look for the letter and when I find it I shall give it to you immediately
4. There were pens clips bands erasers etc lying on the desk
5. My friend Julie who is Mr Wilson's secretary is taking her vacation in Hawaii
6. To finish the dictation Jane worked until seven o'clock
7. The dates that the reports are due are March 31 1983 June 30 1983 September 30 1983 and December 31 1983
8. When you finish typing the report give the original to Mr Flint and a copy to Mr Kane
9. I was not as you know able to see Miss Lambert the assistant buyer but I did see Mrs Rath who is Miss Lambert's secretary
10. The speaker ended his report by saying In closing ladies and gentlemen I wish to thank you for the time you have taken to listen to my speech
11. A number of our top employees for example Miss Roberts Mr Hall and Mr Benton resigned this year

12. Did Mr Morse say that he was calling a meeting of the Executive Committee on Friday

13. No he said that the meeting would be held a week from Friday and that he would notify all members by mail

14. The office closes at five o'clock therefore the letters should be signed and ready to be mailed by that time

15. The price of the stock increased 5 points in the first quarter in the second quarter 4 points and in the third quarter 8 points

16. It is not possible Mr Warner wrote to get your entire shipment to you before December 1 by ordinary delivery therefore I suggest he continued that you authorize us to ship to you by air express any items that you need immediately

17. The building contained one modern three-bedroom apartment one luxurious penthouse and three studio apartments

18. He typed the same error through the report that is e for i

19. Please fill out the application blank see the attached form before returning it

20. On December 1 1984 our company will celebrate its twenty-fifth anniversary

21. Two of our best customers Jones and Brown Inc and Robert Hall Ltd did not receive copies of our latest catalog

22. Mr James dictated We sent you the following telegram Send two dozen black typewriter ribbons immediately

23. If you cannot read the dictation you should ask Mr Evans to dictate more slowly

24. He said that he would attend the meeting and that he would make a report of what took place

25. Our new product which was introduced six months ago is proving to be most successful

EXERCISE **48   REVIEW OF ALL PUNCTUATION   II**

1. I read in the paper that General Davis is coming to our school and that he will speak to the student body

2. However late you are call me when you return from the meeting

3. Our products Mr Weston wrote are available in most hardware stores however if you are unable to obtain them in the store nearest you write direct to our regional office

4. On January 1 our firm was ten years old

5. On January 1 1983 our firm was ten years old

6. My father who retired recently is sixty-five years old

7. To read back her notes Julie had to write slowly

8. To read back shorthand notes is not always easy

9. If this total is not correct I shall have to check two pages of entries

10. His itinerary included stops in Santa Fe New Mexico Denver Colorado Oklahoma City Oklahoma and Austin Texas

11. As a matter of fact it was not my intention to sign the contract

12. The letter contained three misspelled words four typographical errors and two comma errors

13. The person who typed that letter obviously did not proofread it
14. In January he withdrew $50 from his account in February $75 and in March $100
15. I cannot attend the meeting on Friday can you
16. Did Mr Adams dictate answers to those letters or did he ask his secretary to answer them
17. Diane who is Mr Wilson's secretary took her vacation in June and Jean who is Mr Page's secretary took her vacation in July
18. I heard Mr Baker ask Can you type this letter by five o'clock
19. Two of the salesmen Mr Lynn and Mr Carson did not receive copies of the memo
20. I do not believe Mr Conrad that you want your subscription to expire
21. If you cannot do the work or if you do not have time to do it ask Barbara to help you
22. Peg did not make the error nevertheless she corrected it for Mr Burns
23. The special-delivery letter has not been received we do not know what could have happened to it
24. I proofread the letter when I was tired and did not find the error
25. Janet was tired irritable and angry by the time the work was finished

CAPITALIZATION I

In the following sentences, underline each word that should be capitalized or that is incorrectly capitalized.

Example: Alice is a Secretary in a large Corporation, Standard manufacturing company.

1. Mr. james stayed at the davenport hotel, which was built last Fall and is across the Street from mr. corbett's office.
2. On friday, october 19, mr. patrick will leave on a united airlines plane for washington, d. c.
3. the republican party held its convention in san francisco; the democratic party held its convention in atlantic city.
4. The city of new york paid the expenses for its mayor last Spring when he attended a meeting sponsored by the united nations.
5. My program for the summer session will include courses in typing, business english, spanish, and geography.
6. The address typed on the envelope read: mr. james grant, president; grant & martin; 2031 ninth avenue; denver, co 41678.
7. mr. scott is the sales manager for the Company; mrs. jameson is the assistant buyer.
8. mr. rogers is a Salesman for Williams & Brown, a Company that sells Office Equipment in the pacific northwest, the southwest, the midwest, and all areas West of the Mississippi.
9. The City of Portland is located on both the Willamette and Columbia Rivers.
10. The decision in the matter was upheld by the federal courts.
11. The Vice President quoted the bible in his speech before The House of Representatives.

12. mr. cain said, "do not remove the letters from the File."
13. the subject of Federal Taxes was discussed in mr. elliott's book, *The American Constitution.*
14. when I read shakespeare I am struck with wonder
    That such trivial people should muse and thunder
    in such lovely language.

                                                    —D. H. LAWRENCE

EXERCISE **50**   **CAPITALIZATION   II**

1. mr. johnson is Production Manager of the atlantic publishing company and travels extensively throughout the southwest.
2. the letter began with this salutation, "My Dear Mr. Hastings"; it ended with "Very Sincerely Yours."
3. The report bore the title "Ways and Means Of Handling Office Correspondence."
4. Betty bought Coffee, Milk, Kleenex, Coca Cola, and Potato Chips at the Grocery Store.
5. I wanted to study both French History and American Literature this summer.
6. The racehorse man o' war was also known as big red.
7. All federal appointments for that Office must be approved by mr. craig, who is the Director.
8. In order to get to salt lake city, it was necessary to travel over highways 5 and 80.
9. My employer wrote, "we cannot find a record of receiving either order no. 475 or order no. 476."
10. The City of Spokane is East of the City of Seattle.

EXERCISE **51**   **CAPITALIZATION   III**

1. Across the Street from our house is a Shell Oil Company Station.
2. Mr. Martin's job as District Supervisor is a federal appointment.
3. Our local Department Store is holding its annual Summer clearance sale.
4. I paid the monthly statement with my Check no. 276.
5. All entering Freshmen are expected to take courses in english, american history, and health.
6. All entering Freshmen are expected to take english composition, history of the americas, and elements of health.
7. I heard mr. martin ask, "when are the Expense Accounts from the Sales representatives due?"
8. The letter was addressed "My Dear Sir" instead of "Dear Mr. King" as mr. hale dictated.
9. The four horsemen of notre dame have no connection with the cathedral in paris!
10. The Range of mountains to the East is called the Blue Mountains.

11. The story about george washington throwing a Dollar across the potomac river is probably no more true than the one about his cutting down a Cherry Tree.
12. The Invitation was printed in italic type and written in french.
13. What ship was nicknamed old ironsides? i think it was The Constitution.
14. The Nurse in the Doctor's Office told us that Doctor Allen was on vacation.
15. To some new yorkers, the west is any part of the united states west of the allegheny mountains.

NUMBERS AND ABBREVIATIONS I   EXERCISE **52**

In the following sentences, underline any words that contain errors in the writing of numbers or abbreviations.

Example: <u>80</u> people attended the <u>5</u> o'clock meeting on <u>Jan.</u> <u>sixteenth</u>.

1. 100 people paid five dollars each to attend the 1st reunion of the Class of Sixty Four.
2. On January 14th the note for five hundred dollars will be due.
3. The interest for 1 year at six percent will amount to $30.00.
4. Mr. Scott lives at Forty West 33d St.; he has lived there for fifteen yrs.
5. The building costs of a mile of Highway Eighty could be as much as $3 million.
6. After July 22d my address will be 12 E. 7th St., Chicago, Ill. 46130.
7. The meeting will begin at 8:15 and will be held in the 1st National Bank Bldg., 214 N. Tenth St., Sacramento.
8. Order Number 71268 was shipped Feb. 10th to: Mr. James Turner, Junior; 252 E. Seventy-fifth St.; Saint Louis, Mo. It was sent C.O.D.
9. Doctor Wilson holds office hours from two until six o'clock every day except Sun.
10. On page three of Policy Number 21438 his age at that time was given as twenty years, three months, and 27 days.
11. Over 500 people answered the newspaper ad. that offered a 50% discount on all paperback books.
12. The date on the 1st Baptist Church read 1955 A.D.
13. Miss. Thompson, Mr. Lowry, and Doctor Taylor did not leave the bldg. until 7:30 o'clock.
14. 5 lbs. of coffee were used by members of the Y.M.C.A. at a recent meeting.
15. Mr. Harris issued Check #250 to pay Invoice #95 for seventy-five dollars.
16. ½ of the people who came to hear Dr. Phillips speak left early.
17. Put three five-cent stamps on a letter to that destination.
18. June's birthday is Oct. 25; she will be 23 years old on her next birthday.
19. Our co. was started over 50 years ago with 3 employees and five thousand dollars.
20. I did not think the no. on the order was important.

NUMBERS AND ABBREVIATIONS II

1. The address was typed "4032 S.E. 3d St."; it should have been "4032 Third St., S.E."
2. Our Check #400 for 25 dollars was issued Jan. 3.
3. Almost 1,000 people came to the park to celebrate the 4th of July.
4. If the dept. store is offering a discount of 50% on typewriters, will they accept trade-ins?
5. The bridge across the Saint Chas. River required 4 years to build and cost two million $.
6. John was born in N.Y. City on Thurs., Nov. 14, 1940.
7. He lives on W. Walnut Dr., but I do not know the house no.
8. Gen. Jones will speak at the commencement exercises that were 1st scheduled to begin at 2 o'clock but are now planned to begin at 4.
9. Over ⅓ of the graduates from this h.s. will attend the nearby university.
10. On the 1st pg. of the letter, the amt. due was given as two hundred and fifty dollars; on the 2d pg., two hundred and forty dollars.
11. When Tom is 21 years old, he will inherit twenty thousand dollars.
12. On August first we will move to our new offices in the Fulton St. Bldg., located at Ten Fulton St.
13. The 2d mortgage on the property is for $50,000, at fourteen percent interest, for a period of 10 years. It is held by the Amer. Bldg. and Loan Assn.
14. Mr. Wm. Hastings, Senior, is president of the co. He will retire next year after 40 years of service.
15. 10 men will be needed at 3 o'clock to distribute one thousand circulars.

ONE-WORD, TWO-WORD, AND HYPHENATED FORMS

Rewrite correctly any incorrect compound words below by hyphenating, or by writing as one or two words.

Example: over look ___overlook___

1. under taking _____	19. airmail _____
2. nonparticipating _____	20. allright _____
3. somewhere _____	21. under take _____
4. can not _____	22. mean while _____
5. re-enter _____	23. withstand _____
6. with-hold _____	24. over paid _____
7. self-confident _____	25. outlook _____
8. semi-indirect _____	26. in-board _____
9. out-going _____	27. nonstandard _____
10. everybody _____	28. anyhow _____
11. antipersonnel _____	29. worth while _____
12. to-morrow _____	30. semigloss _____
13. in as much as _____	31. postmaster _____
14. our selves _____	32. pre-empt _____
15. re-call _____	33. pre-Islamic _____
16. no one _____	34. percent _____
17. over all _____	35. co-ordinate _____
18. anyone _____	

EXPRESSIONS TO AVOID

Underline the correct expression in each set of parentheses.

Example: I do not know (as to whether, <u>whether</u>) the shipment was sent airmail.

1. (Attached, Attached herewith) is my check for $75.
2. Would you (please, be good enough to) answer all questions on the form.
3. Mr. Scott (has, is a man who has) been elected to his office four times.
4. Please send us your check (when, if and when) you receive the merchandise.
5. We will turn your account over to our attorney (if, in the event that) we do not hear from you.
6. We (often, oftentimes) find that our customers forget to enclose their checks.
7. (The above, The above-mentioned, These) products are sold only by our authorized dealers.
8. Please let us know whether it is possible to ship the order (immediately, at your earliest convenience).
9. (Mr. Davis and/or his secretary, Either Mr. Davis or his secretary) will take care of the matter.
10. (During, In the course of) our conference, many questions were answered.
11. The (party, person) who handles such matters is out of town.
12. (After, Subsequent to) his promotion, he no longer handled the account.

WORDS OFTEN CONFUSED

Underline the correct word in each set of parentheses.

Example: I could not (<u>choose</u>, chose) between the two dresses.

1. No one (accept, except) the secretaries is permitted in the supply room.
2. (Passed, Past) experience proved that she was right.
3. Please (bare, bear) in mind that our product is the best on the market.
4. The (capital, capitol) of Idaho is Boise.
5. The building (cite, sight, site) is west of the town.
6. The (wait, weight) of the gem is two (carats, carets, carrots).
7. I do not know (weather, whether) his (advice, advise) is good or bad.
8. The (principal, principle) speaker at the convention spoke on the (affect, effect) of automation.
9. A (role, roll) call vote will be necessary to show (weather, whether) the resolution will be (passed, past).
10. We purchased the property from the Howard (Reality, Realty) Company.
11. The (wait, weight) of the shipment did not (vary, very) from previous shipments.
12. Ready-to-(ware, wear) clothing is sold in most department stores.
13. Let me (complement, compliment) you on the efficient manner in which you typed the report.

14. (There, Their, They're) books are over (there, their, they're).
15. (Capital, Capitol) punishment is no longer in (affect, effect) in many states.
16. The state's (consul, council, counsel) on traffic safety (formally, formerly) met in a room of the (capital, capitol); it now meets in the Highway Building.
17. The (addition, edition) of two secretaries will eliminate much of the overtime work.
18. The (erasers, erasures) on the page are badly made; perhaps the typist needs a new (eraser, erasure).
19. (Access, Excess) to the land was obtained by crossing a creek.
20. (Anyone, Any one) of the salesmen could call on the customer.
21. For (sometime, some time) I have been looking for a secretary.
22. This (maybe, may be) a difficult problem to solve.
23. Doctor Lynn is (always, all ways) prompt in keeping his appointments.
24. The children were (altogether, all together) on the playground.
25. Jane was (already, all ready) late for an appointment when the phone rang.
26. The (loose, lose, loss) of the file will (loose, lose, loss) much time for our company.
27. Mr. Jacobs, who is an (eminent, imminent) attorney, is very (adapt, adept, adopt) in the courtroom.
28. I cannot (advice, advise) you in this matter.
29. He was (conscience, conscious) of a great deal of confusion in the office.
30. The work will not be finished for quite (sometime, some time).

EXERCISE **57** **WORD DIVISION**

In the blanks below, indicate by a diagonal mark where each word can be divided. If a word cannot be divided, write *No* in the blank.

Examples: self-esteem ____self-/esteem____
away _____No_____

1. length _____
2. separate _____
3. beginning _____
4. considerable _____
5. couldn't _____
6. followed _____
7. awhile _____
8. $2,500 _____
9. importance _____
10. parity _____
11. carelessness _____
12. occurrence _____
13. short-term _____
14. sensible _____
15. alleviation _____
16. overcome _____
17. thought _____
18. convenient _____
19. SEATO _____
20. moved _____

REVIEW I

This letter contains a number of different kinds of errors (spelling, punctuation, grammar, letter form, abbreviation, capitalization, numbers). Find the errors and type the corrected letter in *square-block* style with open punctuation.

March 12, 19--

Hill and Scott Inc.
3487 -- One Hundred and Fifth St.
New York, N.Y. 10025
Attn; John McCoy, Personel Manger

Dear Gentlemen,
   I am glad to recommend Miss. Ann Douglas about who you inquired in you letter of Feb. 28.
   Miss. Douglas worked in this Department of our Company as a Secy from June 1976 to Dec. 1977. She left are firm 'to except a better position.
   We found Miss. Douglass to be a acurrate, and rapid secretary. She was inteligent, and assumed responsability easily. We are real sure that she can adept to all most any office situation, and that she will be a valueable em-ployee.
   While Miss. Douglas worked for are firm she and another Secretary deviced a plan for solving one of the filing problems that caused us much lose of time. We are, in fact still using there system.
   I hope that this letter will help you reach a favorable decision conserning Miss. Douglas. If I can supply furthur information I shall be happy to do so.

Very Sincerly Yrs.,

Mr. David L. Baxter
Accounting Division

DLB/xx

EXERCISE **59** **REVIEW II**

Find the errors in this letter; then type the corrected letter in *full-block* style with mixed punctuation.

January 17, 19—

Mr. Thomas M. West
1721 7th Street
San Francisco, Calif. 94140

Dear Sir

On January 7th 1977 you wrote us regarding some property that we had listed for sale. This property which is a 5-acre cite lays approximately 2 mi. West of San Deigo California and is owned by Roger Willis Jr. We replied giving you a complete description of the property including the price and terms for purchase. We also inclosed pictures of the property.

In February of that year Mr. Hall one of our represenatives showed you the property. Since you desided at that time that the property was to expensive we did not persue the matter. Now the owner of the property has desided that he must sell even if it means taking a loss he has therefore cut the price by 20% so that the orignal price of 750,000 dollars is now 600,000 dollars. You relize we are sure that this is a real low price. Real estate prices have not decreased in the passed year in fact in most instances they are actually higher. This cut has been made to merely speed the owner sale of the property.

We are giving you the first opportunity of purchasing this property. Should you still be intrested call Mr. Hall at (619) 461-2900 as soon as possible. He can supply any information, and will be expecting to here from you.

Very truly yours,
Wilson Reality Company

President
ABW/xx
Enclosure

REVIEW III

Find the errors in this letter; then type the corrected letter in *modified-block* style with mixed punctuation.

July 1st, 19—

Mr. A. B. Davis
Pleasant Valley, Wisconsin 53560

Dear Sir;
   We are writing you about our annual 50-pg. booklet, Complete forcast of World Events, which as you probable no is published every July. This booklet is prepared by the editorial staff of this magazine, directed by Mr. J. M. Ray Jr. a well known authority on national and inter-national affairs. This years addition is especially valueable because it covers next Fall's national elections. The booklet discusses the backgrounds of the candidates and assesses their chances for election. Also included is an intriguing report on our Countrys military expenditures and our predictions as to how taxes will be effected by them this year.
   Because you are a subscriber to our magazine, we are extending to you an oppurtunity to order this booklet before it is offered to the public. Just return the inclosed card in the convient postage payed envelope along with one dollar for your reserved copy. If we do not here from you within 10 days, we shall assume that you are not intrested and that you do not want us to hold a copy for you.
   Don't delay: Order now!

                              Very truly yours
                              WORLD EVENTS

                              Circulation Manager

ABR/jm

Key to Exercises

EXERCISE 1　KINDS OF SENTENCES

1. simple
2. simple
3. compound-complex　*Clauses:* to whom you wrote—*adj.;* if I can—*adv.*
4. complex　*Clause:* When Mr. Curtis returns—*adv.*
5. compound
6. complex　*Clause:* which has 87 rooms—*adj.*
7. complex　*Clause:* whom I can trust—*adj.*
8. simple
9. complex　*Clause:* that Mr. Gray was out of the office—*noun*
10. complex　*Clauses:* However late you are—*adv.;* when you return—*adv.*
11. complex　*Clause:* that I saw last night—*adj.*
12. complex　*Clauses:* that he would call me—*noun;* that I should wait for the call—*noun*

EXERCISE 2　SENTENCE FAULTS

1. fragment
   The important customer has been kept waiting in the outer office.
2. comma splice
   I cannot find the Maxwell file; however, I think it has been misplaced in the file.
3. comma splice
   Mary said that she looked for the file yesterday; she also said that she could not find the Martin file.
4. C
5. fused (run-together) sentence
   Although we recently purchased new filing equipment, we seem to have trouble locating files. Our filing supervisor will try to correct the problems.
6. C
7. fragment
   The supervisor plans to improve the filing system.
8. fragment
   Because the supervisor has had many years of experience, she should be able to devise a more efficient system.
9. fused (run-together) sentence
   The filing system for our company must be able to store a large number of records. Many employees use the files every day.

10. comma splice

 The files contain our records for the past ten years; we need to be able to find records quickly and easily.

EXERCISE 3   CHOICE OF PRONOUNS

1. This	6. I	11. That
2. me	7. that	12. him
3. Those	8. his or her	13. which
4. one another	9. each other	14. Those
5. this	10. his	15. their

EXERCISE 4   PLURALS OF NOUNS   1

1. plural	datum		11. plural	mouse
2. singular	alumni		12. singular	turkeys
3. singular	sisters-in-law		13. singular	halves
4. singular	Mses.		14. plural	safe
5. plural	self		15. plural	fox
6. either	none		16. singular	lunches
7. singular	F.O.B.'s		17. singular	vetoes
8. singular	cupfuls		18. plural	businesswoman
9. singular	Marys		19. singular	none
10. singular	companies		20. singular	branch managers

EXERCISE 5   PLURALS OF NOUNS   II

1. plural	boss		11. singular	none
2. singular	universities		12. plural	none
3. singular	chimneys		13. plural	appendix
4. singular	analyses		14. plural	staff
5. singular	portfolios		15. singular	district managers
6. either	none		16. plural	bookcase
7. singular	attorneys general (or		17. singular	lives
	attorney generals)		18. singular	Joneses
8. plural	#		19. singular	airlines
9. singular	teaspoonfuls		20. plural	potato
10. plural	bunch			

EXERCISE 6   GENDER, PERSON

1. masculine	she	6. masculine	Mmes. (Mesdames)	1. **1**	6. **3**
2. masculine	businesswoman	7. masculine	hostess	2. **1**	7. **3**
3. feminine	alumnus	8. neuter	none	3. **2**	8. **3**
4. feminine	him	9. feminine	groom	4. **1**	9. **3**
5. masculine	sister	10. masculine	landlady	5. **3**	10. **3**

EXERCISE 7 CASE OF PERSONAL PRONOUNS I

1. they	8. she	17. they	26. We	35. we	44. he
2. she	9. them	18. them	27. he	36. him	45. they
I	10. he	19. me	28. him	37. him	46. her
3. her	11. him	20. her	29. us	38. she	47. him
4. I	12. he	21. me	30. her	39. she	48. her
5. they	13. he	22. me	31. she	40. her	49. us
we	14. they	23. he	32. me	41. him	50. him
6. him	15. she	24. me	33. him	42. her	
7. me	16. I	25. her	34. I	43. He	
		him			

EXERCISE 8 CASE OF PERSONAL PRONOUNS II

1. her	6. me	11. him	16. us	21. him	26. he
2. We	7. him	12. him	17. she	22. her	27. her
3. she	8. he	13. I	18. she	23. him	28. we
4. I	9. I	14. she	19. he	24. I	29. him
5. me	10. him	15. me	20. him	25. her	me
				him	30. he

EXERCISE 9 CASE OF PERSONAL PRONOUNS III

1. I	5. her	8. we	13. her	17. him	22. I
2. us	6. I	9. him	him	18. him	23. me
3. she	7. he	10. she	14. he	19. she	24. her
4. he	I	11. her	15. myself	20. I	25. her
		12. me	16. I	21. me	
		me			

EXERCISE 10 POSSESSIVES OF NOUNS I

1. company's	companies'	14. accountant's	accountants'
2. editor in chief's	editors in chief's	15. wife's	wives'
3. season's	seasons'	16. year's	years'
4. man's	men's	17. hostess'	hostesses'
5. attorney's	attorneys'	18. Henry's	Henrys'
6. sister's	sisters'	19. stenographer's	stenographers'
7. sheriff's	sheriffs'	20. committee's	committees'
8. boss's	bosses'	21. army's	armies'
9. businesswoman's	businesswomen's	22. month's	months'
10. nation's	nations'	23. architect's	architects'
11. vice president's	vice presidents'	24. child's	children's
12. doctor's	doctors'	25. fox's	foxes'
13. employee's	employees'		

EXERCISE 11   POSSESSIVES OF NOUNS II

1. actress'	actresses'	14. baby's	babies'
2. lady's	ladies'	15. policeman's	policemen's
3. navy's	navies'	16. merchant's	merchants'
4. brother's	brothers'	17. mouse's	mice's
5. week's	weeks'	18. father's	fathers'
6. calf's	calves'	19. professor's	professors'
7. airline's	airlines'	20. racketeer's	racketeers'
8. secretary's	secretaries'	21. family's	families'
9. lawyer's	lawyers'	22. astronaut's	astronauts'
10. wolf's	wolves'	23. student's	students'
11. girl's	girls'	24. gentleman's	gentlemen's
12. dog's	dogs'	25. stepson's	stepsons'
13. ballplayer's	ballplayers'		

EXERCISE 12   POSSESSIVE PRONOUNS

1. my	1. Whose
2. hers	2. Who's
3. your	3. Whose
4. his	4. Who's
5. their	5. Who's
6. his	
7. Our	
8. our	
9. yours	
10. Their	

EXERCISE 13   AGREEMENT I

1. its	7. her	13. are	20. was
2. its	8. are	14. his	its
3. his or her	9. were	15. are	21. his
4. his or her	10. is	16. is	22. is
5. are	11. is	17. are	23. is
they	his	18. were	24. is
6. their	12. are	19. is	25. are
		his or her	

EXERCISE 14   AGREEMENT II

1. his or her	6. are	11. has	17. was	22. have
his or her	7. was	12. are	18. is	23. has
2. was	8. has	13. was	19. are	24. has
3. were	its	14. are	20. is	25. its
4. are	9. is	15. their	21. he or she	
5. has	10. have	16. were	signs	

EXERCISE 15   AGREEMENT   III

1. decides	8. was
2. is	9. know
3. are	10. is
4. is	11. is
5. are	12. teach
6. knows	13. has
has	14. are
7. are	15. has

EXERCISE 16   WHO/WHOM   I

1. who	11. who	21. who	31. whom	41. whom
2. who	12. who	22. whom	32. whom	42. who
3. who	13. Who	23. who	33. whom	43. who
4. Whom	14. whom	24. who	34. whom	44. who
5. who	15. whom	25. who	35. whom	45. whom
6. who	16. who	26. who	36. Who	46. who
7. Who	17. who	27. whom	37. who	47. who
8. who	18. whom	28. who	38. who	48. whom
9. Whom	19. whom	29. whom	39. who	49. Whom
10. who	20. who	30. whom	40. who	50. who

EXERCISE 17   WHO/WHOM   II

1. Who	7. who	13. Who	19. who	25. who
2. who	8. whom	14. who	20. Whoever	26. who
3. who	9. Who	15. Whoever	21. whoever	27. whom
4. who	10. who	16. who	22. who	28. who
5. Whom	11. who	17. whom	23. Whom	29. Who
6. whom	12. who	18. whomever	24. Whoever	30. Whoever

EXERCISE 18   REVIEW OF PRONOUNS

1. me	9. I	17. whom	26. who
2. his or her	10. me	18. who	his or her
3. We	11. I	19. whom	27. his
4. she	12. she	20. who	28. her
who	13. he	21. who	29. he
5. who	who	22. they	who
his or her	14. them	whom	30. whoever
6. him	me	23. its	
who	15. she	24. her	
7. he	whom	25. he	
who	16. who	who	
8. she	his or her		

EXERCISE 19   VERBS AND VERB PHRASES

1. was seen
2. Have, read
3. walked
4. played, laughed

5. dictated, typed
6. has been dictating
7. do, want

8. shall have finished
9. did, believe, had finished
10. taught

EXERCISE 20   TRANSITIVE/INTRANSITIVE   I

1. takes dictation, T
2. sets, I
3. received, bill, T
4. contained, addresses, T
5. were, I
6. do, have, paper, T
7. am, I
8. is, I
9. laid, papers, T
10. arrives, I

11. did, believe, story, T
12. begins, I
13. Close, door, T
14. was, I
15. made, speech, T
16. is, I
17. were, I
18. does, need, papers, T
19. rang, I
20. rose, I

EXERCISE 21   TRANSITIVE/INTRANSITIVE   II

1. rolled, I
2. rolled stone, T
3. began, I
4. began concert, T
5. Check figures, T
6. are, I
7. Whom did, see, T
8. waited, I
9. left, books, T
10. left, I

11. am, I
12. was, I
13. needs, ribbon, T
14. were, I
15. laid, letters, T
16. lay, I
17. is, I
18. looks, I
19. saw myself, T
20. is, I

EXERCISE 22   VERB TENSE

1. dived
2. begun
3. froze
4. grew
5. left

6. spoke
7. chosen
8. hung
9. rose
10. lent

EXERCISE 23   ACTIVE AND PASSIVE VOICE   I

1. Read, A
2. read, A
3. should be read, P
4. is posted, P
5. drove, A
6. drove, A

7. is bringing, A
8. brought, A
9. were brought, P
10. were made, P
11. received, A
12. have been made, P

13. have made, A
14. am finishing, A
15. was finished, P
16. finished, A

17. grew, A
18. are growing, A
19. planted, A
20. was planted, P

EXERCISE 24   ACTIVE AND PASSIVE VOICE II

1. was offered, P
2. begins, A
3. has been said, P
4. waited, A
5. was found, P

6. found, A
7. was, A
8. set, A
9. was laid, P
10. was lying, A

EXERCISE 25   TROUBLESOME VERBS I

1. Lie
2. lying
3. Lay
4. lain
5. lay
6. laid
7. Lay
8. lay (or lies)
9. lay
10. lain

11. laid
12. lying
13. laid
14. laid
15. laying
16. lay (or lies)
17. lying
18. lying
19. lay (or lies)
20. laid

21. lay (or lies)
22. laid
23. lay
24. laid
25. lay
26. lying
27. lies
28. lying
29. lying
30. laid (or lay)

1. raise
2. risen
3. raised
4. rising
5. rose
6. rise
7. raising
8. rise

9. risen
10. raise
11. raised
12. raising
13. raise
14. rise
15. raise

1. sits (or sat)
2. set
3. sat
4. set
5. sitting
6. sit
7. setting
8. set

9. sat
10. setting
11. set
12. Set
13. set
14. set
15. sit

EXERCISE 26   TROUBLESOME VERBS II

1. laid
2. lying
3. lying
4. lay (or lies)
5. lying

6. laid
7. laid
8. lying
9. lie
10. Lay

11. laying
12. lying
13. lie
14. lying
15. lay

1. raised
2. rose
3. rose
4. raise
5. rose

1. set
2. set (or sets)
3. sit
4. set (or sets)
5. sat

EXERCISE 27   SHALL/WILL; SHOULD/WOULD; MAY/MIGHT; CAN/COULD

1. will
2. will

3. will
4. May

5. should   11. can
6. would   12. shall
7. should   13. could
8. cannot   14. shall
9. will   15. will
10. will

EXERCISE 28   VERBALS I

1. to complete	infinitive	adverb
2. numbering	gerund	noun
3. typed	participle	adjective
4. to take	infinitive	adverb
5. to take	infinitive	noun
6. to quit	infinitive	noun
7. Hurrying	participle	adjective
8. to pay	infinitive	adverb
9. call	infinitive (*To* is understood.)	adjective
10. correcting	gerund	noun
to mail	infinitive	adverb
11. To fetch	infinitive	adverb
tumbling	participle	adjective
12. sizzling	participle	adjective
13. aided	participle	adjective
14. taking	gerund	noun
15. Daydreaming	gerund	noun
to spend	infinitive	adjective

EXERCISE 29   VERBALS II

1. to see	infinitive	noun		5. interesting	participle	adjective
2. to pass	infinitive	noun		6. to raise	infinitive	adverb
cheating	gerund	noun		7. to leave	infinitive	noun
shooting	gerund	noun		8. operating	participle	adjective
3. selling	participle	adjective		9. to take	infinitive	adverb
4. watching	gerund	noun		10. injured	participle	adjective

EXERCISE 30   DANGLING PARTICIPLES[1]

1. <u>Careening wildly down the highway</u>, the motorist was unable to control his car∧.
2. <u>Crowded to capacity</u>, the girl was unable to get on the <u>bus</u>∧.
3. ∧<u>Mr. Rand</u>∧ worked frantically on the report, <u>faced with a two-hour deadline</u>.
4. ∧<u>Jane</u>∧ could not see the movie, <u>having lost her contact lenses</u>.

---

[1] Some of these sentences might be better written by changing the participial phrase to another kind of adjective modifier.

5. Striking midnight, ∧Cinderella∧ ran from the ballroom at the sound of the <u>clock</u>∧, <u>losing her slipper</u>.
6. <u>Breaking his leg in two places</u>, the freshly waxed floor caused <u>Mr. Davis</u> to fall∧.
7. ∧<u>Mary</u>∧ <u>raced down the hill</u>, <u>riding on the skate board</u>.
8. The library is not open in the evenings, <u>causing problems for many students</u>.
That the library is not open in the evenings causes problems for many students.
9. Many famous paintings were donated to the museum, <u>requiring more space than was available</u>.
The many famous paintings donated to the museum required more space than was available.
10. <u>Blinded by the headlights</u>, the car plunged over the embankment.
Blinded by the headlights, the driver plunged the car over the embankment.

EXERCISE 31   POSSESSIVE CASE BEFORE GERUNDS

1. Jane's	6. my	11. his
2. you	7. him	12. him
3. my	8. Senator's	13. his
4. Mr. Smith's	9. Bill's	14. our
5. speaker's	10. Betty	15. Your

EXERCISE 32   REVIEW OF NOUNS, PRONOUNS, AND VERBS

1. believes	17. cupfuls	36. Your
2. hung	18. Paul, the tailor's	37. should
3. have	19. him	were
4. laid	who	38. is
5. rose	20. who	39. was
6. is	21. checks	40. were
7. mother-in-law's	22. is	he
sits	its	41. him
8. are	23. is	who
9. laid	24. are	42. she
10. Is	25. are	whom
11. are	26. her	43. lying
raise	27. I	Mr. Ross's
12. knives	who	44. whom
make	28. lying	45. is
13. who	29. did	46. is
writes	30. was	47. is
14. he	31. its	48. boils
whom	32. Whose	49. ran
15. Messrs.	33. his	50. his or her
are	34. Senator Smith's	
16. she	35. him	

EXERCISE 33   ADJECTIVES

1. smaller	6. worst	9. better	13. easier
2. larger	7. more difficult	10. most beautiful	14. best
3. youngest	8. bigger	11. funniest	15. cleverest
4. tallest	faster	12. more up-to-date	
5. less	better	earlier	

1. three-story, old-fashioned	6. three- four-room
2. first-rate ten-page	7. past-due
3. one-way	8. past-due
4. sixty-day cooling-off	9. *None*
5. do-it-yourself self-teaching	10. 45-inch fourth-class

1. C	other
other	6. any∧machine
2. any∧girl	7. *Cross out* other.
other	8. C
3. any∧newspaper	other
4. *Cross out* other.	9. any∧candidate
5. C	other
	10. any∧class

1. *Cross out* the *before* manager.	6. *Cross out* a.
2. C	7. C
3. *Cross out* a.	8. *Change* an *to* a.
4. C	9. C
5. C	10. *Cross out* a *before* white.

1. That	3. those	5. those
2. These	4. That	

1. The fugitives needed a place <u>where they could hide</u>. C
2. Do not use any abbreviations in your writing <u>that cannot be easily understood</u>.
   <u>In your writing do not use any abbreviations that cannot be easily understood.</u>
3. He said that my overtime pay would be included in my weekly check, <u>which is actually</u>
   <u>half of my salary.</u>
   <u>He said that my overtime pay, which is actually half of my salary, would be included in</u>
   <u>my weekly check.</u>
4. Many of our company executives fly in private jet planes, <u>who must travel a lot.</u>
   <u>Many of our company executives, who must travel a lot, fly in private jet planes.</u>
5. Writing is good writing <u>that cannot be misunderstood.</u>
   <u>Writing that cannot be misunderstood is good writing.</u>

EXERCISE 34   ADVERBS

1. very	6. surely	11. somewhat	16. easily
2. sour	7. real	12. well	17. neat
3. somewhat	8. well	13. very	18. had
4. bad	9. very	14. surely	19. could
5. badly	10. real	15. real	20. anyone

1. Mr. Stevens teaches evening classes∧.
2. ∧Mr. Stevens teaches evening classes.
3. Mr. Stevens teaches∧ evening classes (or∧).
4. The salesman said that he had∧one car for sale.
5. I wrote to Mr. Wilson∧.
6. He paid∧half the bill.
7. I∧wrote to Mr. Wilson.
8. Mr. Curtis is∧late for work.
9. I∧use that typewriter.
10. ∧My car (or∧) will not start in the morning.
11. He spoke∧about the topic.
12. He drove∧over the crowded freeway.

EXERCISE 35   REVIEW OF ADJECTIVES AND ADVERBS

1. I feel bad about Jane's resigning.
2. This detergent is more economical than any other detergent on the market.
3. C
           (or really)
4. I am very∧glad that Jane is feeling somewhat better today.
5. C
6. C
7. Mr. Hayes read only the last paragraph of the letter.
8. C
9. The company furnishes cars for Mr. Scott and Mr. Brown, but Mr. Scott's car is newer.
10. Does the car have a four- or a six-cylinder engine?
11. This kind of eraser works best.
12. C

EXERCISE 36   PREPOSITIONS

1. at *Cross out* up.	11. with
2. to	12. me
3. after	13. with
4. with *Cross out the first* to.	14. into
5. about	15. with
6. among	16. from
7. about	17. at
8. with *Cross out* of.	18. in
9. her	19. for
10. onto *Cross out the first* of.	20. by

1. I live in the white house∧at the end of the street.
2. The pages∧were on my desk.
3. After his car ran out of gasoline, he walked∧to the gas station.
4. He climbed∧to rescue the cat.
5. Mary worked∧for four hours.

EXERCISE 37   CONJUNCTIONS

1. as	4. to	7. unless	10. as if
2. nor	5. like	8. but	11. to
3. that	6. Because	9. when	12. but

1. I wish him both a Merry Christmas and a Happy New Year.
2. Finding the letter in the file and answering it took all afternoon.
   or To find the letter in the file and to answer it took all afternoon.
3. I have neither the time nor the money to pursue the matter.
4. C
5. Not only all the secretaries had extra work, but also many of the file clerks had additional tasks.
6. When hiring new employees, we hope you will give our agency the consideration that both its reputation and record have earned.
7. Joan is a pretty girl with red hair and blue eyes.
8. Since there was a storm, I expected him to be late and to call me.
   or Since there was a storm, I expected that he would be late and that he would call me.
9. C
10. I want him either to take care of the matter or to transfer it to someone else.

EXERCISE 38   REVIEW OF CONJUNCTIONS AND PREPOSITIONS

1. that	8. onto
2. by	9. with
3. Although	10. from
4. whether	11. upon
5. into	12. Since
6. in	13. with
in	14. Before
7. as if	

EXERCISE 39   REVIEW OF THE PARTS OF SPEECH I

1. father-in-law's	10. whomever	18. We	27. any other
2. cupfuls	11. Betty and	19. week's	28. as if
3. Whose	Alice's	20. his	29. him
4. companies	12. its	21. my	me
5. were	13. I	22. past-due	30. are
6. know	14. she	23. has	31. is
7. his or her	15. lay	24. who	32. rising
8. them	16. lie	25. Who	33. sit
9. whoever	17. have	26. lying	34. did

35. Karl, the weaver's	44. laid	55. nor is	65. Lynches'
36. Those	45. Mary's	56. best	66. boss's
37. is	46. is	57. somewhat	67. is
38. children's lying	47. those	58. him	68. Who
39. Whose	48. kind of	59. is	69. hanged
40. she	49. comfortable	60. he	70. haven't
41. are	50. very	61. Who	71. about
42. Messrs.	51. bad	62. me	72. rising
43. him	52. Since	63. lying	73. they
	53. with	64. Harrys	74. he
	54. to		75. older

EXERCISE 40   REVIEW OF THE PARTS OF SPEECH   II

1. he whom	13. him about past-due	22. are	37. is
2. Their		23. are	38. Who
3. who his or her	14. into without	24. brother-in-law's	39. are
4. him	15. as if bad	25. lying	40. his
5. have	16. I	26. me	41. its
6. laid	17. to	27. any other	42. Smiths' sits
7. are	18. weeks'	28. newly formed	43. rising
8. Who's	19. Those	29. surely	44. hanged
9. he who	20. has its	30. real	45. with
10. is	21. Bill and Tom's	31. him	46. each other
11. are		32. she who	47. well-known
12. rose		33. he	48. Fewer
		34. lying	49. her
		35. its	50. he whom
		36. somewhat	

EXERCISE 41   END-OF-SENTENCE PUNCTUATION

1. C
2. . . . isn't he?
3. . . . start? six o'clock? seven o'clock? eight o'clock?
4. C
5. . . . 4 P.M. ⊙
6. . . . November 1 ⑦.
7. Congratulations! . . . set.
8. . . . five o'clock?
9. . . . five o'clock.
10. . . . is it not?
11. . . . office.
12. . . . $50 ⑦.
13. . . . 1900 (?).
14. . . . immediately! . . . late.
15. . . . files ①.
16. . . . see me ⑦.

17. . . . new car? red? blue? white?
18. No! . . . again!
19. . . . work.
20. . . . to me.

EXERCISE 42   COMMAS THAT SEPARATE

1. Mr. Kay is out of the office, but he said that he expected to return by five o'clock.
2. I saw many beautiful tables, lamps,[1] and chairs at the furniture store.
3. C
4. We wish to fill your order promptly, but it is impossible to do so.
5. I read two books, four magazines,[1] and several newspapers while on vacation.
6. C
7. C
8. This key unlocks the doors to Mr. Scott's office, the reception room,[1] and the supply room.
9. Doctor Hall did not say when he would return, nor did he leave a number where he could be reached.
10. Birthdays, anniversaries, holidays, etc., can be remembered by using our calendar pad.
11. This special plastic typing shield helps make erasing easier, quicker,[1] and neater.
12. His life-long ambition was to own the biggest, shiniest,[1] and brightest automobile in town.
13. No one uses the manual typewriter, for everyone prefers the new electric.
14. C
15. I walked across the campus, through the library,[1] and up the steps of the Chemistry Building.
16. Mr. James paid for the invoice by Check No. 500, but he later stopped payment on it.
17. Janet typed the letters, Mr. Scott signed them,[1] and Beth mailed them at five o'clock.
18. C
19. The children shouted, laughed,[1] and sang on the playground.
20. In 1930 the company was near bankruptcy, but it now has assets of over a million dollars.

EXERCISE 43   COMMAS THAT SET OFF

1. If you do not accept this offer immediately, you will lose the opportunity of a lifetime!
2. My uncle, who is retiring in June, has worked thirty years for one company.
3. You will, I think, find the booklet that we sent you most interesting.
4. Mr. Adams, who will be out of the office until Friday, left detailed instructions for signing the contract.
5. Because Mr. Adams will be out of the office until Friday, he left detailed instructions for signing the contract.
6. This is not, after all, a matter that I think is of great importance.
7. As the amount involved is so small, Mr. Harper, we are sure you have forgotten to send us your check.
8. All returns must be filed by Friday, April 15, in order to avoid penalties.

[1] optional comma

9. John Russell, Jr., lives in Pittsburgh, Pennsylvania; his father, John Russell, Sr., lives in Pittsburg, California.
10. Sitting high on a hill, the house commands a spectacular view of the city.
11. When I heard the phone ring, I knew that Janet would answer it.
12. I received an A on the first test; on the second test, a B; and on the third, a D.
13. Inside, the house was alive with people who seemed to be rushing in all directions.
14. Before Mr. Ash returns and after Mr. Shaw gives you the information, type a rough draft of the report.
15. This report, as you probably know, must be finished by Monday, July 31.

EXERCISE 44 ALL COMMAS

1. Jones and Wellington, Ltd., and Scott Manufacturing Company, Inc., are the companies handling our product.
2. If we do not hear from you by Friday, Mr. Hastings, it will be necessary to turn your account over to our attorneys.
3. Fortunately, we are in a position to settle this matter immediately.
4. You have placed our company, its stockholders,[1] and its employees in an awkward position.
5. I do not believe that, assuming these figures are correct, the costs could have been so high.
6. C
7. My sister Janet, who is employed in New York, was here recently.
8. However, unless Mr. Mason signs the letters immediately, it will be too late to get them into the outgoing mail.
9. The sales contract, containing many complicated clauses, was not signed by the customer.
10. Paintings, lithographs, etchings, etc., were on display in the gallery.
11. June 30, 1979, and July 31, 1979, were mentioned as possible meeting dates.
12. Mr. Brady made 25 percent of the total sales; Mr. Harris, 18 percent; and Mr. Wills, 13 percent.
13. This is not, as you know, the best way of handling the situation.
14. To leave the office early, Jerry had to work through the lunch hour.
15. C
16. I wanted to get to the meeting early, but the traffic was so heavy that this was impossible.
17. Before the secretary left, she covered the typewriter and locked her desk.
18. At any rate, Mr. Watson, you will be pleased to know that our product lives up to our advertising claims.
19. Mr. Hill, who recently left our company, is now working in Chicago.
20. C

EXERCISE 45 COMMAS AND SEMICOLONS

1. This is the best pen for writing shorthand; however,[1] it is no longer being manufactured.
2. I do not believe Mr. Perry wrote that letter; in fact,[1] I am sure he did not.

[1] optional comma

3. The letters dated January 21, 1977; March 21, 1977; May 29, 1977; and August 17, 1977, are missing from the file.
4. Careless errors—(*or ,*) for example, typographical errors, omission of words,[1] and uneven margins—(*or ,*) are inexcusable.
5. It is inexcusable to have careless errors; for example, typing errors, omission of words,[1] and uneven margins.
6. When Mr. Dawson returns, ask him to call me; for it is necessary that he sign the contract before five o'clock.
7. I must find Mr. Dawson immediately; he did not sign the contract.
8. The check is for $50,000; however,[1] unless it is presented for payment by July 1, it will be worthless.
9. After Mr. Sherman read the mail, he said that he would dictate the letters and that he would sign them before he left.
10. Marian did not read the directions; therefore,[1] she had difficulty using the machine.
11. Since Connie is ill today, it will be necessary for someone else to take Mr. Lee's dictation; for it is important that his mail be answered promptly.
12. The shipment was not in the afternoon delivery; we do not know where it is.
13. His typing errors are transposition errors; that is, *hte* for *the*, *ofr* for *for*,[1] and *fo* for *of*.
14. Friday, October 29; Saturday, October 30; and Monday, November 1, are the dates of our annual sale.
15. Molly did not file the Morrison letters; nevertheless,[1] she found them quickly for Mr. Hanna.

EXERCISE 46 QUOTATION MARKS, COLON, DASH, PARENTHESES

1. "Collection letters," Mr. Parker wrote, "should be carefully planned before they are dictated. They should also," he continued, "be read very carefully before they are signed and mailed."
2. He did not say that he had not done the work; he said that he would not do it.
3. I stopped abruptly—I could not believe what I saw—when I entered the room that was devastated by the fire.
4. Did he say, "George is late for work again"?
5. Mrs. Evans told the editors the following story: "When Winston Churchill was criticized on a printer's proof for having ended a sentence with a preposition, he is supposed to have commented, 'This is the sort of impertinence up with which I will not put.'"
6. While you were at the Louvre, did you see the "Mona Lisa"?
7. I follow this plan: always proofread a letter before it is removed from the typewriter.
8. The question that was used in the examination was taken from the text (see page 94). *Or* . . . text. (See page 94.)
9. Please omit the following items from the report: paragraph 6, page 8; paragraph 2, page 12; paragraph 1, page 20.
10. Abraham Lincoln paraphrased the Bible (Mark 3:25) when he said, "A house divided against itself cannot stand."
11. Mrs. Palmer asked, "Did you proofread the letter to Mr. Rhodes before you signed it?"
12. Mr. Day told his secretary, "Do not ever mail a letter without first checking all names and addresses." Then he added, "In fact, it would be a good idea to check names and addresses on anything that is written."

[1] optional comma

EXERCISE 47 REVIEW OF ALL PUNCTUATION I

1. Mr. Richards is not in his office, is he?
2. I cannot find the letter that gives the amount of the invoice, but I am sure that it was filed recently.
3. I shall continue to look for the letter; and when I find it, I shall give it to you immediately.
4. There were pens, clips, bands, erasers, etc., lying on the desk.
5. My friend Julie, who is Mr. Wilson's secretary, is taking her vacation in Hawaii.
6. To finish the dictation, Jane worked until seven o'clock.
7. The dates that the reports are due are March 31, 1983; June 30, 1983; September 30, 1983; and December 31, 1983.
8. When you finish typing the report, give the original to Mr. Flint and a copy to Mr. Kane.
9. I was not, as you know, able to see Miss Lambert, the assistant buyer; but I did see Mrs. Rath, who is Miss Lambert's secretary.
10. The speaker ended his report by saying: (or ,) "In closing, ladies and gentlemen, I wish to thank you for the time you have taken to listen to my speech."
11. A number of our top employees—(or ,) for example, Miss Roberts, Mr. Hall,[1] and Mr. Benton—(or ,) resigned this year.
12. Did Mr. Morse say that he was calling a meeting of the Executive Committee on Friday?
13. No, he said that the meeting would be held a week from Friday and that he would notify all members by mail.
14. The office closes at five o'clock; therefore, the letters should be signed and ready to be mailed by that time.
15. The price of the stock increased 5 points in the first quarter; in the second quarter, 4 points; and in the third quarter, 8 points.
16. "It is not possible," Mr. Warner wrote, "to get your entire shipment to you before December 1 by ordinary delivery; therefore, I suggest," he continued, "that you authorize us to ship to you by air express any items that you need immediately."
17. The building contained one modern three-bedroom apartment, one luxurious penthouse,[1] and three studio apartments.
18. He typed the same error throughout the report; that is, "e" for "i." (In print, e and i may appear in italics.)
19. Please fill out the application blank (see the attached form) before returning it.
20. On December 1, 1983, our company will celebrate its twenty-fifth anniversary.
21. Two of our best customers, Jones and Brown, Inc., and Robert Hall, Ltd., did not receive copies of our latest catalog.
22. Mr. James dictated, "We sent you the following telegram: 'Send two dozen black typewriter ribbons immediately.'"
23. If you cannot read the dictation, you should ask Mr. Evans to dictate more slowly.
24. He said that he would attend the meeting and that he would make a report of what took place.
25. Our new product, which was introduced six months ago, is proving to be most successful.

---

[1] optional comma

EXERCISE 48 REVIEW OF ALL PUNCTUATION II

1. I read in the paper that General Davis is coming to our school and that he will speak to the student body.
2. However late you are, call me when you return from the meeting.
3. "Our products," Mr. Weston wrote, "are available in most hardware stores; however, if you are unable to obtain them in the store nearest you, write directly to our regional office."
4. On January 1 our firm was ten years old.
5. On January 1, 1983, our firm was ten years old.
6. My father, who retired recently, is sixty-five years old.
7. To read back her notes, Julie had to write slowly.
8. To read back shorthand notes is not always easy.
9. If this total is not correct, I shall have to check two pages of entries.
10. His itinerary included stops in Santa Fe, New Mexico; Denver, Colorado; Oklahoma City, Oklahoma; and Austin, Texas.
11. As a matter of fact, it was not my intention to sign the contract.
12. The letter contained three misspelled words, four typographical errors,[1] and two comma errors.
13. The person who typed that letter obviously did not proofread it.
14. In January he withdrew $50 from his account; in February, $75; and in March, $100.
15. I cannot attend the meeting on Friday, can you?
16. Did Mr. Adams dictate answers to those letters, or did he ask his secretary to answer them?
17. Diane, who is Mr. Wilson's secretary, took her vacation in June; and Jean, who is Mr. Page's secretary, took her vacation in July.
18. I heard Mr. Baker ask, "Can you type this letter by five o'clock?"
19. Two of the salesmen, Mr. Lynn and Mr. Carson, did not receive copies of the memo.
20. I do not believe, Mr. Conrad, that you want your subscription to expire.
21. If you cannot do the work or if you do not have time to do it, ask Barbara to help you.
22. Peg did not make the error; nevertheless, she corrected it for Mr. Burns.
23. The special-delivery letter has not been received; we do not know what could have happened to it.
24. I proofread the letter when I was tired and did not find the error.
25. Janet was tired, irritable,[1] and angry by the time the work was finished.

EXERCISE 49 CAPITALIZATION I

The following words—shown here correctly capitalized or lower cased—should be underlined:

1. James, Davenport Hotel, fall, street, Mr. Corbett's
2. Friday, October, Mr. Patrick, United Airlines, Washington, D.C.
3. The, Republican Party, San Francisco, Democratic Party, Atlantic City
4. New York, spring, United Nations
5. English, Spanish

[1] optional comma

6. Mr. James Grant, President, Grant, Martin, Ninth Avenue, Denver, CO
7. Mr. Scott, company, Mrs. Jameson
8. Mr. Rogers, salesman, company, office equipment, Pacific Northwest, Southwest, Midwest, west
9. city, rivers
10. Federal
11. Bible, the
12. Mr. Cain, Do, file
13. The, taxes, Mr. Elliott's
14. When, Shakespeare, In

EXERCISE 50   CAPITALIZATION   II

1. Mr. Johnson, production manager, Atlantic Publishing Company, Southwest
2. The, dear, sincerely yours
3. of
4. coffee, milk, potato chips, grocery store
5. history, literature
6. Man War, Big Red
7. Federal, office, Mr. Craig, director
8. Salt Lake City, Highways
9. We, Order No., Order No.
10. city, east, city

EXERCISE 51   CAPITALIZATION   III

1. street, station
2. Martin's, district supervisor, Federal
3. department store, summer
4. No.
5. freshmen, English, American
6. freshmen, English Composition, History, Americas, Elements, Health
7. Mr. Martin, When, expense accounts, sales representatives
8. (the first) dear, Mr. Hale
9. Four Horsemen, Notre Dame, Paris
10. range, east
11. George Washington, dollar, Potomac River, cherry tree
12. invitation, French
13. Old Ironsides, I, the
14. nurse, doctor's office
15. New Yorker, West, United States, Allegheny Mountains

EXERCISE 52   NUMBERS AND ABBREVIATIONS   I

These words should be underlined:

1. 100, five dollars, 1st, Sixty Four
2. 14th, five hundred dollars
3. 1, six, $30.00
4. Forty, 33d, St., yrs.
5. Eighty
6. 22d, E. 7th St., IL

7. 1st, Bldg., N., St.
8. Number, Feb. 10th, Junior, E. Seventy-fifth, St., Saint, MO
9. Sun.
10. three, Number, twenty, three
11. 500, ad., %
12. 1st, A.D. (*goes before year*)
13. Miss., bldg., o'clock
14. 5 lbs.
15. #, #, seventy-five dollars
16. 1/2, Dr.
17. three
18. Oct, 23
19. co., 50, 3, five thousand dollars
20. no.

EXERCISE 53   NUMBERS AND ABBREVIATIONS II

1. 3d, St., St.
2. #, dollars, Jan.
3. 1,000, 4th
4. dept., %
5. Saint Chas., 4, two million $
6. N.Y., Thurs., Nov.
7. W., Dr., no.
8. Gen., 1st, 2, 4
9. 1/3, h.s.
10. 1st, pg., amt., two hundred and fifty dollars, 2d pg., two hundred and forty dollars
11. 21, twenty thousand dollars
12. first, St., Bldg., Ten, St.
13. 2d, fourteen, 10, Amer. Bldg., Assn.
14. Wm., Senior, co., 40
15. 10, 3, one thousand

EXERCISE 54   ONE-WORD, TWO-WORD, AND HYPHENATED FORMS

1. undertaking
2. C
3. C
4. cannot
5. reenter
6. withhold
7. C
8. C
9. outgoing
10. C
11. C
12. tomorrow
13. inasmuch as
14. ourselves
15. recall
16. C
17. overall
18. C
19. C
20. all right
21. undertake
22. meanwhile
23. C
24. overpaid
25. C
26. inboard
27. C
28. C
29. worthwhile
30. C
31. C
32. preempt
33. C
34. C
35. coordinate

EXERCISE 55   EXPRESSIONS TO AVOID

1. Attached
2. please
3. has
4. when
5. if
6. often
7. These
8. immediately
9. Either Mr. Davis or his secretary
10. During
11. person
12. After

EXERCISE 56   WORDS OFTEN CONFUSED

1. except
2. Past
3. bear
4. capital
5. site
6. weight
   carats
7. whether
   advice
8. principal
   effect
9. roll
   whether
   passed
10. Realty
11. weight
    vary
12. wear
13. compliment
14. Their
    there
15. Capital
    effect

16. council
    formerly
    capitol
17. addition
18. erasures
    eraser

19. Access
20. Any one
21. some time
22. may be
23. always
24. all together

25. already
26. loss
    lose
27. eminent
    adept

28. advise
29. conscious
30. some time

EXERCISE 57 WORD DIVISION

1. No
2. sepa/rate
3. begin/ning
4. con/sid/er/able
5. No
6. fol/lowed
7. No
8. No
9. impor/tance
10. par/ity
11. care/less/ness
12. occur/rence
13. short-/term
14. sen/sible
15. alle/vi/ation
16. over/come
17. No
18. con/ve/nient
19. No
20. No

EXERCISE 58   REVIEW I

Hill and Scott, Inc.   March 12, 19--
3487 - 105 Street
New York, NY 10025

Attention Mr. John McCoy, Personnel Manager

Gentlemen

I am glad to recommend Miss Ann Douglas about whom you
inquired in your letter of February 28.

Miss Douglas worked in this department of our company as a
secretary from June, 1981, to December, 1982. She left
our firm to accept a better position.

We found Miss Douglas to be an accurate and rapid secretary. She was intelligent and assumed responsibility
easily. We are very sure that she can adapt to almost any
office situation and that she will be a valuable employee.

While Miss Douglas worked for our firm, she and another
secretary devised a plan for solving one of the filing
problems that caused us much loss of time. We are, in
fact, still using their system.

I hope that this letter will help you reach a favorable
decision concerning Miss Douglas. If I can supply further
information, I shall be happy to do so.

Very sincerely yours

David Baxter
Accounting Division   DLB/xx

EXERCISE 59   REVIEW II

August 1, 19---

Mr. Thomas M. West
1721 Seventh Street
San Francisco, CA 94140

Dear Mr. West:

On January 7, 1983, you wrote us regarding some property
that we had listed for sale. This property, which is a
five-acre site, lies approximately two miles west of San
Diego, California, and is owned by Roger Willis, Jr. We
replied, giving you a complete description of the property, including the price and terms for purchase. We also
enclosed pictures of the property.

In February of that year Mr. Hall, one of our representatives, showed you the property. Since you decided at that
time that the property was too expensive, we did not pursue the matter. Now the owner of the property has decided
that he must sell, even if it means taking a loss; he has,
therefore, cut the price by 20 percent so that the original price of $750,000 is now $600,000. You realize, we are
sure, that this is a very low price. Real estate prices
have not decreased in the past year; in fact, in most
instances, they are actually higher. This cut has been made
merely to speed the owner's sale of the property.

We are giving you the first opportunity of purchasing this
property. Should you still be interested, call Mr. Hall at
(619) 461-2900 as soon as possible. He can supply any
information and will be expecting to hear from you.

Very truly yours,

WILSON REALTY COMPANY

President

ABW/xx

EXERCISE 60   REVIEW III

July 1, 19—

Mr. A. B. Davis
Pleasant Valley, WI 53560

Dear Mr. Davis:

We are writing you about our annual 50—page booklet,
"Complete Forecast of World Events," which, as you prob—
ably know, is published every July. This booklet is pre—
pared by the editorial staff of this magazine, directed by
J. M. Ray, Jr., a well—known authority on national and
international affairs. This year's edition is especially
valuable because it covers next fall's national elections.
The booklet discusses the backgrounds of the candidates
and assesses their chances for election. Also included is
an intriguing report on our country's military expendi—
tures and our predictions as to how taxes will be affected
by them this year.

Because you are a subscriber to our magazine, we are
extending to you an opportunity to order this booklet before
it is offered to the public. Just return the enclosed card
in the convenient postage—page envelope along with $1 for
your reserved copy. If we do not hear from you within ten
days, we shall assume that you are not interested and that
you do not want us to hold a copy for you.

Don't delay; order now!

                            Very truly yours,

                            WORLD EVENTS

                            Circulation Manager

ABR/jm
Enc.

Index